CULTURE SHOCK!

USA—The South

Jane Kohen Winter

Graphic Arts Center Publishing Company
Portland, Oregon

In the same series

Argentina	France	Malaysia	Sweden
Australia	Germany	Mauritius	Switzerland
Bolivia	Greece	Mexico	Syria
Borneo	Hong Kong	Morocco	Taiwan
Britain	Hungary	Myanmar	Thailand
Burma	India	Nepal	Turkey
California	Indonesia	Netherlands	UAE
Canada	Iran	Norway	Ukraine
Chile	Ireland	Pakistan	USA
China	Israel	Philippines	USA—The South
Cuba	Italy	Singapore	Venezuela
Czech Republic	Japan	South Africa	Vietnam
Denmark	Korea	Spain	
Egypt	Laos	Sri Lanka	

Barcelona At Your Door	Paris At Your Door	Living and Working
Chicago At Your Door	Rome At Your Door	Abroad
Havana At Your Door		Working Holidays
Jakarta At Your Door	A Globe-Trotter's Guide	Abroad
Kuala Lumpur, Malaysia	A Parent's Guide	
At Your Door	A Student's Guide	
London At Your Door	A Traveller's Medical Guide	
New York At Your Door	A Wife's Guide	

Illustrations by TRIGG
Photographs from Jane Kohen Winter, unless otherwise indicated

© 1996 Times Editions Pte Ltd
© 2000 Times Media Private Limited
Reprinted 1996, 1997, 1998, 2000

This book is published by special
arrangement with Times Media Private Limited
Times Centre, 1 New Industrial Road, Singapore 536196
International Standard Book Number 1-55868-246-5
Library of Congress Catalog Number 95-79457
Graphic Arts Center Publishing Company
P.O. Box 10306 • Portland, Oregon 97296-0306 • (503) 226-2402

Printed in Singapore

CONTENTS

To my little girls,
Emma, Molly, and Claire,
and to their dad, Arthur

ACKNOWLEDGMENTS

Most of the information in this book came from the mouths of the people I interviewed. My job was simply to get it all down and organize it. I was lucky to find so many eloquent new and old Southerners who very generously gave of their time and spoke so candidly about culture shock and southern ways of life.

I would especially like to thank Rae Aeberli of Mountain View, Arkansas, who spoke with me at length and then sent me regular packets of fascinating articles from her extensive personal clippings file. Anne and Don Plosser of Birmingham, Alabama, provided some very amusing and insightful material, showed me around Birmingham, and even took me to Irondale for ribs. Edwina Thomas of Memphis, Tennessee, expended a great deal of energy sending me source material and setting me up with prospective interviewees, as well as giving me lots of encouragement.

Many, many thanks to the following people for their time, frankness, wisdom and anecdotes:

Moriah McStay Lee and Betsy McStay for their help in Chicago and Memphis; Colleen Miller of Evanston, Illinois; Barbara Cranner of New Orleans, Louisiana; Donene Schiel, Stephanie Schiel and Linda Maslow, all of Montgomery, Alabama; Jay and Sheri Weber of Mobile, Alabama; Mary Mulherin of Memphis, Tennessee, who led me to Kay P. Williams of the Town and Country Cotillion in Richmond, Virginia; Malcolm Anderson and Heather Hildreth of Columbia, South Carolina; Dr. Mike Marshall of Memphis, Tennessee; Arlene Isaacson of Raleigh, North Carolina; Tony Magnetti, also of Raleigh, North Carolina; Allison Buckner, formerly of Arkansas and now of Gurnee, Illinois (a special thanks for the Rotel tomatoes); Erin Garton of Nashville, Tennessee; Nancy Goodman, formerly of

5

Prospect, Kentucky (and places East and Far East); Donna Burks, temporarily of Vicksburg, Mississippi; Janice Carrington, restaurateur in Atlanta, Georgia; Marcia Retchin of Charlottesville, Virginia; Nelson Kane, also of Charlottesville, Virginia; Melanie Birk and Jennifer Wheeler, both former Southerners; Marcella Werblow of Miami Beach, Florida; Sandi and Julius Nessel of Tucker, Georgia; Dannia Southerland of Durham, North Carolina; and two very helpful sources in Charleston, South Carolina and Miami, Florida, who preferred to remain anonymous. I also wish to thank the individuals who referred me to some of the above interviewees: Kathie McGarrity, Karen Melbinger, Nancy Ancrum, Shauna Runchey, Lizzie Graham, Judy Cottle and Sarah Miller.

I thank Donna Burks, Kay P. Williams and Nancy-Pace Newton, Keano Atwood of Ocean Springs Distributors, Gulfport, Mississippi, Dan Veroff of the Center of Southern Folklore Archive in Memphis, Tennessee, and Barbara Taylor of the Museum of the City of Mobile, Alabama, for help with photographs.

I am especially grateful to my sisters, Elizabeth Kohen Martinez and Amy Kohen Cohn, my parents, Helen and Rolly Kohen, and my friend, Jill DuBois, for sending me material, helping me find interviewees, reading my chapters, taking or finding photographs, and listening to my writer's lamentations. You too, A.W., for all of the above times ten, for your sense of adventure and for your unparalleled trip planning skills.

INTRODUCTION

Welcome to the South! The region you have chosen to live in or visit for an extended period is possibly more culturally complex than any other region in the United States. It is steeped in history, mythology and stereotype, and is probably the nation's most misunderstood collection of states.

When people think of the American Midwest, images come to mind of endless seas of corn and wheat, and maybe a flash of a gangster-run Chicago in the twenties. California brings to mind loopy, sunburnt youth and ego-driven Hollywood types, while the Northeastern states call up clapboard houses and tight-lipped people with formal customs. The West evokes cowboy images. But these impressions are simplistic and dated.

The images of the southern United States perpetuated by non-southern Americans and foreigners alike (as well as Southerners themselves) are far more extensive and fleshed out. People react to the South with gut-felt passion, downright horror, or derision.

If you turn on the television *anywhere* around the country, *any* day of the week, you will see commercials that play with people's romantic notions of the South as a region of hoop-skirted ultrafeminine belles, movies that work on people's fears of the South as a land of fat white males out to lynch black folk, and situation comedies that make Southerners out to be funny-talkin', barefoot hillbillies that don't know nothin'.

What I hope to do in this book is to help you, the newcomer, avoid pitfalls brought on by culture shock, misinformation and preconceived notions. I aim to teach you to sort the real South from the ridiculous South, to make you familiar with the common regional stereotypes, and to give advice on how to act when you meet them. The chapters that follow include information on subjects such as proper and taboo topics of conversation, manners at dinner parties, what to do if people knock on your door and ask you to join their church, and what to wear to work and various social functions.

I also give background on southern "culture," in the historical, religious, and artistic sense of that word, so that you'll know your Old South from your New South, your Baptists from your Church of Christs, what great southern writers gave to American literature.

You will also find sections on southern obsessions like football and hunting, leisure activities like gardening, and celebrations like tailgate picnics, Atlanta's Freaknik weekend, and debutante balls. Other chapters discuss the southern accent and southern expressions, southern food, and what Southerners think of the rest of us.

Now for the disclaimer: the South is an *enormous* region nearly the size of Europe, inhabited by millions of people, *each one different*, and I make no attempt to understand or describe all of them. My goal is merely to give you a good many reference points to enrich your stay in the South and to educate you about your surroundings and some of the people you will come in contact with. A little knowledge about one's neighbors can go a long way towards making one feel a little more at home in a strange and wonderful land.

Chapter One

JUST WHERE IS THIS PLACE CALLED "THE SOUTH"?

Just where the South actually starts and stops—its geographic boundaries—has been a matter of dispute and excited opinion for many generations. There are people who believe that the true South consists of only the original states that made up the Confederacy. Others say that the real South is the Deep South, and should not include any states to the north and west. Texas, many people believe, should not be considered the South, but rather its own planet (one which, by the way, is not covered in this particular volume). To some, Atlanta, the historic capital of the South, is not truly a part of the region because it is a large city filled with non-southern transplants.

To others, the southerly parts of states such as Missouri, Indiana, and Illinois are part of the South, because people there have a small-town, southern way of life and speak with a watered-down version of a southern accent. A person from Georgia, however, would think this notion utterly ridiculous. And some wonder about Florida, the most southern state on the Eastern seaboard: is it part of the South even though it is full of retirees from the North and Latin American immigrants? Others don't even believe the South, as a distinct region with a separate cultural identity, exists at all anymore, rather that it has been smothered by mainstream American culture. Because Southern-ers feel so strongly about their homeland, it is probably wise to get the boundaries of the South sorted out before we proceed to discuss what's inside them.

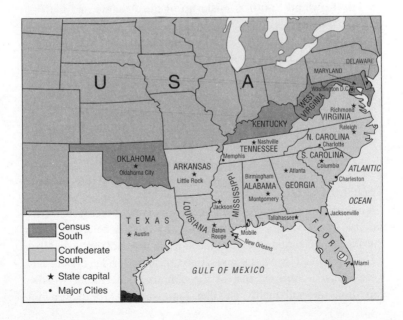

SOME IMPORTANT GEOGRAPHIC TERMS

On a map, the southern region of the United States stretches from East Texas on the west to the Atlantic Ocean on the east, and from the Potomac River in the northeast to the Ohio River in the northwest and then south to the Gulf of Mexico. Within these enormous boundaries lie several subregions whose names are useful to know:

The Deep South is made up of Alabama, Louisiana, Georgia, South Carolina, and Mississippi;

The Carolina Piedmont incorporates North and South Carolina;

The Tidewater usually refers to the historic coastal area of Virginia;

The Upland South refers to the northern region of the South, not including the northern coastal areas;

The Lowland South is made up of the Atlantic and Gulf coastal areas;

Appalachia refers to the mountainous areas of Maryland, Virginia, West Virginia, North Carolina, Kentucky, Tennessee, and Georgia;

The Mason-Dixon Line currently refers to a boundary that separates the South from the rest of the country; the phrase "below the Mason-Dixon line" is used to describe the South; Mason and Dixon were actually British astronomers hired in the 1760s to resolve a border conflict.

THE OLD SOUTH

Technically, this term refers to a grouping of states that were settled early on in our country's history, mostly by English colonists. South Carolina and Georgia were the first states in the Old South, and they were later joined by Mississippi, Alabama and Florida. These states were isolated from the rest of the country, had similar weather conditions and soil quality, and their land was ideal for the growing of cotton. That particular crop was difficult to harvest and clean, so intensive slave labor was used. In fact, by the time the Civil War started, some two million slaves lived in the Old South. Hence, the states of the Old South were the first to secede from the Union.

The white Southerners who lived in the Old South had certain common personality traits. They all took pride in owning land and felt that local decisions should be made by local gentry, not by a central authority living outside the immediate region. Contrary to popular belief, most of the whites in the Old South were not enormously wealthy plantation and slave owners—although such people did exist—but relatively small farmers or members of the poorest classes.

The upper and lower classes were separated socially, as they were in England, but all whites, whether they owned slaves or not, generally agreed that they were superior to black laborers. Landowners in the Old South had a deep-rooted sense of their differentness from their northern neighbors and banded together whenever they felt their way of life was threatened, either by European authority, rebellious black slaves, or Northerners who wished to abolish slavery.

Today, when people refer to the Old South, they often mean the mythical antebellum (or pre-Civil War) South they've seen in the movies. This South is infused with romance and features genteel, pale-skinned women in elaborate costumes whose virtue is protected by gentleman farmers and who are looked after by loyal and happy black slaves who always "know their place." It brings to mind a fictional time when society was governed by certain rules that everybody followed and when people of all races lived in harmony.

To black people, as well as to many whites, the Old South refers to a time of enslavement and injustice, when black people were without rights and forced to live lives of persecution and indignity.

Given these two disparate definitions, it would not be wise, while living in the South today, to sigh wistfully when discussing the Old South, and to wish, as I have heard some people actually do, for things to be "the way they used to be."

Antebellum houses are often turned into inns or bed and breakfasts. This one, The Harbour Oaks Inn, in Pass Christian, Mississippi, is owned by Tony and Diane Brugger.

THE CONFEDERATE SOUTH

The Confederate South was made up of 11 slave-holding states that seceded from the Union in 1860 and 1861, after the election of Abraham Lincoln. South Carolina was the first state to leave the Union and was followed by Mississippi, Florida, Alabama, Georgia, Louisiana, Texas, Virginia, Arkansas, North Carolina and Tennessee. Even though the border states of Missouri, Kentucky, Delaware, and Maryland were slave-holding states, they opted to retain allegiance to the Union, as did the people of western Virginia, who created a new state named, aptly, West Virginia.

THE NEW SOUTH

The term "New South" was popularized in 1886 by the managing editor of the *Atlanta Constitution* newspaper, Henry Grady, in a speech given to members of New York's New England Society. Grady's New South referred to a post-Civil War South that, Grady and other hopeful New Southerners believed, was dedicated to economic progress, free from racism and accepting of its defeat at northern hands.

Since that time more than a century ago, the term has been in constant use. The words have no strict technical or geographic designation, the way Old South did, but are used metaphorically to refer to an outlook held by the entire region. You hear New South used in the media by businessmen trying to encourage potential northern investors to bring industry to the region, by tourist agencies luring people southward to spend their money, by anyone trying to convince people that the South is not what it used to be: poor, backward, culturally bereft, segregated by race, and closed to outsiders.

THE CENSUS SOUTH

The United States Census Bureau currently classifies the South as a region encompassing almost 1 million square miles and 16 states as well as the District of Columbia. The 16 states are Florida, Georgia, Mississippi, Alabama, Tennessee, Louisiana, Kentucky, North Carolina, South Carolina, Virginia, West Virginia, Delaware, Maryland, Oklahoma, Arkansas, and Texas.

Most scholars and followers of southern culture would be more than happy to throw Maryland, Delaware, and Washington, D.C. out of this official definition of the South, by the way, but this is the one the government insists on using to calculate population statistics and economic growth. Be aware then that these states are included in the statistics about the South given in this book.

JOHN SHELTON REED'S SOUTH

John Shelton Reed, a sociologist at the University of North Carolina at Chapel Hill, might be called the country's best (and funniest) cartographer of southern culture. In his many books, magazine and newspaper articles, and speeches he has charted the region of the South in some unusual ways.

15

First and foremost, Reed believes and has devoted his academic career to proving that a distinctive place called the South does indeed exist and that the region is inhabited by people with a distinctive way of looking at the world. He even goes so far as to say that Southerners should be considered a separate ethnic group like Italians or Polish Americans.

In his 1991 book, *The South for New Southerners*, Reed says that the South is a "shared concept ... an idea that people can talk about, think about, use to orient themselves and each other. People know whether they're in it or not." The South, he asserts, is basically "a poor, rural region with a biracial population, reflecting the historic dominance of the plantation system." It is this shared history of poverty and racial tension that makes the South and Southerners different.

Reed deals with the location issue of the South using maps of the United States and shading them in various ways. One particularly fascinating map charts the South in terms of where a plant called kudzu grows. Kudzu is a type of weed or vine originally from Asia that was planted in the South in the early 20th century to enrich the soil. What southern farmers didn't know then was that kudzu had the ability to grow as much as a foot a day and could completely cover unsuspecting cars and small buildings, as well as smother other plants. (Poet James Dickey called it "a vegetable form of cancer.") This evil weed still grows and is cursed throughout the South. According to Reed's map, it is found in all the usual southern states, as far west as East Texas, as far south as northern Florida and as far north as the southern tips of Illinois, Ohio, and Indiana. I think that if you traveled around the country and listened and talked to people you would come away believing that all these states (and pieces of states) should indeed be called the South.

Reed also charts the South in terms of the states where the most lynchings occurred, those that have the highest concentration of blacks, and even the states mentioned most in country music songs.

In the latter map, the results indicate that Texas, Louisiana, and Tennessee are the most southern states. When he maps the South according to states having businesses that use the word "Dixie" rather than "America" in their names (as in the Dixie Doo beauty parlor), he comes up with a South that looks a lot like the kudzu South, only without Atlanta, Appalachia, East Texas, and southern Florida.

[As an aside, I am truly baffled by the fact that "Dixie" is still used at all in so many business names in the South, although the word appears to have lost some ground in the 1990s. The term is synonymous with the slave-holding Old South and carries all that era's negative connotations. The word was originally popularized, by the way, in a song called "Dixie's Land" written by a Northerner (!) named Daniel Emmett in 1859. It was performed by a minstrel troupe who donned plantation garb and sang the following in black dialect: "Den I wish I was in Dixie, Hooray! Hooray! In Dixie Land I'll took my stand, To lib an die in Dixie." This song, still played regularly at the Stone Mountain amusement park outside Atlanta, would not be the one I'd choose to whistle aloud as I walked the streets of today's New South.]

Reed's map of the South in which he charts the states that use the word "southern" rather than "American" in their business names is the one he considers to best define the physical boundaries of the region. This map, devised using urban telephone directories, includes the 11 states of the Confederacy, only the most eastern edge of Texas, parts of Oklahoma, Kentucky, Florida, and Arkansas, but none of Missouri.

THE ATLANTA ISSUE

If you study the most recent statistics from the U.S. Census, you will see that southern metropolitan areas experienced tremendous population boosts during the 1980s. Nearly four million people migrated from the Midwest and Northeast to the South in the last ten years, most of them to the city and suburbs of Atlanta. Whether these people have come to Atlanta for the jobs, the weather, or the reasonable cost of living, their presence has been seen by many as a negation or at least a dilution of the culture.

One woman I know who migrated from the Midwest to a suburb of Atlanta about two years ago says that her neighborhood or her "subdivision" is made up of so many transplants that it is easy to find yourself living in a completely non-southern world in the midst of the historic South. Another transplant, a black businesswoman from New York who has lived in Atlanta for five years, told me that the notion of southern good neighborliness is completely unknown to her. When she came South, she thought her neighbors would invite her in for coffee or out bowling, but in five years she has only nodded or said hello to a few of them on the street. She doesn't even know their names. She did add, however, that most of her neighbors were also from points north.

Part of the problem with Atlanta is that it is a big city that looks like any American big city anywhere, with tall glass buildings, expressways, corporate headquarters, and their accompanying executives. Atlanta also has a high percentage of blacks in positions of power within the corporate world and in local government. Southern culture, to many, is not associated with a large, relatively new, impersonal city with a strong black influence.

Southerners have typically lived in small, rural towns where everybody knew everybody and families lived close to each other for many generations. Like all big cities, Atlanta provides a certain anonymity that small southern towns do not. But Atlanta does still have elements of southern culture and behavior that obviously become more profound if you leave the subdivision (and its nearby malls and supermarkets) and get the opportunity to work or socialize with people born in that part of the South.

The businesswoman I mentioned above, for instance, owns a restaurant located in the midst of five black colleges. During her five years in Atlanta, she has experienced an ongoing if not severe case of culture shock. Her southern employees, she says, always use "ma'am" when addressing her; some even call her "Miss —," much to her surprise. And when she goes into stores, she finds that her New York-bred impatience gets the best of her as she waits for the cashier or salesperson to chat politely and familiarly with each and every customer ahead of her in line. When she drives, she must force herself not to lean on the horn and scream out the window as the man in the car in front of her lets the fourth and fifth cars turn ahead of him. She finds herself yearning for the taste of ethnic foods and the look of ethnic neighborhoods she saw in New York; she can't get good ricotta cheese in the grocery store or a decent hot pastrami sandwich. She has had a few run-ins with the locals over the issue of race and the part slavery played in the Civil War. She has seen Confederate flags flying and been to Stone Mountain to see the Confederate war heroes come to life.

Big city or no big city, she is very much in the South.

WHAT ABOUT SOUTH FLORIDA?

By anybody's definition, northern Florida is truly a part of the South. It was settled by Southerners and still contains people who consider themselves southern. But South Florida is an entirely different story, especially the Miami metropolitan area, which includes Miami Beach.

The primary reason why Miami and cities north of it are not southern is because the area is filled with transplants, from New York City, from Cuba and other Latin American countries, and from Haiti, not to mention everybody's grandparents from the Northeast and Midwest. There used to be a joke in Miami that the Broad Causeway, a bridge going from one ethnic neighborhood in Miami Beach to another one in Miami, was the longest bridge in the world because it connected Israel with Cuba. Miami is now more than 55 percent Cuban, and Miami Beach is predominantly Jewish. Culturally, then, at least for white and Hispanic people, the region is not the least bit southern.

South Floridians almost universally speak without a southern accent, although you will find older people who grew up there calling the city "Miamah." Not many people have grown up there, however. People in Miami are not typically southern in that they have little feeling for the land, few family roots, don't eat traditional southern food, are not quick to defend their homeland, know nothing of the Civil War, and absolutely do not view themselves as Southerners.

Black people who grew up in South Florida, however, probably have more in common with black Southerners than white South Floridians do with white Southerners. In the 1930s and '40s, there used to be signs on Miami Beach hotels that said, "No Blacks, No Jews, No Dogs." Jews and blacks were not permitted to join certain country clubs or to live in certain neighborhoods. One woman remembers being escorted from the dining room of such a club when she was a little girl because the maitre d' recognized her name in the guest book and knew she was a Jew.

In the late 1950s and early 1960s, black people were subject to curfew laws and could not be on Miami Beach soil after a certain evening hour. Famous black entertainers who came to "the Beach," as it is called, to perform in hotels would have to cross the bridges and sleep over in Miami after the show. And people who wanted to keep their household help around after nightfall built back houses or small one- or two-room buildings behind their own large homes so the help could stay when evening fell and not be considered technically "on the property." (If you are currently in the market for an old South Florida house, you'll find many with former servants' quarters, but now these are considered "income properties.")

Schools were segregated in Miami Beach until the late 1960s, when busing laws were established. In one all-white elementary school, rather than bus the children in one direction or another, they ordered the teachers to switch schools. So a white teacher was sent to a black school and she was replaced by a black teacher. In a year, however, the white teacher was back, telling anyone who would listen how she had threatened to quit the school system if she wasn't sent back to her old school where the children "knew how to behave." Busing was successfully carried out at the junior high and high school levels, however.

SOUTHERNERS OUTSIDE THE SOUTH

Southerners are often described as people with a very loyal sense of place. They yearn for the South when they're not there and manage to come back several times a year for holiday celebrations. They hate to hear their region trashed by anyone, in any way. I can safely say that few people from other regions in the United States feel this way about where they live (except maybe diehard New Yorkers).

When Southerners are forced to pick up and go elsewhere, to further their careers for instance, they do unusual things like form clubs with other Southerners so they can have a few hours every month with their own kind, eating familiar foods and talking in their own special code language. Some white Southerners living outside the South in other *American* cities even call themselves "expatriates," equating their situation to that of an American living in say, Taiwan or Geneva! There is a woman's group in Chicago called the Southern Alliance that has been meeting regularly for more than fifty years, and some Southerners living in New York City are so tight that they have been dubbed the "Magnolia Mafia" by a journalist for the *New York Observer*.

In addition, there are large numbers of Southerners living in Ypsilanti, Michigan, working in the auto industry, as well as many descendants of Southerners in Bakersfield, California, where their families went to get work in agriculture during the Depression.

THE DISBELIEVERS

There are many people, both southern and otherwise, who don't believe that the South has any special sort of regional identity anymore, rather that all of America has become one giant strip mall

21

(with a McDonald's at one end and a Gap at the other), that teenagers nationwide now talk the same way (with a California-cool accent peppered with lots of "likes" and "awesomes"), that there are so many outsiders in the South now that it's no longer the South. In 1991, Hodding Carter III, a television producer from the South, said the region, "as a living, ever-regenerating mythic land of distinctive personality, is no more."

It is surely true that mainstream American popular culture (the kind developed by corporate executives in board rooms) has taken the fancy of people from all the regions of the United States, as well as masses of Asians and Europeans who eat Big Macs, wear Michael Jordan T-shirts with their Air Jordans, and watch episodes of "L.A. Law" and "Melrose Place."

Somehow, this Americanization of the globe has not totally trampled or replaced southern culture. The South still has its own delicious but rather unhealthy cuisine, despite efforts by nutritionists to abolish fried foods. It is still responsible for giving the nation its best college and professional football players. Becoming a debutante, cheerleader, or beauty queen are still things southern girls aspire to, even if much of the rest of the country isn't very interested in such pursuits.

Southerners are absolutely better mannered and more hospitable than other Americans. They often can recite their family trees back many generations, they have annual family reunions and go to church as a family every Sunday. They are often conservative politically and vote for candidates according to certain patterns. And the southern accent and Southerners' special way of putting words together persists.

In addition, academics all over the world find it worthwhile to study southern culture, past and present, and to publish their findings in the many academic journals devoted to that subject. In 1989, the University of North Carolina Press at Chapel Hill and the Center for the Study of Southern Culture at the University of Mississippi at

Oxford published a 1,634-page volume called *The Encyclopedia of Southern Culture*. This fascinating book divides its enormous subject into reader-friendly sections that go into great detail about Southerners and southern culture, both historical and current. (If you are interested in purchasing the *Encyclopedia* at a reasonable rate, watch for it in book club promotions, often advertised on the back covers of Sunday book review sections.)

I may be wrong, but I have never seen an encyclopedia of this magnitude devoted to the culture of California or the Pacific Northwest, or as many non-southern states with entire departments devoted to regional studies. Aside from the Southern Studies department at Ole Miss (as the University of Mississippi at Oxford is called), there is one at Florida International University in Miami, at the University of North Carolina at Chapel Hill, at universities in South Carolina, Alabama, Kentucky, and Arkansas, even one at Lake Forest College in Lake Forest, Illinois!

A WORKING DEFINITION

Now that you have heard all the various opinions concerning the existence or nonexistence of the South as a region, let's come up with a working definition of the area, at least for the purposes of keeping a solid image of the South and the Southerner in mind while reading this book.

Geographically, it would be reasonable to say that the South is still made up of all the Confederate states and at least the edges of all the states bordering this region. More accurately, however, the South is simply *where Southerners and southern culture are found,* whether that happens to be a typical small southern town, a large city like Atlanta, a northern area like Chicago where black Southerners migrated to, or anywhere where Southerners have formed social networks with fellow Southerners. In his writings, John Shelton Reed often mentions that an excellent definition of the South is what a lawyer friend of his calls the "Hell, yes!" line; in other words, where a person will answer "Hell, yes!" when asked if he or she is a Southerner. (I cannot picture Midwesterners answering with such enthusiasm when asked if they are from their region.)

The South, then, is truly a state of mind rather than a place with a hard and fast latitude and longitude. All the transplants to the region whom I interviewed for this book felt a sense of foreignness when they first found themselves in the South; they initially defined their culture shock simply by saying they were "in another world." After being in the region for a while, transplants found this "other world" to be more religious, more friendly, more patriotic, more food-focused, more family-oriented, more sports-obsessed, more color-conscious than other areas of the United States. In the rest of the book, I will try to provide insight into these essentially southern behaviors and personality traits.

THE SOUTH IS ALIVE AND WELL IN THE AMERICAN IMAGINATION

As historians, geographers, sociologists, and Southerners try to prove or disprove the existence of the South as a physical place and to define its borders, the rest of us know that the South and the Southerner remain alive and well in the American imagination. More than any other region in these United States, the South is steeped in myth and its people victims of stereotyping perpetuated by television, newspapers, films, and books, by Southerners and non-Southerners alike.

Many southern stereotypes are cruel and unfair, while others contain elements of truth. For the newcomer to the South, however, wholehearted belief in any stereotype can be a dangerous thing. At best, it can lead to tremendous disappointment ("You mean all southern women don't wear hoopskirts and spend their days choosing potential beaux on the porches of their ancestral homes?") and, at worst, to terrible offense and rejection.

If you move South with the attitude that everyone you meet is a hick, eats possum, knows nothing of fine art and culture, and wants to marry his cousin, you will be making a grave error and few southern friends. Despite all those old episodes of "The Beverly Hillbillies," "Green Acres," "Gomer Pyle," "Petticoat Junction," "The Andy Griffith Show," and "The Waltons" that many of us grew up watching, Southerners are not all gun-toting, moonshine-drinking fools with thick heads to match their accents. Even if you do love Harper Lee's *To Kill a Mockingbird*, old Shirley Temple movies with their faithful black servants, and those nice blond farm girls from "Hee Haw," you must get it out of your head that all white southern men have white sheets in their closets, all black people in the South "know their place," and all southern girls have full chests and vacant minds.

One of the most important ways to prevent yourself from being taken in by stereotypes is to watch television—the worst perpetrator of this particular crime—with a critical and sensitive eye. Advertising executives use southern stereotypes on a regular basis to sell their clients' products. Little Caesar's Pizza, for instance, is now buying lots of airtime to promote their Crazy Bread, which is supposed to be good for dipping. Their spokesman is an older white man with a thick southern accent who is called a "Crazy Dippin' Fool" because he likes to dip everything in bronze to preserve it. His former pet has been dipped, a bronzed squirrel falls out of his tree with a clonk, and even his deceased wife, complete with working garden hose, is now solid metal. This ad lets the audience know that people with southern accents are eccentric—even crazy—old fools.

Then there's the old commercial for Shake 'N Bake that has recently been revived where the little girl, complete with thick southern accent, is proud to proclaim, "And I helped!" when her mother gets credit for making a good supper. Ever since this commercial came out when I was a child, little kids have been running around imitating this little girl's southern accent, and making fun of her momma's-little-helper attitude in the kitchen.

Have you seen the commercial for Polaner All Fruit where the aristocratic British ladies and gentlemen gasp, faint, and freak out all together when the thick-accented, ignorant southern hick at the table refers to this classy fruit spread as common "jelly"? What about the one for flavored Coffeemate where the gracious and sexy southern belle flirtatiously encourages everyone to try this delicious new product? Why is it that millions of dollars are being spent to portray Southerners as backward and trashy and nobody is putting up a stink?

Advertisements are not the only thing on television that convey negative southern stereotypes. The host of VH-1's Stand-Up Spotlight comedy show recently did a whole (unfunny) number on his trip to North Carolina where everyone is deformed in some way and stares at you with an ignorant look on their face, unable to follow the simplest conversation. Jay Leno even lapsed into a southern accent recently on his late night talk show to indicate that he was playing stupid. The South would need a 20-man, 24-hour anti-defamation league to police the airwaves, radiowaves, film reels, books, magazines, and newspapers and ferret out all the defamatory statements made against it.

Somehow, ad executives, entertainers, and members of the general public who take pains to be politically correct (and perhaps overly sensitive) toward many other groups have decided that Southerners—primarily white ones—are still acceptable targets to mock, criticize, and demean. Perhaps the people who perpetuate these stereotypes feel that regional identity is open to ridicule because it is too impersonal to cause real offense. Maybe they are so accustomed to making

Southerners the butt of their jokes that they have ceased to notice what they are doing. Or maybe they just find Southerners colorful, lovable, and entertaining. (Who didn't adore Forrest Gump?) Probably, though, the real reason why we are confronted with the Crazy Dippin' Fool on a daily basis is that the marketing geniuses who thought him up have found that southern stereotypes *sell*.

THE TABULA RASA *APPROACH*

What you must do as a newcomer to the region is to try to rid yourself of all your preconceived notions about Southerners before you interact closely with them. This will probably prove to be impossible, ultimately, because some of these stereotypes are funny, nice, romantic, even fascinating, not to mention partially true, but it is certainly worth a try. (I have personally spent far too much time fantasizing about *Gone with the Wind*, and wondering if I would have been more like the sickly but angelic Miss Melanie or the cut-throat, surviving, and triumphant Miss Scarlett had I lived in those times.)

When it comes to the particularly evil stereotypes, it is wise to try the *tabula rasa* (or "clean slate") approach when you go South, or anywhere foreign for that matter. This takes a good deal of control on the part of the newcomer as well as a true interest in coming to terms with and integrating into the new culture. The first thing you must do is to identify the stereotype and recognize it to be dangerous. Then train yourself to keep the negative myth or image from creeping into your consciousness while you are interacting with the new culture. Most importantly, learn to keep your predetermined beliefs private, your mind open, and—here comes the crucial part—*your mouth closed* until you are able to make your own judgments and draw your own conclusions.

One of the primary reasons that Southerners find it so difficult to get along with outsiders is because non-Southerners seem to think they already know everything about Southerners and do not hesitate to tell them so.

EXAMINING THE STEREOTYPES

Don't feel guilty. It is human nature to allow stereotypes to enter our belief system, especially when they are so well drawn by such creative people, and the images are so powerful. According to John Shelton Reed in *Southern Folk, Plain and Fancy*, we are quick to adopt stereotypes—southern or otherwise—because they help us understand our world, categorize people or "pigeonhole" them so we know (or think we know) how they will behave. Reed says that white southern stereotypes, or what he calls "social types," such as the belle, the redneck, the good old boy, and the gentleman are "cultural artifacts, like unicorns and trolls, elves and werewolves; they are social constructions that Southerners use to amuse each other and mystify the Yankees." Reed goes on to say that southern social types are more than imaginary creatures, that they "signify ... collections of real people, who resemble one another in ways that could be quantified and measured if we wanted to."

Reed also tells us that white southern social types *originated* in the South (even though the rest of the country has used and abused them ever since) and were used primarily by the upper class to differentiate themselves from and hold themselves superior to the lower class. According to historian C. Van Woodward, Northerners later used white southern stereotypes to release aggression and bolster their own status, the way Europeans commonly stereotype Americans. Black social types, Reed says, are a wholly different animal; they are far more complicated than white ones, in a constant state of flux, and less evident to people living outside the region.

In the following sections, we will define and describe some of the more well-known white and black southern stereotypes, placing each in a historical context and, where possible, attempting to determine how much reality lies in each one.

POOR WHITES: REDNECKS, CRACKERS, HILLBILLIES, AND TRASH

The stereotype of the poor white Southerner, particularly the male variety, has probably produced more fear in non-Southerners moving South than any other. During the course of doing research for this book, many of the people I talked to admitted that initially they had had irrational fears about driving to the South. They were worried that a group of rednecks in a mud-splattered pickup truck would spot their out-of-region license plates and harass them in some way.

One Korean-American man from Chicago making a trip to Memphis had been told that he should gas up at the Illinois border and go straight through Missouri and Arkansas without stopping until he reached the big city on the Mississippi River. A black woman traveling to Vicksburg, Mississippi, was frightened that she would meet up with a toothless racist en route; so was a Jewish woman going from New York to Raleigh, North Carolina.

Although the term **redneck** was not widely used until the 1930s, the figure behind the term, the yeoman farmer of Scotch-Irish descent laboring in the fields, hoe in hand, head bent, until his neck got sunburned or red, has been around since the region was settled. Yeoman farmers were proud, God-fearing small farmers (with few slaves) who believed fiercely in the American idea of freedom, and were willing to fight against the British in the American Revolution and again against the Yankees in the Civil War. According to scholars, the yeoman farmer was the average Southerner and his unrefined lifestyle was much more representative of the antebellum South than that of the wealthy plantation owner.

Today, when somebody uses the term redneck (or its nasty synonyms, *peckerwood*, *linthead*, *woolhat*, or *coonass*), he is not referring to the independent yeoman farmer (who is no longer with us), but to a poor, uneducated white male of the lower classes who has a vivid and defined set of characteristics. The term is derogatory, no doubt, but is used so frequently by Southerners—redneck or otherwise—and non-Southerners that it has lost some of its sting. There is even a certain amount of pride among rednecks about being rednecks, as evidenced by the lyrics of country music songs and by books such as *The Official Redneck Handbook* by Jack S. Moore, published in 1983. Once a stereotype is embraced like that, it both loses its power to wound and reinforces its own validity.

According to Moore's dialect-ridden book (which was probably written to contrast the amazingly popular *Official Preppy Handbook* by Lisa Birnbach which came out in 1980):

> ... bein' a Redneck is somethin' special. ... Bein' Redneck ain't a putdown; it's a celebration of life! It's pride and determination, and Rednecks is resourceful; never resentful. Redneck means bein' American and damned glad of it. ... They is always the first to stand up when the National Anthem is played, and is always the first who stop an' help ya when your car's broke down on the highway. ... Rednecks is close to their family. Goin' to the drag races with the kids and gettin' a Big Mac 'n Fries afterward is the type of simple pleasure Rednecks was suckled on.

Moore goes on to tell us that "This here country was built on Redneck sweat!", that there are High Rednecks and Low Rednecks (the former "has at least one vehicle that runs," the latter "has six vehicles that don't run—all in front of the trailer"), and that the official "Redneck Tuxedo" is a pair of overalls stained with pork gravy. If you read this book you will notice how the author gives rednecks a class hierarchy, and how the most evil quality of redneckhood—a fierce intolerance for others—is not mentioned.

When a woman moved from up north to Mississippi, one of her office colleagues gave her a printed list of redneck characteristics that was entitled, "You will do well in Vicksburg if ..." According to the sheet, people from the area would accept you if "you owe the

In the South, people proudly proclaim their devotion to religion and the past on the back of their pickup trucks.

taxidermist more than your annual income," "you prominently display a gift you bought at Graceland," and "your wife's hairdo has ever been ruined by a ceiling fan," among other things.

The Encyclopedia of Southern Culture devotes a good amount of space to the redneck, his barbaric English, greasy diet, love of country music, and his women companions who "chew gum vigorously and wear plastic hair curlers in public." Redneck men have names like "Bubba," "Leroy," and "T.J.," and women are called "Billy Jean," "Peggy Joe," and "Mavis," says the *Encyclopedia*. Redneck women, by the way, are usually derided for their appearance, but not for their character. They are usually the breadwinners in the family, going off to work early while their husbands sleep off the booze they drank the night before.

What sets the redneck apart from other white southern men who eat the same foods, also love to drink beer and to hunt, and have an equally macho disposition, is his laziness, his taste for violence for violence's sake, and what the *Encyclopedia* calls his "incorrigible" racism. The redneck is the lower class "villain," Reed says. (Just watch how the redneck is portrayed in the 1970 film "Deliverance" if you want to see him at his most despicable.) Will D. Campbell, a preacher, writer and self-proclaimed redneck, says that the poor white Southerner became a closed-minded racist because he never had an established place in antebellum society. He was neither the master nor the slave, and was never asked to participate in society until the Civil War, when the white aristocracy had him give his life to preserve the system of slavery. During the Reconstruction period, Campbell says, the redneck watched while the government handed out land and food and other aid to newly freed blacks while poor whites got nothing. Some people believe that the hatred, anger, and fierce suspicion of others that rednecks are accused of today began during those times.

The **cracker**, another poor, white, uncultured southern character of Scotch-Irish descent, is a cousin to the redneck, but he usually lives in northern Florida or southern Georgia. The term, used as early as the mid-18th century, was not necessarily a derogatory one until the 1960s, when it was adopted by blacks to refer to a white person with racist tendencies. In fact, the state of Georgia was formerly called the Cracker State and the baseball team was named the Atlanta Crackers.

A redneck or cracker who lives at a higher altitude (in Appalachia or the Ozarks) is a **hillbilly**, a mountain person who is known for his insulated lifestyle, his laziness, and his lack of education, but who does not have the menacing quality of the redneck or the cracker. Many of us got our image of the hillbilly from "The Beverly Hillbillies," that sitcom about those innocent, family-oriented folk who got rich and went to California with all their backward notions on the back of their broken-down truck.

Granny, Uncle Jed, Jethro, and Ellie May Clampett called the swimming pool in their new mansion the "cement pond," thought the billiards room was a "fancy eatin' room" and that the cast-iron kettles

they brought to the table were to be passed using the pool cues. They wore funny clothes, loved possum, made their own moonshine, which they drank out of a jug, and had constant cultural clashes with the natives, who usually had dollar signs for eyeballs.

"The Beverly Hillbillies" may have given us the most vivid version of the hillbilly stereotype, but it was not the first. The comic strips *L'il Abner* and *Snuffy Smith* showed southern mountain people to be poor, stupid, and happy fools, sometimes drunk and sometimes feuding. Hillbilly music became popular in the 1930s, thereby adding to the image of the mountain folk with their twangy voices and homemade instruments.

While the derivation of *hillbilly* is obscure, Gene-Gabriel Moore, an Atlanta writer, says that many Scotch-Irish settlers named their sons William after William of Orange. William became Bill, Bill became Billy, Billy lived in the hills, so he became "hillbilly." (Even Moore admits that this notion may be "far-fetched," but it sounds good.) The word hillbilly appeared in a cartoon as early as the 1830s,

Moore says, where it was used to refer to someone from southeast Kentucky.

While some people may call themselves hillbillies these days, the term is still considered offensive and not to be used off the cuff. If you travel through Appalachia, you might run across little shops selling hillbilly merchandise like a bag of Cheerios marked "Hillbilly Donut Seeds" or t-shirts with pictures of toothless, barefoot people on them. Mountain folk, then, see the humor in their image, just as long as they are doing the name-calling.

The term **poor white trash** is probably the most offensive label you could give a poor white Southerner, and one poor whites rarely use to describe themselves. Dorothy Allison, a native of South Carolina, described the life of the poor white Southerner in her beautifully written, semi-autobiographical novel, *Bastard Out of Carolina*. Bone, the young girl who tells the story, is a member of the Boatwright clan, a classic "trash" family complete with drunken, fighting uncles, loving but exhausted aunts raising a host of wild children, a toothless but wise granny, and a sexually abusive step-father. Bone struggles with her white trash identity throughout the novel, hoping to find a way out of the brutal life her family has mapped out for her.

Many poor white Southerners feel tremendous shame about their origins. As writer Lloyd van Brunt said in a piece for the *New York Times Magazine* that appeared in March of 1994, "This shame, this feeling of worthlessness is one of the vilest and most self-destructive emotions to be endured. To be poor in a country that places a premium on wealth is in itself shameful. To be white and poor is unforgivable."

The only time I've ever seen a person make light of his poor white trash background is Ernest Matthew Mickler in his *White Trash Cooking* (1986) and its sequel, *Sinkin' Spells, Hot Flashes, Fits and Cravin's* (1988). In the introduction to the first volume, Mickler explains the subtle class differences between "white trash" and "White Trash":

Manners and pride separate the two. Common white trash has very little in the way of pride, and no manners to speak of, and hardly any respect for anybody or anything. But where I come from in North Florida you never failed to say "yes ma'm" and "no sir," never sat on a made-up bed (or put your hat on it), never opened someone else's icebox, never left food on your plate, never left the table without permission, and never forgot to say "thank you" for the teeniest favor. That's the way the ones before us were raised and that's the way they raised us in the South.

The white trash image many of us associate with the South was developed in Margaret Mitchell's *Gone with the Wind* (1936) in the character of Emmy Slattery, the lower-class woman who gave Scarlett's momma the disease that killed her, in Erskine Caldwell's *Tobacco Road* (1932) and *God's Little Acre* (1933), and in James Agee's *Let Us Now Praise Famous Men* (1941), illustrated with the powerful photographs of Walker Evans.

MORE WHITES: GOOD OLD BOYS, BUBBAS/ BUBBETTES, AND BUDDIES/BARBARAS

The **good old boy** has something in common with each of the characters mentioned above, but he is usually a working- or middle-class man who is fun-loving, likeable, masculine, outdoorsy, and quick-witted; he's not as wicked as his redneck relation nor as willing to start a fight for no good reason. The writer Tom Wolfe, a Southerner from Richmond, Virginia, now living in New York City, first used the phrase *good old boy* to describe stockcar racer Junior Johnson in a piece he wrote for *Esquire* magazine in 1967.

Former President Jimmy Carter's brother Billy was an oft-quoted member of the club who once claimed that the difference between a good old boy and a redneck was that a good old boy drives around in a pickup drinking beer and puts the empty bottles in a bag, while a redneck drives around in a truck and throws his empties out the window. (Sounds a little like the difference between white trash and White Trash, eh?)

Roy Blount, Jr., a southern humorist, once likened the good old boy to the Jewish "mensch," a loyal, reliable, inherently honest figure who can be counted on to do the right thing by his family and friends. John Shelton Reed says that the archetypal good old boy was the character portrayed by actor Burt Reynolds in the two *Smokey and the Bandit* films (1977, 1980). In *Myth, Media, and the Southern Mind*, author Stephen A. Smith tells us that the good old boy "operates on the premise that 'life is nothing to get serious about,'" and is a contemporary "cultural hero."

The stereotypical good old boy is named **Bubba**, which is a southern nickname for "Brother." There are many men actually called Bubba in the South, but not all conform to the stereotype. Most often, the word Bubba is used in political terms by non-southern reporters, as in, "Which candidate will get the Bubba vote?" i.e., "Who will the typical working- or middle-class, white southern male vote for in the next election?" Bubba tends to be politically conservative, a registered Republican, although he may once have voted Democrat. He typically likes Jesse Helms and the military; he dislikes gays, environmentalists, politicians from the Northeast in loafers, blacks who don't know their place, pro-choice advocates, and handgun control laws. Bubba thinks things should be the way they used to be when life was simpler, when criminals went to jail and children were born to two married people.

Humorist Maryln Schwartz says that, among other characteristics, Bubba is obsessed with football, "raises a lot of hell, drinks a lot of beer and has a gun rack on the back of his pickup truck." His female counterpart is **Bubbette**, who "for years ... devoted herself to taking care of Bubba, cooking his pot roasts and making dip for the bowling league auxiliary. She also sold cosmetics on the side." Schwartz calls Marla Maples, wife of zillionaire Donald Trump, a Bubbette.

Ted Turner, Bill Clinton, and Al Gore, as well as Arkansas television producer and presidential pal Linda Bloodworth Thomason, Schwartz says, are a step above Bubbas and Bubbettes: they're **Buddies** and **Barbaras**—more polished, better schooled, more ambitious versions of the stereotype, southern yuppies for the '90s. According to the bitingly clever Schwartz, Buddy watches football, not from the couch like Bubba, but from the stadium skybox owned by the company he works for. Bubba dumped Bubbette when he became Buddy, so he could marry his second wife, Barbara, also a corporate exec. Bubbette went to law school, became a Barbara herself, and now lives with her nutritionist, a younger man. Get it?

UPPER-CLASS WHITES

Southern stereotypes are rarely from the solid middle class (aside from a few Bubbas). Scholars theorize that this has happened because the middle class is not nearly as colorful as the upper and lower classes, and southern and northern purveyors of stereotypes would therefore have little interest in them. The upper-class stereotypes, the southern gentleman and his female counterparts, the belle and the lady, are especially beloved by Americans. We admire their magnificent homes, their excellent taste, their beautiful manners, their flawless appearance. They are our aristocracy and we want them to be real. How did we formulate our vision of them and why has it stuck? Are these people real or fantasy? To what extent?

Gone with the Wind:
What Havoc You Have Wreaked

To understand upper-class stereotypes, one must first examine the primary source of our images, what might be called the mother of southern stereotypes, *Gone with the Wind*. This big, fat epic novel about a southern plantation family and its heroine Scarlett O'Hara before and after the Civil War was written by Atlantan Margaret Mitchell and published in 1936. After only three weeks on the market, it had sold almost 200,000 copies, a huge amount in those days. In 1937, Mitchell won the Pulitzer Prize for Literature. By 1938, sales were more than 2,000,000. The book still sells almost 250,000 copies a year nationally, and 100,000 a year in other countries. Something like 30 million copies have been sold to date. The movie, directed by David O. Selznick and released in Atlanta in 1939, was a tremendous hit all over the country, seen and loved by millions.

There has been a bestselling sequel to the novel, made-for-television sequels to the film, movies about the making of the movie, biographies of the author, biographies of the director, biographies of the actors, movies about the actresses, and on and on. The story has become an American classic; its characters are so believable and so beautifully portrayed on the screen that readers and viewers have lost the ability to judge whether or not they are real, or if things really happened that way in the South during that terrible time.

On one level, *Gone with the Wind* is so compelling because of the magnificent picture it paints of life at the top of society. We are wowed by Scarlett's beauty, her tiny waist and the gorgeous hoop-skirted dresses she wears to show it off, the life of balls and barbecues she leads. She's clever and quick, willful and self-centered, but she gets what she wants and besides, all the guys fall all over her. We adore the fiercely protective and loyal Mammy who raises Scarlett and stays with the family after the war. The other slaves in the movie seem equally well treated and apolitical.

We admire Ashley's manners, his sense of duty, his education, and we think the world of the angelic Miss Melanie who sees the good in all human beings. Rhett Butler is incredibly handsome and sexy, and like Scarlett, a survivor. We die over those houses they live in with their dramatic columns, European furniture, and grand double staircases.

Watercolor of Rhett Butler, that rogue, taken from an original movie program from Gone with the Wind, *circa 1939. Photograph by Jill DuBois.*

What impressive stuff this is to read about or, better, to watch, but how dangerous and misleading. As writer and television journalist Charles Kuralt says, Mitchell "captured the popular imagination with a portrait of the vanished southern aristocracy as mystically righteous, religiously genteel, tragically doomed from the start. Her tale is as well established in the American mind today as the legends of King Arthur in the British mind, but it's also about as well grounded in fact."

Yes, some people did live like the O'Haras and the Wilkeses, and some slaves were contented to be slaves, but most didn't and weren't. Unfortunately, when it comes to *Gone with the Wind*, we can't help ourselves. We are taken in by Mitchell's vision, blinded by its beauty. We don't let ourselves see how hot and restricting those dresses must have been, how useless gentlemen like Ashley were, how most slaves weren't as naturally obliging as Mammy and didn't have such cushy house jobs, how ugly and empty all those mansions and things are when bought with the labor of an enslaved people.

Mitchell makes the masters out to be basically good, moral people and the slaves to be pretty simple and content. The Yankee soldiers are the bullies; the scalawags, carpetbaggers, and poor whites are the scum. We believe Mitchell because we want to understand history the way she does, with clearly defined good and evil, innocent and guilty. It's a tidy package and, at least at first, nice to look at, too.

On a different level, writer Tom Wicker says that our fascination with and love for *Gone with the Wind* center around the idea of loss the movie leaves us with, the fact that the South was changed forever after the Civil War. Of course, the abolition of slavery was essential, but with it went a genteel society and an idyllic landscape that many Americans cannot help but mourn, especially the way it was portrayed by Mitchell and Selznick.

According to Wicker, after the war the southern region would never again conform to "the Jeffersonian ideal of an agrarian America free of the infections of big cities and large commerce, and the insatiable drive for industry, money, power" that the North represents. He says that the "sense of loss" experienced by the South, as personified in Scarlett O'Hara, the loss "of youth, of innocence, of faith, of confidence, of the hope for a better tomorrow that will surely come, of something ineffable we thought we had a right to expect—is at the heart of American life."

THE GENTLEMAN, THE LADY, AND THE BELLE

The myths of the **southern belle**, the more mature **lady**, and the **gentleman planter** have been with us since the first plantation novels were written in the 19th century and the first plantation movies came out in the 20th century. Although the traditional southern gentleman stereotype has been left behind as society has changed, the female figures have managed to adapt to the modern world quite well. In fact, they are still alive—in their mythical and actual forms—to this day.

A novel called *Swallow Barn* by John Pendleton Kennedy, published in 1832, gave us one of the first literary examples of the southern lady and the southern gentleman. In this and other plantation novels, the planter, usually from the aristocratic Tidewater region of Virginia, is portrayed as gracious, educated, and honest. He is comfortable in all social situations and the gentle master of all he surveys.

The lady is self-sacrificing, pious, and pure to the point of saintliness. She supports her husband, the patriarch, in all things, but she is not weak. She has responsibility within the home and for the children, and she is an amiable, capable hostess. In a plantation film like *Gone with the Wind*, Scarlett's mother and Melanie Wilkes are good examples of southern ladies; Ashley Wilkes and his father are typical gentlemen.

The mythical belle is not as quiet or as dignified as her older manifestation. In historic literature and film, she is a terrible flirt who loves male attention but who is innocent of experience. She looks and acts very, very feminine; she giggles, she babbles, she plays dumb. As

Anne Firor Scott writes in *The Southern Lady: From Pedestal to Politics*, the lady is "the most perfect example of womankind on earth," while the belle is "beautiful, graceful, accomplished in social charm, bewitching in coquetry, yet strangely steadfast in soul ... perhaps the most winsome figure in the whole field of our fancy." Somehow, when the belle marries and has her first child, she miraculously matures into the lady.

The belle image has stayed with us throughout this century. Novelist Anne River Siddons, who grew up in the South in the 1950s, says she was raised to think that winning a good husband who could provide a good, steady life was a southern girl's goal. She explained the particularly southern desire for male protection eloquently when she was interviewed by writer V.S. Naipaul for his book *A Turn in the South*:

> I can tell you why Southern women teach their daughters ... that they must have a man to protect them. After the Civil War those women had lost their entire worlds. And I think they perceived that this had happened through the sheer folly and childishness of these men of theirs. ... And they determined then to control those men by guile and charm and feminine wiles, because those were the only weapons they had ... You can't aspire to what you can't imagine. And so, to survive, we had to hook up with a man.

Siddons talks about the pain of being a brainy woman in a South where it was more important to be pretty and compliant: "We never prized our minds. We never prized our individuality. It was all right to make good grades. It was all part of being a good little girl. But to be a great thinker, to have a great talent and pursue it, would cut you right out of the herd. And that was the thing we were most afraid of. It could send you walking alone."

In the 1990s, southern girls are probably much more like other American girls than ever before, but there is still at least a hint of the belle in many of them. Northerners who have elected to attend southern colleges and universities often find that the female coeds there dress in a more feminine style than students elsewhere do. They wear big bows in their hair, lots of makeup, even large jewels. They are bright and studious, but many come to school to find a career *and* a suitable mate. Belles still giggle, they still flirt, and they concern themselves with the formal social scene of sorority and fraternity parties more than many of their northern counterparts. Their relationships with boys tend to be traditional in nature: girls don't have boy friends in the South, they have boyfriends.

Florence King, who writes with tremendous insight and great humor about southern stereotypes, tells us in her *Southern Ladies and Gentlemen* that "today's belles are ... brides and debutantes." According to King,

> All brides crave their moment of glory, but in the South there is a *name* for a woman who dazzles multitudes—a belle. For many Southern girls, a big wedding is the only chance they will ever have to be this legendary creature that all Southern women are supposed to be. A big wedding is much more than a moment of glory; it is a storybook fable come to life.

Maryln Schwartz has written a hilarious guide to belle weddings and belle behavior that leaves us with no doubt that the belle is still alive all over the South. Many southern women I interviewed for this book swear that Schwartz is telling the truth in *A Southern Belle Primer*. Here are some of her belle facts:

- Southern belles have real names like Lady and Fancy, and many are called "Sister."
- Southern belles always send thank-you notes, never wear ankle bracelets, don't chew gum or smoke in public.

- Southern belles never curse; their favorite words are lovely, precious, darlin', cute, sweet, and nice (the last two are really used to mean something is just okay or even awful); the worst thing a belle can call someone is "tacky."
- Southern belles start looking at silver patterns when they are in grammar school.
- Southern belles love iced tea, hairspray, beauty contests, theme parties where everything matches (e.g. the dress matches the napkins, matches the punch, matches the husband's tie).

In the 1990s, does the belle still marry the gentleman and become the lady? The mother of a belle is surely a lady and her grandmother is a grande dame, but no, sad to say, the real southern gentleman seems to have all but disappeared from the South. He was a bit too cultured, intellectual, too sissy in an English uppercrust way for today's macho, hunting, fishing, football-watching South. No, the belle probably marries a kind of refined good old boy—someone with excellent manners and solid family connections, of course—but someone with business savvy, various sports obsessions, and a confident macho disposition.

John Shelton Reed tells us that you still see the upper-class southern man on television or in the movies, but he is usually cast as the "evil aristocrat" (J.R. Ewing, the cruel slaveowner) or the "white-suited buffoon" (usually named "Colonel"). The evil aristocrat social type appeared recently in the very mediocre 1994 film *Lassie*, set in Virginia. This upper-class meany, a rich sheep farmer, tries to cheat Lassie's "family," who have recently moved to the area, out of their land. He even sends his two bratty junior aristocrats over to rough up the boy and his dog and let them know who's boss. Of course, Lassie and the boy triumph.

A recent example of an upper-class gentleman buffoon is the character of the uncle in the movie *Passion Fish*, set in Louisiana

Cajun country. Wearing a pastel suit and a Panama hat, the uncle comes to visit his just paralyzed and very depressed niece, a former soap opera star, and regales her with funny stories before drinking himself into a stupor and snoring it off on her couch.

BLACK STEREOTYPES

Contemporary southern black stereotypes are not often found in the media, although African-Americans in general suffer from all kinds of pigeonholing. These days, blacks usually appear on television and in the movies in blighted urban settings as crack dealers, drug addicts, gangbangers, and evil, violence-loving degenerates. Black males in particular are so often linked in the media with senseless, violent crime that they cannot walk in white neighborhoods without people crossing the street or policemen stopping them for questioning. Among blacks themselves, there are many character types based on color shade, attitude, class, and income, but these are rarely documented by scholars.

Southern black stereotypes are found most often in a historical context, especially in older movies or books written or directed by whites about the antebellum or Reconstruction South. The plantation romance that gave us the gallant gentleman and the girlish belle also gave us the **happy darky** stereotype. This stock character was usually a very friendly, loyal, unaggressive slave who knew his role in the grand scheme and accepted it without question. Sometimes, the simple, happy darkies would sing and dance in musicals set in the South, giving the impression that their talents were innate and that all they needed was a good banjo to keep them happy.

Northerner Harriet Beecher Stowe's novel, *Uncle Tom's Cabin*, written in 1852, provided America with vivid black stereotypes, including that of Uncle Tom, a faithful black servant. Today, an older black man who eagerly defers to white authority or appears to believe in his own lesser status is derogatorily referred to as an **Uncle Tom**.

The black buffoon or **Sambo** has been used countless times in the media. The word sambo, according to the *Encyclopedia of Southern Culture*, "is Hispanic in origin, deriving from a 16th century word *zambo*, which meant a bowlegged person resembling a monkey." Sambo usually had a large toothy smile on his face and was a kind of black court jester. His type appeared in many books and films and his image could be found on all kinds of household knickknacks from salt and pepper shakers to lawn ornaments, the *Encyclopedia* says. The lawn ornaments were made out of iron and usually featured a very black-skinned, white-eyed boy dressed up in jockey silks; they were found all over many neighborhoods a few decades ago. Now you see them at antiques shows in their original state, or still on well-manicured lawns, but painted to look Caucasian.

Probably the most harmful and distorted black stereotypes created by whites had to do with sex. Often, writers and filmmakers made young black female slaves out to be easy and sultry, a direct contrast to the rather stiff, inexperienced, and ladylike white belle. In books and films dealing with both antebellum and Reconstruction themes, the black man was made out to be a sex-crazed rapist, who, if the white man let his guard down, would go out and steal the virtue of every white woman in sight. This latter character was brought to the public most vividly in D.W. Griffith's pro-Ku Klux Klan silent film, *Birth of a Nation* (1915), which played on white people's fears of a post-Civil War South dominated by aggressive, lustful blacks.

The **mammy** stereotype, a product of the plantation novel and other southern books and films, often had many positive characteristics. She was usually a large, motherly woman wearing an apron and a kerchief who provided comfort and love to white children, and who had a certain strength and wisdom surpassing that of the white family. The mammy worked hard and knew profound suffering but, through faith, managed to keep going. Dilsey, the black housekeeper in William Faulkner's *The Sound and the Fury,* is an excellent example of the strong mammy figure, as is Hattie McDaniel's Mammy in *Gone with the Wind.*

In general, these historic black stereotypes have become taboo in the media in the past few decades, at least compared to southern white stereotypes. Plantation dramas, Civil War and Civil Rights films, and television shows featuring strong, independent, proud black characters (e.g. *Roots*, "The Autobiography of Miss Jane Pittman," "I'll Fly Away") are more the norm now. Fortunately, as Nancy M. Tischler writes in the *Encyclopedia*, "The slave over the years has gone from 'darky' to 'nigger' to 'Nigra' to 'Negro,' from 'person of color' to 'colored' to 'black,' from 'boy' and 'gal' to 'man' and 'woman.' The shift is clearly from stereotype to individualized human being."

— Chapter Three —

NORTHERNERS EXPOSED

In the South, the breeze blows softer than elsewhere through the pine trees and the accents fall softer on the ear. Neighbors are friendlier, and nosier, and more talkative. (By contrast with the Yankee, the Southerner never uses one word when ten or twenty will do.) The spring is prettier, the summer hotter and happier, the fall longer and sadder, the winter shorter than elsewhere on the continent. This is a different place. Our way of thinking is different, as are our ways of seeing, laughing, singing, eating, meeting and parting. Our walk is different, as the old song goes, our talk and our names. Nothing about us is quite the same as in the country to the north and west. What we carry in our memories is different, too, and that may explain everything else ...

—Charles Kuralt in *Southerners: Portrait of a People*

Newcomers to the South have a good deal of reprogramming to do to smooth their transition into southern society. They must sensitize themselves to the southern stereotypes fed them by the media and learn to separate truth from fiction. But they must also realize that Southerners, like all of us, are perpetrators as well as victims of stereotype. For centuries, Southerners have cherished their identity as separate and distinct from Northerners and other outsiders. Southerners, in other words, are as adept as anybody else at the game of "us" and "them."

In this chapter we will learn what the collective southern "us" thinks of the collective northern "them" and give advice on how to behave more like the natives.

THE HOMOGENOUS SOUTH

Bluntly stated, many Southerners living in areas where migrants tend to flock feel *invaded* by outsiders and their foreign ways, and sometimes wish they didn't have to deal with them. Wouldn't we all feel uneasy, even displaced, if the comfortable, familiar place we grew up in was suddenly peopled by a whole lot of *strangers*?

Until quite recently, the South was an extremely homogenous region. Most white Southerners were Protestants of English, Irish, or Scotch-Irish descent. Most lived in rural areas or towns where families had known each other for generations. Most did not have the resources to move away from home when they became adults (many, in fact, had never been outside their state or county) and so the region was not characterized by mobility. Most Southerners were not well off—many were poor—but they received satisfaction from their common religion, their food (when it was plentiful), their shared value system.

While the Northeast, Midwest, and West were receiving immigrants who spoke many different languages, believed in many different gods and ate a range of exotic foods, the South had basically two types of people—blacks and whites. With neither an influx of strangers nor an outpouring of Southerners, the region was able to stay the way it had always been longer than anywhere else.

In its pre-Sunbelt days, few people wanted to live in the South, few even wanted to *go* there—unless they were speeding through (or flying over) the rural parts and heading straight for the sunny coast. The South, don't forget, had long been looked down upon by the rest of the country, even the world, for its position on slavery, its defeat in the Civil War, its closedmindedness, its insularity, its perceived lack of high culture, its poverty, and its supposed rural backwardness. In an article called "Fear of Dixie" written for the *Atlanta Journal-Constitution* in February 1991, writer Drew Jubera said,

> I grew up in Pennsylvania during the '60s thinking "Southern hospitality" was a trick phrase manufactured to lure Yankees South so they could *get us*. Before the Sun Belt Boom, we thought of the region as America only by constitutional decree. It was the Heart of Darkness, an unfathomable place of unspeakable nastiness, a slyly drowsy landscape still populated with freckled Johnny Rebs who picked off Yankees from tree stands. ...

The negative image attached to the South all those years before the region became the desirable place it is today caused the southern psyche to develop in interesting ways. Some Southerners, feeling that their opportunities for economic success or personal achievement were limited in such a place, left for the North. Millions of African-American Southerners, in particular, left the South after World War II, a period known as the Great Migration.

Most Southerners, however, those who had the wherewithal to leave and those who didn't, stayed in the region and developed or maintained a different idea of their homeland. Some felt tremendous shame in being southern; others felt shame mixed with love for the land. But still others turned their regional inferiority complex on its head: they took a tremendous pride in being southern, they valued their way of life, their land, their homes, their community.

SOUTH FOR SALE

In the last three decades or so, since the Civil Rights Movement, migration from south to north has fallen off tremendously, and a second migration, from north to south, is taking place. In fact, between 1980 and 1990, the Census Bureau reported that the South gained approximately 4 million new residents and about 4 million more new Southerners are expected in the 1990s. (These figures include Texas, Washington, D.C., Delaware, and Maryland, as well as what are considered the true southern states.) The primary areas of growth have been in North Carolina, Virginia, Florida and Georgia. Between 1980 and 1987, the population in the Atlanta metropolitan area alone increased by almost 25 percent. In particular, African-Americans of southern origin are today returning to the South in great numbers.

It seems that everybody these days wants to get a piece of the South, to enjoy its climate (made pleasant by that blessed invention, air-conditioning), buy up its land, and take advantage of its beauty and ease of living. Vacationers adore every part of it, and retirees come in droves to live out their lives with neither down jackets nor potentially dangerous patches of ice. Corporations relocate to the Southland so they can take advantage of the wide open spaces, the quality of life, the low cost of labor.

What happens when development (an evil word to many a Southerner) takes place? Malls are built. Subdivisions spring up. Housing costs go up. Traffic problems develop. Small businesses

TRIGG

run by people who know you disappear. Big businesses come in and non-Southerners are hired for all the top executive positions. This happens everywhere in America, no doubt, but it is a particularly painful transition for Southerners, who have always valued simplicity and familiarity, and who have taken such pride in their strong sense of who they are.

Some of this development is good, of course, and many Southerners welcome the addition of new faces and new businesses. The economy improves and, at the middle and lower levels, there are more jobs. The Gap and Barnes & Noble move into the mall and give people the chance to buy into that casual all-American look and to hang out in coffee bars surrounded by bestsellers. In southern cities like Charleston and Savannah, for instance, wealthy newcomers have been credited for the restoration of some of those cities' finest historic homes. But what has been lost, Southerners wonder? Why does this place not look and feel like home anymore? Wait, some Southerners ask themselves, are these outsiders trying to *take over*, the way they tried to after The War Between the States?

This fear of losing their way of life is nothing new to many Southerners. In different ways and for different reasons, they have been fighting to maintain themselves for nearly 150 years. To combat the latest assault on their identity, their fear of being assimilated, if you will, into the great American mass, Southerners have reacted by becoming even prouder of their land, their homes, the places they were raised. They can't say enough about their climate, their food, their local football heroes, their closeness to one another, their religious fervor, their old-fashioned values. The boosterism in the South is truly unmatched by any other region of the country.

Southerners expend great effort to keep things the way they used to be, to keep the past alive. They join genealogy clubs, host grand family reunions, preserve historic homes and sites, stage serious Civil War re-enactments and—this is key—they talk about the past, all the time, as if it just happened last Tuesday. While the rest of the country seems to be characterized by a wandering from city to city, a nonchalance about home, an ignorance about the past, and a search for the best lifestyle to acquire, the South is a region filled with people who love and revere their home and who don't want to lose it.

WHAT THE CRITICS SAY

Several notable southern writers have taken the newcomer invasion very seriously. In Ann Barrett Batson's *Having It Y'all: The Official Handbook for Citizens of the South and Those Who Wish They Were*, she repeatedly refers to non-Southerners as Folks Not From Here (the caps. are hers). Florence King, in an article for the *New Republic* magazine (March 1, 1993), calls outsiders "Damnyuppies," which I assume is a variation of Damn Yankees. She blames them for changing the face of the South. Their "lust for relocating," she says, "is turning our gothic paradise into a homogenized Sunbelt."

King also picks up on a newcomer quality that many Southerners dislike: their rootlessness. "... Damnyuppies have no *from*," she claims. "Most of them seem to have no distinctive traits, habits, or accent—just master's degrees. Higher education, which bestows mobility, has made Damnyuppies *fromless*." Because of the Damnyuppy invasion, King says that "Southerners, perhaps the only Americans still capable of homesickness, can now experience it without leaving home."

Sociologist John Shelton Reed feels so homesick when he is out of the region that he refers to himself as an "expatriate" when away from home, a word usually reserved for someone living outside his native country, not his state! Reed's main beef with northern invaders is not as hostile as King's, but he does say that Northerners make him "tired." It *is* tiring to talk to people who come from different cultures, who don't share the same background, don't sound the same or use the same expressions, who don't have that insider information that comes from growing up inside a close-knit community where most people are pretty much like you.

Reed probably feels that spending time with northern outsiders is like having someone from a faraway place like Uzbekistan or Mongolia in your home. If you are a caring, sensitive, hospitable host (which many Southerners are), you would probably wear yourself out trying to make that person feel comfortable and making sure not to cause offense.

Josephine Humphries, a native of Charleston and a fine southern writer, is troubled that the rapid development of the South will cause the death of the small town, the most fertile setting for the southern novel. Humphries, quoting another great southern writer, Reynolds Price, has stated that "fiction is best set in a town of fewer than ten thousand souls, a town from whose center open country [can] be reached by a fifteen minute walk." Places like these, with both natural beauty and a community of like souls, are being replaced, Humphries laments, by "fake towns." "Places called 'Seaside' and 'Charleston Place' in Florida," she says, "are merely developments costumed as towns" which will in turn provide settings for disconnected, mediocre, fake southern fiction.

The late southern humorist Lewis Grizzard was very vocal about the changing South in the columns he wrote regularly for the *Atlanta Journal-Constitution*. In one column, Grizzard recounted a conversation he had with a transplanted northern woman in his doctor's office. When the woman, noticing Grizzard's southern pronunciation of a word, remarked that Southerners "have a language all [their] own," Grizzard retorted (in the column only, I think): "Yeah we do. If you don't like it, go back home and stick your head in a snow bank."

He went on to say that transplanted Northerners have the audacity to "want to tell us how to speak, how to live, what to eat, what to think and they also want to tell us how they used to do it back in Buffalo." In another column, Grizzard exhorts his fellow Southerners to secede from the Union. "No more heavy taxes to bail out decaying northern cities. No more stupid federal regulators," he wrote.

To Grizzard and to many passionate Southerners, the North still represents The Government and its attempt to control the individual states, all those cheatin', lyin' politicians living in Washington, D.C., the I.R.S., and all the problems that go along with big city life and crowded, industrialized urban areas.

Some concerned southern citizens have written to their local newspapers blaming outsiders for an increase in criminal activity in their areas, the proliferation of malls at the expense of old, less glamorous hangouts, for trying to steal the southern personality and call it their own.

Many Southerners are horrified at the look of all those new housing developments, their sameness, their silly names, their poor workmanship and heavy price. Reed tells us that developers build homes like these because they are "fungible, easily assessed by realtors for sale to succeeding generations of transferred professionals and executives. ... not the kind of thing you buy with the thought of bequeathing it to your eldest son."

Where, the natives ask themselves, are the old neighborhoods where everybody knew everybody, where family homes carried a volume of stories with them, where houses were allowed to look less than perfect and where kids ran around barefoot causing trouble with their buddies and cousins? Often, locals say, new and better schools are built within or close to these new communities to serve the children of the newcomers while older schools suffer from lack of resources. Other Southerners blame northern transplants for taking from the community without giving something in return: eagerly moving into new subdivisions filled with other transplants, for example, but taking little interest in local government or community organizations.

OUTSIDERS: A SOUTHERN PERSPECTIVE

Southerners have plenty of opinions about Americans from other regions coming to the Southland. Of course, these are stereotypes and not universally held, but they do have some truth to them and should be given some attention. In Columbia, South Carolina, some people refer to natives as "Been Heres" and newcomers as "Come Heres." In Charleston, a native of that old southern city is called a "From Here," while someone from another southern locale is a "From Away." If you are not southern at all, you are a "From Off." (From off *what*? the planet?)

Southerners particularly love to label those from the North, especially those from evil urban dens like New York City. New Yorkers are brash, say many Southerners, mean even to their friends, uncouth to all. They are so used to averting their eyes that they look at nobody and appear to be standoffish, snotty, even insincere.

To a Southerner from a rural area, all urban, upwardly mobile Northerners—those Damnyuppies—are thought to like money and career more than their families. They are always on the move, putting in extra hours at the office, rushing here and there to maintain their competitive edge. They don't know how to relax and enjoy themselves; when they hear a joke, they state dryly, "That was funny," rather than crack up laughing.

Yuppies from Atlanta, by the way, are not exempt from this kind of criticism. Atlanta, the capital of the New South and a showpiece of steel and glass, is considered the South's North; Southerners think its citizens are pushy and forthright, racing around town to make power breakfasts and do lunch. And Charlotte, many Southerners fear, is on its way to becoming the next Atlanta.

Urban male Yankees are thought by some Southerners to be fancy folks, trying to look so sharp in their Italian suits and girlish loafers, wasting their time at the opera of all places or at gallery openings where they sip Chardonnay and discuss abstract art. They're soft when it comes to macho displays and couldn't do hard labor if their lives depended on it. And so what if they went to Yale?

According to the prevailing stereotype, professional northern women are not true females at all but bitchy feminists always trying to compete with men. They wear those dark masculine suits and have such blunt, businesslike haircuts. They have no manners, no softness, and they don't know how to make a man feel special. Writer Bo Whaley, in his politically *in*correct *Field Guide to Southern Women,* says that northern women are inferior to southern women because they would rather make reservations than dinner every night. According to Whaley:

Status is also a priority with northern women, whereas southern girls are content to dine in any establishment that features an all-you-can-eat buffet for $3.99 and high chairs for the younguns. The women of the North have a tendency to want to be seen in spiffy restaurants that provide Monday morning conversation at the club or office, whereas the women of the South want to eat and status be damned ... Southern girls are content with backyard barbecues, a quick trip to the river or the beach. ...

If you're a native of California, some Southerners might categorize you as a major flake, apt to eat miniature artichokes and drink designer water by the costly gallonful, quick to adopt any new religion or cult that comes your way. Trend-worshipping, you wear any grungy rag that's hot and pierce your body in all kinds of ungodly places.

If you are from the Midwest, to some Southerners you are oh-so-dull and colorless. Your best clothes are jeans and t-shirts, you have pasty white skin and you don't know how to use makeup. Furthermore, you have no notion whatsoever about entertaining and hospitality. Your food is tasteless, your manners not particularly good and you cannot keep a conversation going—probably because you have so little to say. In short, you're a bore.

If you are a Canadian spending the winter in Florida, as millions do each year, you are known statewide for your stingy ways. You never learned the custom of tipping in a restaurant and you are first in line for the 5 p.m., three-buck buffet special. You go in for the blotchy, sunburnt tourist "tan," accented by tacky, loud-colored shorts and the fatal socks 'n sandals combo. And oh yeah, you drive like an old lady.

If you are not American (or Canadian) at all, Southerners may treat you a bit more gently, although many may never truly and deeply accept you. As one woman from an old southern family explained, southern Americans unthinkingly expect other Americans to be like them, and when they are not, the Southerners are amazed, disappointed, turned off. But if you are from an entirely different culture, she said, you have a certain appeal, an exoticism, that may entice the Southerner to take an interest in you. Good luck.

NEWCOMER NO-NOS: A GUIDE TO INCONSPICUOUS BEHAVIOR

Now that we know the ugliest things Southerners are saying about the rest of us, how do we dodge the stereotype, alter our behavior so that we don't get pegged as the Pushy New Yorker, the Fruitcake from Fresno, the Dullard from Des Moines? How do we learn to fit in? Here are a few key guidelines to being a little bit less conspicuous in the South:

1. Slow down

The pace of life in the South is slower than elsewhere in America. Americans from other regions, as well as many Europeans and Asians, are used to making every minute of the day count. They thrive on tight schedules; their appointment books are crowded with meetings, lunch dates, conference calls. Many people love being frantic—it makes them feel vital, wanted, necessary. And these same people despise inefficiency, laziness, and a lack of urgency in others.

When non-Southerners move South, they often find themselves waiting for things they never waited for before. One newcomer remarked that car washes in the South take an hour, even the automatic ones, and that even getting a fill-up at the gas station can be a lengthy process. Another mentioned that saleswomen in the South chat with every customer in the store and, instead of throwing your purchases at you without a glance, they take the time to carefully wrap your clothing in crisp white tissue paper, place it gently in a shopping bag, and tell you how they look forward to seeing you again. Repairmen promise they will come Thursday at eleven, but come two hours later, or at eleven the next day, or the next week.

After five minutes of waiting, the non-Southerner feels a creeping annoyance. After ten minutes, his temper begins to rise. My time is important to me, the person says to himself, and you are wasting it. After fifteen minutes, the outsider boils over. He says and does things he wouldn't normally do: complains in a loud voice, shakes his head, rolls his eyes and mutters, maybe even screams irrationalities at the slow guy. Not the best way to make friends or develop relationships with colleagues, eh?

An Arkansas woman told a story about a newcomer who did not care to wait her turn in a long grocery line, so she decided to make a place for herself at the front, just behind the storyteller. After the others in the line politely protested and the newcomer said, "Too bad," the Arkansas native and the checker gave each other a knowing glance and made a silent pact to teach the newcomer a lesson. Very, v-e-r-y slowly, the native reached into her basket and placed her first item onto the conveyer belt. The checker slowly reached for the item, looked at it hard, turned it this way and that, read the label. Then she ever-so-slowly keyed in the price and slowly extended her arm to place the item in the bagging area. Then the native unloaded her second item, the checker reached for it and repeated the process. Needless to say, the newcomer, fuming and grumbling under her breath, got the message.

Southerners, you see, don't care to hurry. They don't know what all the fuss is about, why things need to be done yesterday. They know how to stroll through life appreciating the small things, taking a moment to greet a stranger, to say hello to the salesclerk, to stop and catch up with a neighbor. As one newcomer to Kentucky put it, "This place is full of simple pleasures and everybody here knows how to enjoy them."

If someone is sick or in the hospital, the typical Southerner will take the time to visit or to prepare a dish for the family. Southerners stop to help people, even strangers, change a flat; they gladly let a driver get ahead of them on the highway if he's misjudged an exit. If

61

Relaxing, southern-style, on the breezy porch.

a Southerner needs a favor from a friend or to discuss something important with a colleague at work, he will spend several minutes, maybe even a half hour or so, chatting with the person first, asking about family members or mutual friends. Non-southern urbanites don't spend time on trivialities before getting right to the point. "They simply don't understand the meaning of social lubrication," one Southerner said.

It is ironic that many outsiders move South to change their lifestyles, to resign from the rat race or at least to ease up on it, but when they arrive they find that they cannot stop running and that the slow southern pace is making them crazy. As one newcomer to North Carolina put it, "The first few weeks I was here, I spent my life at the drugstore sticking my arm in those blood pressure machines and found that my frustration was making my blood pressure sky-rocket!"

The best way to avoid this is to leave yourself extra time to do things in the South, to prepare yourself for waiting, to talk yourself out of impatience, and to forcibly make yourself slow down. Most non-natives adjust nicely to the southern pace after a year or so and then realize how pleasurable it is to take the time to stop and smell the coffee.

2. Don't be a know-it-all

Whatever you do, Southerners say, don't come to our region and tell us how things are done up North, or out West, or in London or Tokyo. Newcomers to any region or country naturally like to discuss their former homes and jobs. In the South, the land of the inferiority complex, it is fine to reminisce, but it is not wise to give advice in a superior manner, to try to "'larn' us better," said a native.

Urban outsiders often assume that they are more worldly than their southern hosts. They've seen more foreign films, visited finer museums, eaten in better restaurants, traveled to more exotic places, worked for larger, richer companies that are run more efficiently than southern ones. Outsiders are often quick to point out that the fund-raising committee they sat on in Chicago used more sophisticated tactics than southern organizations to raise money; that the hairdressers up north were better trained in the newest hairstyles and highlighting techniques; the stores in Los Angeles carried more fashionable clothing; the restaurants in San Francisco had special low-fat, low-cholesterol entrées on the menu; and finally and most potently, that the schools *everywhere* were better.

Of course, much of this is absolutely true, but outsiders need to realize that just because the people they meet have always *lived* in the South does not mean they never *go* anywhere and don't know how to appreciate fine wines, French manicures, and designer clothing. Many upper-class Southerners have traveled everywhere, gone to fine schools, and shopped Rodeo Drive—they just prefer to live in the South. And the ones who have not had the opportunity to leave home don't want to hear how much better it is outside the area, unless the newcomer can tell him in a gentle, constructive way that causes no offense.

One southern native got especially peeved when, at election time, a northern newcomer working for a local organization called to remind her about the coming election and to encourage her to go out to the polls. The native was insulted because she interpreted the newcomer's tone to be that of an urban sophisticate to a backward hillbilly. "I've been voting in this county since I was 21 years old," the native replied, "but thank you very much for the call."

3. Don't be so direct

Consider these true stories: A newcomer to Mississippi, while dining in a local restaurant, found her food to be quite undercooked. When the waitress came over and asked, "So, how is your fish?" the newcomer said bluntly, "Raw." The waitress, to the newcomer's surprise, stormed off in a huff, obviously taking the criticism personally.

An Italian-American from New York moved to the Research Triangle and was invited to a southern home for a party. Upon entering the house and seeing the hostess's very overweight dog, he couldn't help but mention, in a friendly way of course, how "fat" the animal was. The hostess, however, took offense. "Well, what should I have said?" asked the blunt New Yorker, trying to right his wrong. "If you had to say anything," said the hostess, "you should have said, 'My, isn't your dog *well-nourished!*'"

Many Northerners don't go in for so much nonsense. They are very upfront and take pride in their "tell it like it is" attitude. Southerners, however, decorate their speech with niceties to make others feel good and to avoid unpleasantness and ugly behavior. From a very young age, Southerners of all classes are taught to use language to put boundaries on conversation so it stays where it should be: in a defined area of gentility where nobody is made to feel uncomfortable, insulted, or embarrassed.

It is not that Southerners don't recognize that the world and its people are less than perfect, it's that they have been raised with the old adage "If you don't have something nice to say, don't say anything at all." Of course, in a language where everything has to be pleasant, the word "nice" takes on a different meaning. When a Southerner tells you your new couch is "nice," he or she really means that it ain't so great. If a Northerner says the same thing, you know he means it, because if he didn't, he would say something blunt like, "Well, it's not *my* taste, but different strokes for different folks, ya know?"

4. Don't be aggressive and overbearing

Northerners, particularly the urbanites among them, live by the notion that "Those who scream the loudest get the most" or that "You have to grab what you can get out of this world, or somebody else will get it first." Their behavior is aggressive because they have to survive in cities overrun with ambitious, busy people competing for taxis, apartments, promotions, notice of any kind. They tend towards self-promotion, bragging even, which frankly has no place in polite southern society.

A southern woman confronted this problem when she had a party for a newcomer to welcome her to the community. During the party, the guest-of-honor repeatedly drew attention to herself by discussing where she had gone to school, the degree she had earned and her professional accomplishments. This behavior did not endear the newcomer to the Southerners present, and the party, in short, was not a success. The newcomer did not realize that in the South your manners, family name, and family history define you more than your credentials. For some Southerners, mentioning your education in particular is a sore spot, because it implies a certain superiority.

It is fair to say that if the newcomer had been a man, the party might not have turned out to be a bomb. Southerners especially dislike aggressive, self-promoting behavior in women, and many a northern female has found that her manner of speaking was a "little too crisp," as one outsider put it, for the local populace. "If you're an aggressive woman, do not come to Alabama unless you want to change," advised a transplant from California. "You will spend a great deal of time

learning to keep your mouth shut," she warned. It's not that southern women aren't powerful—they just go about getting what they want in subtler ways.

Southerners are known for their self-deprecating, ultra-modest behavior. They would rather appear uneducated and unsuccessful than to assert themselves by saying something like, "I'm Harvard Business School ... you know, the class with the most CEOs in Harvard history." According to southern writer Sibley Fleming, "In the South ... we march forward by holding back," a trait she says stems from the religious belief that all men are "corrupt" compared to God.

5. Learn how to interpret southern friendliness

Non-Southerners have problems interpreting southern warmth and politeness. They are often initially impressed by it and might remark to their friends up north how nice and welcoming Southerners are. Many female newcomers in particular, probably because they place greater importance on making friends in their new home, find themselves dismayed or hurt a month or so into their stay because they realize that southern warmth does not guarantee instant intimacy or lasting relationships. Many female newcomers end up bitterly remarking to their friends at home how southern women are a bunch of two-faced phoneys who say meaningless things and make empty promises.

Cultural misunderstandings like these come about because Southerners and Northerners have different ideas about how to treat strangers. Southerners, you see, are friendly *on the surface* to everybody, while Northerners reserve their friendliness for their trusted friends. Ann Barrett Batson, the author of *Having It Y'all*, says that Southerners "smile especially kindly" to their enemies, treat strangers "as if [they've] known them since [they] were born," and "if the passerby is friend, family, or even mere acquaintance, the encounter should become a reunion of sorts" ending with a "fond farewell, such as 'Now, you tell your sweet mama I said hello.'" Northerners, on the other hand, treat their enemies with disdain, ignore strangers completely, and upon running across a friend in an unlikely place, say a quick "How goes it?" followed by a mere "Take care."

When an outsider moves into a primarily southern neighborhood, he or she often receives visits from a few families on the block who ring the doorbell with homemade cookies in hand, stop to chat for awhile, and leave by saying, "Y'all come see us!" In such a situation, the non-southern newcomer is likely to interpret her neighbors' actions to mean that she has already been accepted into the group and is free to stop by whenever she likes. That is absolutely untrue. Southerners dislike unplanned visits from strangers as much as everybody else; they expect such liberties to be taken by only their closest friends and family. It is important for newcomers to realize that friendships in the South take just as long to develop and solidify as they do everywhere—they just appear to start more quickly.

The same care should be taken by outsiders when it comes to assessing romantic intentions in the South. Many a northern man has moved to the Southland only to find himself thrilled by the attention given him by southern women. Up north, he thinks, women flirt either not at all or only if they have the hots for you, so these southern girls must all find me charming and attractive. Not so. Flirting is another type of friendliness used by southern women and girls for members of the opposite sex. It's a natural form of casual banter and implies nothing as exciting as the Northerner imagines. As Florence King said so humorously in *Southern Ladies and Gentleman*:

> Southern women flirt so automatically that half the time they don't realize they are doing it. Batting your lashes is a Pavlovian reaction as soon as you say word one to any man, and so is that rapt gaze called 'hanging on to his every word.' In the South, it's all a game and everyone plays it. …"

Southerners understand the rules of the game, but Northerners, being so literal and so *un*versed in the art of indirect expression, usually do not. The northern man who learns to play along in the spirit in which southern flirting is intended will no doubt save himself great embarrassment.

6. Don't make comments about the southern accent

Children who move south from other regions sometimes make inappropriate comments such as, "The people here sure talk funny," while their mothers are standing in a crowd of Southerners. It is easy to forgive children for speaking their minds, but what about all those adult newcomers who also err in this area? Outsiders often have trouble understanding the southern accent, and unfortunately some of them criticize the speaker to his face. "The people here don't speak English," newcomers mutter, or "People here speak so slowly it takes them two minutes just to say hello."

Some completely insensitive newcomers mimic the southern accent to amuse their friends or mock a native who has just said something that made him angry. Big no-nos, these. Some non-Southerners, on the other hand, find the accent beautiful and easy on the ear and then, being so direct, they say, "Wait, I like the way you said that. Could you do that again for me?"

All such notice of southern speech is considered rude, even if it is intended to be complimentary. It makes Southerners self-conscious and at the very least stops the flow of conversation. These days especially, when television and its accent-free newscasters and actors have begun to influence the speech patterns of southern youth, the accent is, for many, another source of southern pride. Most newcomers get used to the accent over time and even find themselves picking it up, unconsciously or otherwise. If they don't (or won't), then their children certainly will.

7. Don't comment when Southerners don't fit the stereotype

A southern writer, Sue Monk Kidd (who related this true tale in an article for the *Atlanta Journal-Constitution*), sat next to a northern man on an airplane. He, thinking she was a typical adoring southern wife and hence a good audience for his anti-feminist views, spouted off about how women in the North don't know how to take care of their men. When she proclaimed herself a southern feminist he said, "I thought southern feminist was an oxymoron." Another outsider, a black woman, was surprised when a group of white Southerners stopped to help her when her husband got suddenly ill on a small Georgia road. She commented that she didn't think they would stop because she was black.

Outsiders who come to the South thinking they already know Southerners—in all their manifestations—are likely to be surprised when they find them to be as varied as other people. It is fine and dandy to notice this, even to delight in it, but it is not fine to announce your surprise to the Southerner in question. In other words, don't say, "You're not as southern as I thought you were" or "You don't act southern." (Conversely, it is equally unwise to make remarks when a Southerner *is* acting particularly southern, for example "All you people have good manners around here.") It not only makes the Southerner feel uneasy, as if he's been pegged, it makes the newcomer look ignorant and narrow-minded.

TRUE ACCEPTANCE?

Even if I avoid the social indiscretions outlined above, the newcomer might wonder, will I ever lose my otherness? In certain areas of the South, old communities like Charleston, Savannah, New Orleans, and Mobile, outsiders are forever outsiders, even if they're from the next town or another southern state. One woman who was born in Kentucky but who has lived in Mobile, Alabama, for close to 40 years says that her close Mobilean friends *still* say things to her like, "Well, you wouldn't understand, not being from around here" to distinguish her from the group.

A New Orleans native explained that old New Orleans society is "closed to Northerners and outsiders because people here are put off by them. It is okay for an outsider to be a spectator, but not a participant." The native went on to say that she knew of only one new family that had got into the upper echelons, and that was because the couple came from prominent northeastern families, were wealthy, well-educated, and well-mannered, and most importantly, were taken under the wing of a prominent New Orleans woman who introduced them to all her close friends.

Yankees and other non-Southerners, therefore, are probably always going to be different, no matter how much they change their "Yankeefied" ways, as a transplant to Birmingham put it. However, those who truly want to fit in and who have the adaptability, personality, patience, and sensitivity to do so (and don't mind *not* being accepted by the oldest and most prominent southern families) will be welcomed into the fold in time.

— Chapter Four —

MANNERS, DRESS, AND ENTERTAINING IN THE SOUTH

Good manners are what make Southerners different (a euphemism for "better") from those who Aren't From Here, a distinction of which Southerners are *very* aware and *very* proud. You simply can't take good manners too seriously Down South. While an occasional trifling with the law of southern manners can be tolerated (but not excused), those who blatantly defy it will soon find themselves about as warmly received as secular humanists or carpetbaggers. After all, we Southerners wrote the bible on good manners and believe in practicing what we preach.

—Ann Barrett Batson in *Having It Y'all*

When you are in the southern region, even if it is for a short amount of time, you get a strong sense that Southerners subscribe to a code of behavior that has certain defined rules. There is form and structure to entertaining, dressing, and social behavior. Ritual is revered, ceremony and pageantry persist, and "shoulds" and "shouldn'ts" are important topics of discussion. Good manners at the table, in church, and at school are expected by Southerners of all races and social classes, although the rules may be especially elaborate among members of the upper classes.

If you are not southern, this realization might make you uneasy. At home, you think, nobody but my grandmother makes a fuss if she doesn't receive a thank-you note after sending a gift, if the children leave the table without asking to be excused, if the bridesmaids wore black satin to my cousin's afternoon wedding. Outside the Southland, you wouldn't necessarily judge someone by his behavior at the dinner table. If he slurped his soup or didn't thank the host and hostess for a delicious meal, you might notice (and you might disapprove), but you wouldn't think it had bearing on his true character.

In the South, people believe that there is a relationship between exterior forms of behavior (manners) and interior beliefs (morals). According to the *Encyclopedia of Southern Culture*, "… in the South, moral codes, laws, and manners have been intertwined, with the aim of curbing individual aggressiveness and maintaining social order through a combination of external community pressures and internalized motivation."

Manners also reflect on your family name and family history. When someone slurps at the table or transgresses the code of manners in other ways, the Southerners at the table would *never* say anything, but they might think to themselves, "I wonder who brought *him* up?" Outside the region, people are often judged by their job title or by how much money they have. In the South, especially among old southern families, behavior and family name are considered before economic and employment status.

In this chapter, we will discuss how Southerners do things—how they act, how they give parties, what they wear—and how such customs came to be so important to them.

MANNERS IN A HISTORICAL CONTEXT

Why is it that the South followed and maintained this code of etiquette and behavior when much of the rest of the country either never did or abandoned it a generation ago? The wealthy planters in the colonial South were of English origin and therefore followed rigid English customs regarding proper behavior. Some planters were of aristocratic birth (and more aspired to be) and, seeking to identify and separate themselves from other settlers and slaves, behaved as they thought proper noblemen and noblewomen should. Much of the northeastern region of the country was settled by Puritans, who were fiercely religious and hard-working, but lived simple, anti-materialistic lives.

The Encyclopedia of Southern Culture tells us that the planters in the Tidewater region exemplified the highest standards of behavior, while the frontier settlers and planters of lower status were less adherent to the code. In colonial days, planters and their ladies aimed to conform to the ideals of chivalry and honor as exemplified in English myth and behavior. Southern men in particular took pride in being able to handle a myriad of situations, both pleasant and unpleasant, in a calm, collected but decisive manner, as true gentlemen should. Women tried to be pure and virtuous, and men sought to protect their women and children at any cost. When insulted, the southern man took to dueling to preserve his honor.

Practically speaking, planters obviously had the time and the wealth to play Gracious Noblemen. They had house slaves, who enabled them to host grand parties complete with silver, crystal, music, silk gowns, and glorious food, and field slaves, whose labor gave them leisure time. The wealthy behaved well and held each other to high standards of behavior because they had the luxury to do so. Also, the communities of the South were (and in many instances, still are) small enough so that bad behavior would be noticed by friends and neighbors who, in turn, would spread the word to their friends and neighbors.

According to one theory, the code of behavior (and only some of the silver and crystal) persisted after the Civil War because it was the only structure left after the region was devastated physically and economically by the Union soldiers. A previously wealthy family that found itself destitute after the war could always fall back on manners and proper upbringing as a source of pride and identity.

During the century and a third between the war and the present day, many southern communities remained isolated and relatively unchanged. The pace in southern towns was slow, people stayed in the community to raise their families, and citizens had the time to be nice to each other. Good behavior toward others has also been linked with southern religious devotion. In other words, Southerners take the Bible's direction to love thy neighbor and to do unto others seriously (although serious contradictions in this theory arise when relations between races are considered). In addition, the teaching and practice of good manners continued to be an important tradition in the South because good manners could be put to use. Southerners, remember, love and have always loved to party.

MANNERS AND RACE

In the South, manners and correct behavior were used by some to keep the races separate. White people often demanded respect and deferential treatment from blacks; this behavior kept whites in a superior position, took the edge off the essential brutality of the relationship, and for the most part, kept violence and chaos at bay. Blacks valued manners between themselves as well; many slaves came from African cultures in which manners, especially respect for elders, was an essential element of everyday life.

In many instances, blacks complied with demands for submission to whites in order to survive. In both antebellum and post-Civil War periods, blacks bowed and scraped and yes-ma'amed and no-ma'amed whites to avoid economic hardship and physical harm to themselves and their families in a white-dominated society. Of course, the behavior blacks were forced to adopt was only a mask and did not reflect their true feelings.

The degrading position blacks were obliged to take lasted well into the 20th century. Up until the later stages of the Civil Rights Movement, according to the *Encyclopedia*, the rules regarding black behavior toward whites were still rigid.

> Blacks should address all whites with respect, should not crowd whites on sidewalks, should enter the home of a white person through the back door, should sit at the back of the bus, and should stand or wait at the end of a line for service until all whites had been served.

Whites, on the other hand, were not required to use respectful titles such as Mr. and Mrs. for blacks, but called them by their first names (or even "Boy" or "Uncle"). In addition, they did not shake their hands when greeting them or sit at a table to eat together.

Many whites in the South, however, were taught to treat the blacks who worked for them with love and respect. Often you will hear a white Southerner say that blacks in the South have always been treated better than blacks up North. Statements like these often refer to personal employer/employee relationships in which blacks had or have essential roles as laborers within a household or family business.

In his *Civilities and Civil Rights*, a history of the Civil Rights Movement in Greensboro, North Carolina, author William Chafe discusses the community's code of civility and its effect on social change. According to Chafe, whites in Greensboro had long used rules of etiquette to maintain the paternalistic status quo, to keep blacks "in their place." The white commitment to civility, which Chafe defines as "courtesy, concern about an associate's family, children, and health, a personal grace that smooths contact with strangers and obscures conflict with foes," made "good manners more important than substantial action."

Regarding black behavior, Chafe asserts that "blacks know well the meaning of civility. As much as any group, they have given meaning to the ethic of hospitality. No people are more generous to victims of misfortune, none more open toward strangers." But blacks also were unaccustomed to and afraid of causing trouble during that period, and therefore used great caution in claiming their constitutional rights. Undoubtedly, Chafe implies, if the code of civility in the South had been less powerful, changes in the community would have occurred sooner.

THE MANNERS MAVENS

As mentioned in the previous chapter, the code of etiquette in the South is primarily designed to make people feel good, to keep discourse on a pleasant path, and to keep discomfort and disagreeable conversation at bay. Southerners will go out of their way, or even stretch the truth, to prevent another's feelings from being hurt. Similarly, like the Japanese, Southerners prefer to say "yes" rather than "no" when asked for a favor (even if they are unable to oblige) because "yes" fosters goodwill and "no" closes the conversation. In the South, rules are valued because they help everyone know what is expected of them and avoid hurt feelings.

The southern code of manners is embodied in the woman of the household, and it is she who is responsible for teaching it to the children (with reinforcement from fathers, aunts, grandmothers, housekeepers, and elders of all kinds, of course). According to the Southern Life Poll done in 1993 by the *Atlanta Journal- Constitution* and the University of North Carolina, black Southerners in particular are strong adherents to the code of manners taught by their elders. Based on a pool of approximately 1,500 people (1,000 of them Southerners), the pollsters found that a higher percentage of black Southerners were taught to use "sir," "ma'am," "Mr.," and "Mrs." when speaking to adults than white Southerners were, although both groups were considerably more polite than non-Southerners.

Southern mothers do not use a book on etiquette, nor does she need to enroll in a course; she knows what to do because her mother taught her, as her grandmother taught her mother, and so on. Southern mothers begin teaching manners to their children as soon as the little ones are old enough to understand. As a mother from New Orleans said, "I began to teach my son about using a spoon the right way when he was sitting in the high chair eating his grits in the morning."

SOME SPECIFICS

If you are completely unfamiliar with Western rules of etiquette, as a newcomer, you ought to read a classic text on manners to set the framework for your own education. (Books by Judith Martin a.k.a. "Miss Manners," Letitia Baldrige, and Marjabelle Young Stewart are all recommended.)

In general, southern rules of etiquette are really just old-fashioned, formal good manners, the kind some of our parents and grandparents used to live by but which, these days, have fallen out of use in other regions of the country. For those of us who have a general knowledge of good manners, but did not have the benefit of a southern upbringing, here are a few specific rules that Southerners tend to adopt in the following situations. By the way, if you ever find yourself at a loss as to what to do in the South, one Southerner recommended that you simply do what makes you and the other guests comfortable.

at the table...

- A short prayer giving thanks for the meal is commonly recited before anyone touches his napkin or lifts his fork.
- Nobody starts eating until everybody is properly seated and served, even at a dinner party where the hostess repeatedly urges everyone not to wait.
- In a restaurant or at a family gathering, a man will pull a woman's chair out for her when she approaches the table and, again, when she returns after a ritual nose powdering.
- The man (or men) at the table will stand when a woman enters the room, even when the upright individual urges everyone to stay seated.
- Although southern cooks love to see others enjoy their food, it is not considered polite to eat voraciously and/or to thoroughly clean your plate, nor is it polite to reach for the last pork chop before asking everybody at the table if he would like it.
- Using a toothpick after the meal (men only please!) is considered acceptable, Ann Barrett Batson says in *Having It Y'all*, but toothpickers "should not conduct an overly enthusiastic search-and-destroy mission," while in the process.
- Nobody leaves the table until everybody has finished the meal. At a large gathering in someone's home, it is acceptable for young children to leave the table before a lengthy meal is finished, but only if they ask their parents if they may be excused. Some southern children also ask to be excused from the table when eating a casual meal at home. Upon leaving the table, a well-mannered southern child will sometimes say something like, "Thank you for the good supper, Mama and Daddy." A grown person will also compliment the cook on the meal before taking his leave.
- Drinking alone is not good manners. For instance, if a Southerner is drinking a glass of iced tea during the afternoon and a visitor calls, she will offer her guest a glass; if the guest refuses, the host

will refrain from drinking hers as well. On the other hand, if the host is not drinking and the guest requests a drink, the host will also pour one for herself.

- It is *not* polite to ask your guests to refrain from smoking at the table in your home; nor is it polite to ask a neighboring diner in a restaurant to put out his cigarette. Newcomers to the region say that fewer restaurants have nonsmoking sections in the South than elsewhere and that Southerners tend to get miffed if asked to refrain from spreading their secondary smoke.

in public...

- A southern man will open a door for a woman.
- A southern man will give up his seat for a woman, especially if she is pregnant or elderly.
- A southern man will light the cigarette of a woman and help her with her coat.
- A southern gentleman will allow a woman to step out of the elevator first. One Memphis girl who had gone away to Chicago for college forgot about this rule when she returned home; she found herself standing in the elevator wondering why, when the doors opened, all the men remained motionless and stared at her.
- When walking down a busy street, a southern man will take the position nearest the street, thereby shielding his female companion from wayward traffic and mud-spattering vehicles. He will rush to the side of someone who needs help crossing the street.
- A well-mannered Southerner will not walk down the street eating. Ice-cream cones are acceptable, but not Whoppers eaten out of the paper, or hot dogs, or Chinese take out, or any other main courses.
- Southerners do not like to draw attention to themselves while in public. If a child is bawling or having a tantrum, the parent will quickly remove him or her from the public eye to handle the situation in private. Similarly, people do not argue or bicker in places where they will be overheard.

- When walking down a street in the South, Southerners will nod or say hello to the people who pass, even if they've never laid eyes on them before.

in conversation...

- It is essential in the South to use "ma'am" and "sir" when addressing elders or those in positions of authority. Children in the South use them every day when speaking to their parents, teachers, coaches, or any adults with whom they come in contact. Adult Southerners use them constantly when talking to relatives, employers and employees, clients, and customers.
- Children in the South call their parents' friends Mr. and Mrs. to show respect, while children outside the region tend to use first names or, sometimes, Aunt and Uncle. An elderly female in the South (usually the grand dame type) is sometimes addressed as Miss ("Miz") Helen to show deference and respect, although this designation is not universal and offends some older women. In times past, housekeepers in southern families used to call the children in their care Miss Margaret or Master John; occasionally you still hear this among old-fashioned caregivers.
- Using "please" and "thank you" are absolutely required whenever possible, even for the teeniest courtesy. These words ought to be accompanied by a sincere smile and direct eye-to-eye contact with the other person.
- Cursing of any kind is not done in the South—not to the driver who just cut you off, not when you drop the grocery bag on your toe, nor when you run your pantyhose on the chair seat. Southern women will say all sorts of made-up words (like "Sugar!", "Daggummitt!", and "Dang!") rather than use the real thing. A southern man will never curse in front of a lady, although he will in all-male company.

Writer Maryln Schwartz told a funny story about cursing when she was interviewed for *Southern Living* magazine. An 82-year-old grand southern lady, Miss Maybelle, was watching the Clarence Thomas hearings when a feminist on screen shouted out, "It's time we kicked some ass!" As Schwartz puts it, "Miss Maybelle just about had a heart attack. She said she thought that was trashy and terrible. … And I said, 'Well, Miss Maybelle, what do *you* think women should do?' And she said, 'I think they ought to kick some *fanny*.'"

- It is not good manners to say the word God out loud in the South unless you are in church.
- It is common to give compliments to friends upon first meeting. For example, when a woman meets a friend on the street, she will always find something nice to say like, "Oh, I just love your…" Even when a southern woman meets a friend who has just had her hair done in an *un*becoming way, she will go out of her way to compliment the new hairdo. As one woman who has lived in South Carolina for many years said, "The worse she looks, the more nice things the other woman will say."
- When receiving a compliment, the Southerner will thank the person, but then remove the attention from herself by immediately returning the compliment. Southerners, like many Asians, choose to appear modest and self-deprecating rather than needy for notice and attention.
- Southerners love to talk and prefer long, fanciful explanations to short, curt ones. Even if a speech or conversation has become way too long, a Southerner will appear to listen attentively rather than cut off the speaker in mid-sentence.
- It is not proper to discuss money with others in general conversation. A Southerner will ask only his nearest and dearest how much something costs, while a Northerner or an Asian will not hesitate to ask a casual acquaintance or even a stranger, "If you don't mind my asking, how much did…?" Similarly, Southerners do not flaunt their wealth or allude to it in conversation. Often, you have no idea how much a Southerner is worth even after knowing him

or her for years. A Northerner, however, is likely to give you a summary of his net worth on the first date.

- When two Southerners meet for the first time, it is appropriate to ask about family background, i.e., to say, "Who are you kin to?" This is a good conversation starter in the South (it would be considered nosy or strange elsewhere) because often, after doing a little social geography, two Southerners will find that they are connected in some way.

- Similarly, it is *not* considered rude for Southerners to ask each other, "Which church do you go to?" upon first meeting. This helps them place each other and opens up conversational opportunities. Outside the South, religious affiliations are private matters discussed only between people who know each other well.

- Good manners extend to telephone conversations in the South, even if you are talking to a stranger. A Southerner will often chat with the person first—ask how he is, remark on the weather—and then get down to business with something like, "Would you be kind enough to see if your store carries…?"

at a party…

- As a guest, you should greet your host or hostess immediately upon your arrival. Before you leave even an enormous party you should seek him out again to say thank you. Similarly, a host or hostess should greet each guest individually when he arrives.

- It is not polite to discuss politics at a party, as this topic tends to bring out fierce feelings that can spoil the mood. Specifically, many Southerners would rather not discuss abortion rights, gun control, animal rights, gay and lesbian rights, and environmental concerns while in a festive atmosphere. Discussing race or AIDS is not recommended in social settings either. If you are a Northerner or a Californian, you might be accused of being a liberal—not a compliment in the South—if you bring up such things at a social gathering.

- Good (or at least neutral) topics of conversation at a party include the weather, sports (especially if your host's favorite team is winning), the latest crazy news story, food, and/or general local happenings.
- Southern gatherings often revolve around alcoholic beverages, and guests often get pleasantly intoxicated, but it is not quite the thing to get sloppy drunk. Drink should relax your guests and encourage excellent conversation, not make people reveal all their terrible secrets or get violent or violently ill.
- After a fancy dinner party in New Orleans, the women sometimes remove themselves from the dining area according to the English custom, leaving the men to their cigars and manly talk. (This would probably horrify your typical Northern female.)

when introducing people...

- The introduction should begin by addressing the older person, or the person who commands the most respect, first. For example, if a Southerner was bringing a friend home from college, he or she would start the introduction process with, "Mom, I would like you to meet my friend, Emma," and then go on to say, "Emma, this is my mother."
- Southerners rarely leave people in a room *un*introduced, as this causes awkwardness and inhibits the flow of conversation. If your guests do not know anything about each other, in the South, it is proper to supplement the introduction with a little background about the person, e.g. "Molly, this is my friend, Claire, the one who went to Ole Miss with your cousin Elizabeth."
- It is customary for men to shake hands upon meeting, although women do not always do the same.

when someone is in need...

- A Southerner will consider it his duty to visit a sick friend in the hospital each day of his stay. He or she will go out of his way to prepare food for the spouse left at home and to bring something small (a book, a magazine, a particular food) to the one in bed. At the very least, a Southerner will send a get well card.

- When the patient comes home from the hospital, sometimes a friend or relative will stay with him temporarily until he is back on his feet. Others in the community will stop by the house regularly to check up on him, bringing food and conversation and anything else the sick person needs. Southerners try to help the elderly to remain independent and in their own homes as long as possible.
- If a local family is a victim of a tragedy like a fire, the entire community will respond with food, clothing, household items or, if possible, monetary donations. Local newspapers often provide the names and church affiliation of the victims so people will know where to bring donations. Some churches or schools host pie suppers for the needy; for these events, concerned members of the community bake their best pies to be auctioned off for the benefit of the family.

on the road...

- When waiting at a stoplight, it is not nice to sound your horn the second the light changes from red to green if the car in front of you does not immediately move forward. This happens in the North every day, but in the South, where the pace is slower and everyone is not in a hurry, it is considered bad manners. A woman living in South Carolina says that in Charleston, inattentive drivers are allowed to sit through an entire green light without the person behind them tooting his horn.
- Tailgating, cutting drivers off, speeding, passing on the right, and other acts of aggressive driving are not looked kindly upon by southern drivers or by southern policemen. While in Mississippi recently to research this book, I was pulled over within minutes of my arrival and fined $52 (my first ticket!) for going 70 in a 55-mile-an-hour zone; the highway, I noticed, was swarming with

patrolmen ready to catch other transgressors. In the North and Midwest, the authorities only seem to chase the mad demon drivers going 80 and above.

- Needless to say, screaming curses out the window at other drivers is not a southern habit, but as a southern native said recently, "As newcomers move in and the roads get more crowded, we are starting to see more 'third finger salutes' around here than we used to."

- When lost on the road in the South, it is fine to pull over and ask for help, because Southerners usually go out of their way to aid the disoriented. If you stop in a small southern town to ask directions, you might get to hear a little history of the area, find out who built the house you are looking for, who lived there afterwards and what color it used to be painted.

in a business setting...

- Employers treat employees with respect, and vice versa. Bosses make sure to greet their employees in passing and may even stop in to chat and ask about the family. Employees expect to be thanked for a job well done, and to be spoken to in a courteous way whenever possible.

- Business deals are not done in the blink of an eye in the South because getting down to the nitty gritty takes longer; people expect to talk pleasantries at the beginning of each meeting, and to get to know the other party involved before signing anything.

- If the parties already know each other, they might make a deal with a handshake, and no money will change hands until the job is complete. A person's word is trusted in the South until it proves otherwise.

THE SOCIAL SOUTH

Southerners are a gregarious people and they are constantly planning, attending, or thinking up a reason to meet and/or have a party. As

Charles Kuralt said in his *Southerners: Portrait of a People*, "Recognizing that it certainly isn't true of all of us, I would propose that a Southerner is distinguished by a sense of neighborliness, a garrulous quality, a wish to get together a lot." According to the 1992 Southern Poll by the *Atlanta Journal-Constitution*, hospitality and friendliness were the regional characteristics most highly valued by Southerners of both races.

Anne Firor Scott, author of *The Southern Lady from Pedestal to Politics, 1830–1930*, says that in the old days,

> Visiting was the essence of life. ... in towns even busy men spent some part of the day calling on friends, and in the country visits from family or friends were usually overnight and might—in the case of maiden aunts or widowed parents—stretch on for weeks or months.

In *Womenfolks*, Shirley Abbott talks about the "country hospitality" practiced by her family during her Arkansas youth. Even though invitations were rarely formal, she says that "people just showed up and were always made welcome. ... To stay less than an hour was an insult, and there was always a meal. Nobody ever was let out of a house without the goodbye ritual, which could take up to three hours."

SOUTHERN GET-TOGETHERS

Entertaining comes naturally for Southerners because they grew up in homes in which "having company over" was a regular event, and because they still do it so often. In parts of South Carolina, groups of hosts and hostesses arrange Friday night "Drop-Ins," small parties given in multiple homes on the same night so that guests can flit from house to house, drinking and tasting hors d'oeuvres as they go. Cocktails parties are still very big all over the South, although the small dinner party (for 6–10 guests) is probably the most common form of southern entertaining today, at least within a certain social class. Even though Southerners entertain their guests at clubs and restaurants more than they used to, many still prefer to entertain at home, whether they cook or hire a caterer. The atmosphere at home is more intimate and invites open conversation and relaxed behavior.

Many non-southern Americans freak out if they are required to have a dinner party: they have no experience cooking for a group, setting a pretty table, arranging flowers, or creating a mood in which guests feel comfortable and well-treated. Southerners, though, are easy hosts. They plan their parties so well that much of the food is prepared in advance, thereby allowing them to spend time conversing with their guests. Their tables are beautifully laid (often with heirloom china, silver, and crystal) and they even know the proper positions for the salad fork, the fish knife, the soup spoon, the water glass, and the butter plate. Because they have so much practice, their food is often perfectly prepared. Moreover, they have a knack for keeping a conversation alive and maintaining the festive mood of a party. And they make it *look* so easy.

Here are a few tips from southern hostesses on having a successful dinner party and making your guests feel special:

- Ask guests who you think will enjoy and feel comfortable with each other.
- Find out your guests' food preferences beforehand and plan the menu around them.
- Add little touches to the table to please your guests: handwritten place cards, handwritten menus, napkins arranged in interesting shapes, antique or handcrafted table decorations.
- Create your own flower arrangements using uncommon blooms rather than ordering stiff-looking, expensive ones from the florist.
- Make sure you have more than enough food, so that people leave satisfied; the food needn't be fine, just tasty and well-prepared.
- Arrange the seating so that people will feel comfortable conversing with their neighbors; couples needn't sit together anymore.

- Allow guests (of both sexes) to come into the kitchen and help if they choose to; it makes the event more personal.
- Serve light hors d'oeuvres and drinks first, allow for about 45-60 minutes of chatter, then serve dinner.
- Lay the dishes out on a sideboard or buffet so guests can easily help themselves and return for seconds.
- If the main course is a messy one, provide guests with extra napkins or bring out finger bowls or microwave-heated towels after the meal.
- Consider asking musically talented guests to sing or play their instruments after the meal, advises author Sara Pitzer in *Enjoying the Art of Southern Hospitality*; this might sound silly, but it is sure to please.

As a *guest* at a southern gathering, consider these tips:

- RSVP as soon as possible after receiving an invitation. Nothing is more irksome to a hostess than not knowing how many people will be coming to her event, and nothing is more embarrassing to an invitee than receiving a call from the hostess asking whether or not he or she will be attending.
- When invited to a more casual dinner party, offer to bring a dish with you, although the offer may be declined. If the guest and the hostess are close friends, the offer is likely to be accepted, because the hostess is familiar with the guest's culinary talents. If the guest and the hostess do not know each other well, the guest may be asked to bring something easy, like a bottle of wine or a loaf of bread from a bakery. If the guest is uncertain how to handle this situation, he or she can simply say something like, "I make a nice fruit salad. Let me know if you'd like me to bring it." This approach gives the hostess an out if your dish does not fit into her menu plan, while it also shows a willingness to contribute to the event.

- Do *not* arrive at the party on time or the hostess will not be ready! In the South, dinner parties are usually called for 7:30 p.m., so it is proper to arrive between 7:45 and 8 p.m.; any later and parts of the dinner may be spoiled. (You Midwesterners, known for your to-the-second punctuality, and you Southern Californians and New Yorkers, known for your fashionable, make-an-entrance tardiness, take heed!)

- Bring a bottle of wine, a bunch of flowers, or a small hostess gift (a box of notecards, a jar of homemade preserves, a Christmas ornament for a holiday party) to the event. Many Southerners live by the rule that you should never go to somebody's home empty-handed. The hostess may not use the wine that evening, but she will no doubt enjoy it at a later date; the flowers will immediately go into a vase, which will be displayed for all to see.

- Don't worry if you do not know formal table etiquette; just watch your neighbor out of the corner of your eye and do likewise, or ask. It is better to say, "I am not quite familiar with how things are done. Might you lend a hand?" than to eat off your neighbor's bread plate or use your dessert silverware for the fish course.

- Offer to help the hostess during the party, even though she will often decline the assistance. At a dinner party where help has been hired for the evening, this is unnecessary. However, if the host and hostess are doing everything themselves, it is nice to offer to carry in platters, clear the table, or help get the dessert and coffee set up. In many southern homes, men are not expected to help—except in the mixing of alcoholic beverages or the grilling of meat out-of-doors—but it is always nice for them to offer.

SOCIAL RECIPROCITY

When planning a guest list for a party, a southern host will invite people that he or she feels will mix well, but he will also be aware of whom he owes a dinner to. Southerners, perhaps more than many other social Americans, are conscious of the issue of reciprocity in entertaining and are likely to take the discharging of social obligations seriously.

For example, if someone invites a Southerner to a dinner party, he or she will be sure to invite that person back within a reasonable period of time. Similarly, if the first invitation was for a night at the theater or a fancy dinner party at home, the return invitation will be of equal weight. If the recipient of the invitation cannot afford to take his hosts out or doesn't have the skill or table settings to make a fancy meal for them, he can always write a note expressing his appreciation or offer to cook them a simple but tasty meal.

The reciprocity issue also extends to small favors. For instance, if a Southerner drives your child home from school, you should be sure to return the favor within a reasonable amount of time. Also, if a Southerner agrees to help you with a project around the house, you should make definite plans to help him in return.

Southerners are particularly generous with favors and invitations, but they also expect similar treatment, especially if they have helped or invited you two or three times without reciprocation. Other Americans might go to a great party at someone's house and thoroughly enjoy themselves, but they may not necessarily feel obligated to return the invitation.

SAYING THANK YOU

The non-Southerner who enjoys the hospitality of others without giving a thought to reciprocating probably wouldn't send a thank-you note either. In the South, sending a thank-you note is a must, especially after attending an intimate dinner at someone's home or receiving a gift of any kind. Author Maryln Schwartz advises that thank-you notes should be written as soon as possible after (or during!) the event:

> It's never too soon to write a thank-you note. Some belles take the notes and a pen with them to a party. In the middle

of the evening they go into the ladies' room and write a
thank-you note describing how much they enjoyed the
dinner. ... They then put the note in the mailbox as they
leave. The hostess receives it first thing in the morning.

Southern mothers teach their children to write thank-you notes at
a young age: they stand over them spelling out the words and if
something gets crossed out, they make them start over. Outside the
South, it is unfortunately very common *not* to receive a note after
bringing a gift for a child's party or even after sending a wedding gift.

In the South, thank-you notes are appropriate for nearly every
occasion and, as many a southern hostess has said, you cannot go
wrong by sending one. Everybody likes to receive thank-you notes,
even for the smallest favors, even if the note is not really necessary.
Southerners often have their own stationery printed up for such
correspondence: a card with the name printed in a colorful, casual
script is used for most notes of appreciation, while an off-white, heavy
card with the name printed in formal calligraphic style suits a formal
note. Blank cards with reproductions of famous works of art or
architecture are also appropriate.

The words used to express gratitude should not sound as if they
were written by a computer ("Thank you so much for the nice gift. I
love it and will use it often. I hope to see you soon. Sincerely yours,
Unimaginative Ursula"). As Tyler Norman said in a piece about
thank-you notes written for the *Atlanta Journal-Constitution*, "The
writer has to come up with 10 sentences ... that are clever but not
effusive, flattering but not simpering." (She admits that this is not
easy, especially if you don't know the hostess well.) However, as long
as the writer is polite and sincere and has neat handwriting, Norman
assures us that he'll be asked back.

If a Southerner is a close friend or relative of the host or hostess,
he or she does not need to write a note after a party, but she will
undoubtedly call first thing the next morning to ooh and ahh over the

stunning table decorations and the wonderful food (and, sometimes, to do a postmortem on the other guests' attire or behavior). If a guest is not a particularly close friend of the host and hostess, and the party was small and lovely and the hostess went out of her way to make the guest comfortable, it is appropriate to send a flower arrangement to the house the next day.

It is not necessary to send a thank-you note after a very large gathering at someone's home, but it is still a nice gesture. For these events, it is appropriate to show your appreciation by bringing a bottle of wine or champagne or a bunch of flowers with you to the event. The wine should be wrapped up in nice paper and accompanied by a small card with a simple message and the giver's name(s) so the hostess will know who brought it.

GOOD HOUSEGUESTS

Southerners often treat their houseguests like royalty. The southern host makes sure his guest's room is clean and fresh, that the bathroom is well-stocked with fresh towels, shampoo, and toothpaste. More importantly, he also takes time off from his own activities to tour the visitor around the area, seeing historic sites and eating in favorite local restaurants. "We make special plans to please our guests in the South," said one southern hostess. "We prepare special foods to please them, make sure the house is spotless, and let them know that they are a priority." Elsewhere in the United States, houseguests are often given their own key, a map of the area, and a schedule for public transportation, and expected to make their own way.

If a guest is invited to stay at the home of a Southerner, he will bring a small gift with him when he arrives. An appropriate present might be something from the guest's hometown that is unavailable in the host's area (e.g. a food product or a local craft) or something personal that the guest knows the host loves. When the houseguest leaves, he or she should send another gift or write a personal note thanking the host for the lovely time. It is important to choose a gift that is not too expensive or showy, or the host will feel uncomfortable; something small and personal is usually best.

As a houseguest, it is also essential to offer to do household chores to show your appreciation for the host's hospitality. One southern woman who entertained friends from the Northeast for a week every winter found herself exhausted and angry after each visit because the guests did not know how to behave. Although the hostess went out of her way to plan special events for the visitors and to make them feel at home, they repeatedly took advantage of her hospitality by leaving dirty dishes in the sink, and sitting around chatting while she bustled about making meals and cleaning up.

The guests didn't mean to be negligent, they were simply unaware of the rules. They should have cleaned up after themselves, made their own beds, kept the bathroom neat, bought groceries and cooked a meal or two for their hosts, and sent a nice thank-you gift to show their appreciation.

THE ART OF SOUTHERN ADORNMENT

In the South, appearances are crucial. One doesn't step out of one's house without looking clean, neat and, for many women, fashionably dressed, lipsticked and properly coifed. Just as there is a standard for behavior in the Southland, there is a standard for appearance. The grunge look so popular on the coasts (and some cities in between)— dirty, untrimmed hair, wide, baggy jeans, multiple earring holes, no makeup, clunky shoes—does not do in the South, especially among the upper classes. It's thumbs down there also for hippy dresses, crazy hats, thigh-high boots, leather mini skirts, masculine suits on women, nontraditional suits on men, yellow eyeshadow, purple hair, black nailpolish, and so on.

While the rest of the nation dons jeans for a casual day at the office, t-shirts and sweatpants to school, shorts to church (!), and jogging suits on airplanes, the South still believes in understated suits and ties for work, khakis and button-downs for school, dresses, hats, and suits for church, and nice pants outfits at 35,000 feet.

Small women's boutiques specializing in ballgowns and other formalwear still thrive in many old southern cities. When attending football games at large southern universities, it is proper for girls to wear—sit down for this one—*dresses, pantyhose,* and *high heels*, while their dates wear *coats* and *ties*! Everywhere else, this fall ritual calls for team sweatshirts, jeans, and sneakers.

In a February 1995 article in *Newsweek* entitled "Have We Become a Nation of Slobs?" filled with examples of Americans showing disrespect for the dressy in favor of the comfortable, the South is mentioned mostly as a place where formal codes of dress are still popular. In the South, looking nice goes hand in hand with acting nice. Dress also indicates social class. The man who stands when a lady enters the room must dress for his role as gentleman, and the lady who accepts his graciousness must look like a lady.

95

BEAUTY WORLD

For southern women in particular, looking feminine and being thin and pretty are important. Southern women of a certain class religiously apply makeup every morning, get their nails manicured regularly, have monthly haircuts, and exercise regularly to keep their bodies trim.

Plastic surgery is an option for many teenagers and older women who wish to change the shape of a nose, lip, chin, or chest or to temporarily halt the aging process. Gray or mousy colored hair is colored—usually with tints in the blonde family—and hairspray is applied to maintain that "just done" look.

According to Ann Barrett Batson in *Having It Y'all*, "… life Down South is one continuous beauty pageant. Ladies are expected to always look pretty and fresh as a flower, no matter what the circumstances. … Pity the gal who's spied having a bad hair day. It would have been better for her not to leave the house, because she *will* be talked about—and she *will* be mortified."

The pressure for women to look good in the South is so strong that more than a few southern females end up leaving the region so they do not have to conform to gender standards. One southern woman mentioned in Shirley Abbott's *Womenfolks* said that she left the South because she was "plain" and feared that nobody would ever marry her. "… They make it too hard on their ugly ducklings down there," she said, "particularly the ones that never turn into swans."

Perhaps the concern both for ritual and outward appearance, especially in women, is what makes the South the land of the beauty pageant. As one Auburn University coed said, "At our school, there are pageants for everything. There's Miss Homecoming, Miss Fall Rush, Miss Auburn, Miss Auburn University [not the same as Miss Auburn], Miss Glamorata, and Miss Greek Week. The contestants all have to have good looks and a great body." Even little girls—wait, even baby girls—compete in beauty pageants in the South; so do mothers, and mother/daughter teams.

According to the *Encyclopedia of Southern Culture*, southern women are more likely than others to win national beauty pageants. Author Frank Deford, quoted in the *Encyclopedia*, says that this is so because "the modern southern belle has, of course, long been the Pageant ideal ... so that—even in those years when a Southerner does not win—the likely winner is still probably patterned after that type."

A team of sociologists from the University of Southern Mississippi determined in 1986 that southern contestants are more likely to be successful in beauty contests because the southern states have "strong pageant systems," they "encourage beauty contestants," and "pageant officials, judges, and contestants assume, based on past experience, that southerners will do well."

According to Gerdeen Dyer, writing in the September 9, 1990 edition of the *Atlanta Journal-Constitution*, beauty contest judges tend to crown Southerners more readily because they have "poise," which means "the ability to walk and talk gracefully and to keep your head when you're asked the unanswerable question about love, war, or the ozone. It's the art of dignified survival," the writer says, something southern women, having lived through the Civil War, are more than familiar with.

WHAT TO WEAR WHEN

Although dress varies widely within the southern region, there are some commonalities in apparel among men and women of a certain social class. Southern women tend to avoid wearing the grays, forest greens, taupes, and blacks so prevalent in chilly climates. Floral prints and bright or pastel colors are very popular, especially in the summer months. Fabrics such as cotton, silk, linen, wool crepe, and wool gabardine are preferred because of their lightweight quality.

Dress and suit silhouettes tend to be less structured than those seen in New York, and more feminine and formal than in California. (Women who wear manly suits are often accused of looking "hard.") Outfits with coordinating elements are popular in the South, as are matching accessories. Making sure the various elements of apparel go together is a concern.

Dressing up for many southern women includes a flash of glitz or glitter in the form of fabric decorated with beading, sequins, rhinestones or metallic detailing. The jewelry is often large and always real, and even diamonds are worn these days during the daytime. Southern men are generally neat and conservative dressers, and don't choose to draw attention to their clothing.

The southern hostess often gives her guests direction about what to wear right at the bottom of the invitation. This helps the invitee avoid appearing at an event improperly dressed and, therefore, embarrassed and uncomfortable. If a guest is unsure how to dress, it is fine to call the hostess (or another invitee) to ask about attire.

Here are some general hints on how to dress properly in the South in the following settings.

to a "casual" gathering...

- In the South, "casual" does not mean the same thing as it does elsewhere. In the Midwest, for instance, when you are instructed to dress casual, that means you can wear jeans, t-shirts, sandals, even shorts or sundresses, if the weather permits. In the South, however, "casual" really means "nicely dressed," especially for women. For a casual dinner party at someone's home, southern women wear dresses, or blouses and skirts, and *maybe* nice pants, although some southern women claim that they don't wear pants— ever—when they go out at night. At a casual dinner party in the South, men wear nice pants and sport coats, or nice pants and a sweater. Invitations to casual occasions sometimes say "sport jackets and ties."
- If an invitation says "very, very casual" the event is usually being held outdoors, so the guest can wear jeans or shorts and t-shirts.
- At a very casual Christmas party, some Southerners will wear holiday sweatshirts depicting winter scenes, reindeer, decorated

Christmas trees, or Santa Claus. Some holiday revelers go all out and accessorize with tiny Christmas light earrings (that light up) or necklaces made from tree bulbs. At a merely casual Christmas party, women will wear rich colors like deep red and dark green in keeping with the season.

in a business setting...

- Sorry girls, but pantyhose are often required at the office in the South every day of the year, even in August.
- Southern women tend to wear higher heels so they look taller and more feminine. A Midwestern lawyer transplanted to South Carolina found her female co-workers staring at the comfortable flats she wore every day to work; the day she wore relatively low pumps, everyone made sure to admire them.
- Skirts and jackets or nice dresses tend to be the norm among females in the southern office rather than stiff-looking suits; skirts cut many inches above the knee are not quite proper. Pants are a no-no, especially for female executives.
- Makeup should not be too loud at the office, and hairstyles should be neat and conservative; pearls or matching earring/necklace sets are common.
- For men, it's conservative Brooks Brothers-style gray or navy blue suits with white shirts and quiet ties. Shoes should be polished. In the summer, you'll see a handful of older men (lawyers mostly) wearing traditional lightweight seersucker suits, slicked back hair, saddle oxfords, and maybe even a straw hat. How southern.

on the college campus...

- Pretty and feminine are the standards for coeds on the southern college campus; looking "cute" is a widely held aspiration. That means nice pants, nice shoes, and pretty blouses or nice shirts to class, often accompanied by a nice jacket. If a t-shirt is worn, it is often dressed up with pearls. Khakis and topsiders are the norm for boys.

- As mentioned earlier, for football games, it's nice dresses for girls and khakis, dress shirts, ties, and jackets for boys, especially if you are in a sorority or fraternity. (Adult alumni dress similarly.) After the game, many college kids change into jeans and t-shirts for the fraternity dance party (probably because they don't want to get beer on their clothes when things get out of control).
- Many southern college girls have long, straight, silky blonde hair. As far as hair accessories go, it's large hair bows tied around high, neat ponytails. At Auburn, sometimes these bows are so large that the wearers are called "Bow Heads." Boys in the South, of course, do not wear ponytails.
- The jewelry worn by southern college girls is often finer and more expensive than what your grandfather saved to give your grandmother on their fiftieth wedding anniversary. Large diamond stud earrings, heirloom bracelets, pins and pendants, and cocktail rings with weighty precious stones are absolutely the norm among many girls on southern campuses. Pearls, silver beads, charm bracelets, and luggage tag earrings are all popular.
- Monogrammed items of all sorts—backpacks, necklaces, earrings, towels, sheets, purses—are common.
- Sorority girls and frat boys are required to have a selection of dressy clothes for dances and formals. Many girls have a closetful of prom-style dresses that they share with their friends. Boys have a few good suits that look a lot like Dad's.

at school...
- Many children in the South go to private schools that have their own rules regarding dress. However, children who go to public schools or private schools that do not require uniforms should be dressed neatly. Many mothers do not allow their sons to wear sweatpants to school, and others do not permit t-shirts with writing

on them. In one private school in Mobile, the formal dress code contains such rules as: no shorts shorter than 3 inches above the knee, no crop tops, shirts must be tucked in, no cutoffs, etc.

- Clean, nice jeans (without holes) such as those sold at the Gap and button-down shirts or blouses are getting more popular among southern school children.

- Hair for boys should be trimmed regularly and kept short; single pierced earrings and little tails of hair left long at the back are not appropriate at many southern schools.

- Some southern boys still give their letter jackets (leather-sleeved, snap-front jackets with high school letters earned for athletic prowess sewed on them) to their sweethearts as a symbol of teenage "commitment."

to run errands...

- Southern women of a certain social class even appear at the mall or the grocery store in nice clothing, hair in place, makeup applied, jewelry on. In the South, appearances, even at the Piggly Wiggly, are important.

- In spring, a southern woman might wear shorts and a sweater to do errands, but the shorts will be pleated and pressed, and accompanied by flesh-colored pantyhose (perfectly matched to the wearer's skin tone) and expensive loafers.

- In the fall, a southern woman might wear a skirt, blazer and turtleneck to the grocery store; the preppy look (thanks to Talbot's) is big year round.

for babies and toddlers...

- Little children are often exquisitely adorned in the South, especially for nice occasions. From the time a boy is born to about the age of three, he will be dressed in a one-piece suit (or "one-all") with a large and often hand-stitched collar, for family gatherings, birthday parties, and other important events. Some boys wear velvet kneebreeches, à la Little Lord Fauntleroy. Hair is kept short and neat.

- With baby girls it's dresses with lace and frills, tiny baby shoes, lace stockings, bows or forehead bands, and diaper covers or pantaloons to cover the unsightly disposables. When little girls get bigger, they even wear little slips under their dresses so their diapers or panties don't show. There's no mistaking little girls for little boys in the South.
- Even at the playground in places like New Orleans, Birmingham, and Charleston, some southern mothers have their little sweeties in starched cotton or smocked dresses, bows and diaper covers.
- Monogramming on children's clothing is popular in the South.

in church...

- Black southerners, in particular, dress beautifully for church. At one time, church was one of the few (if not the only) places where blacks could wear nice clothes. Today, the men wear suits and ties, the women wear lovely dresses or fancy suits, often accompanied by tasteful hats, bags and high-heeled shoes. Children are dressed in their best clothes: little girls wear frilly dresses, stockings and party shoes, and little boys wear miniature suits and ties. In white churches, congregants usually wear nice clothes also. In New Orleans, parents dress their children well to go to Catholic mass: navy blazers and khakis with saddle oxfords for boys, pretty dresses and shiny, strappy shoes for girls.
- Easter Sunday is the dressiest day in church; girls and women wear brightly colored springtime dresses, often accompanied by hats.
- Although the matter is under dispute, it is generally assumed that white shoes can only be worn to church (or anywhere) between Easter or Memorial Day (in May) and on Labor Day (in September). The same goes for white handbags.

The Thomas Watkins family of Memphis, elegantly dressed to go to church, circa 1940s. Courtesy of the E. Wilson Collection of the Center for Southern Folklore Archive.

- Sometimes, the term "dress for church" is used in the South in connection with a non-religious event; this simply means that the guest should wear to the occasion what he or she would normally wear to church.

to a fancy occasion...
- When an invitation says "black tie" in the South, it means evening dresses for women and black tuxedos for men. "White tie" signifies evening dresses for women and a certain type of white tuxedo jacket for men. A proper gentleman in the South owns— not rents—his custom-made tuxedo, complete with studs, bow-tie, cummerbund and appropriate dress slippers.

- An elegant morning wedding will call for a "morning suit," a gray coat with a special striped neck piece and black pants. (A morning suit is only required for the male members of the wedding party, and can be easily rented at a formalwear shop.) Male guests at a morning or afternoon affair should wear nice but not formal suits, while women should appear in elegant (but not floor-length) dresses or classy suits.
- Southern women wear evening gowns to charity balls, country club events, debutante parties, and Mardi Gras extravaganzas. Southerners adore designer clothes, but tend to trust the biggest names, e.g. Chanel, Donna Karan, and Ralph Lauren, rather than more experimental designers. Sequins, satin, velvet, and silk are acceptable everywhere in the South, in full-length or shorter styles, but cuts tend to be conservative, i.e., not particularly short, tight, or revealing. In New Orleans, however, evening wear tends to be sexier than elsewhere in the region. As far as accessories go, small, expensive evening bags and very high shoes with skinny heels are appropriate, and sometimes even long formal gloves.
- Only the fanciest evening weddings call for long dresses; most weddings require women to wear nice silk or velvet dresses (depending on the season) or designer suits. Velvet is not appropriate after Valentine's Day. According to many Southerners, it is still inappropriate to wear black (or white, unless you're the bride) to a wedding.
- Debutantes wear all white to be presented.

Chapter Five

SOUTHERN FOOD

Within the South itself, no other form of cultural expression, not even music, is as distinctively characteristic of the region as the spreading of a feast of native food and drink before a gathering of kin and friends. For as long as there has been a South, and people who think of themselves as Southerners, food has been central to the region's image, its personality, and its character."

—John Egerton, *Southern Food, at Home, on the Road, in History*

Southern culture manifests itself strongly in southern cuisine. As the previously hard and fast boundaries between the southern region of the United States and the rest of the country start to soften and even disappear regarding other aspects of culture, food culture remains relatively constant.

Eating southern food can throw the uninitiated into severe culture shock, especially if he or she is from a particularly foreign place (like Japan or Israel or Italy, or even southern California). Many outsiders think that southern food is strange, spicy, icky, unhealthy. A great many southern recipes, for instance, depend on the addition of pork, a food avoided by many other Americans and forbidden to people of the Islamic and Jewish faiths. Outsiders cannot understand how Southerners can eat grits, and all types of strange greens, or why Southerners adore buttermilk with cornbread mushed up in it, or all kinds of things containing slimy okra. Southerners can drink coke all day and iced tea so sweet it makes your teeth ache. And they seem not to have heard that cooking vegetables until they're dead robs them of all fiber and vitamins, or that fried foods are terrible for you and can make you really fat.

Unfortunately, southern food is often misunderstood and severely underrated by non-Southerners. Essentially, it is simple, homestyle cooking—what people in the restaurant business call "comfort food"— with an emphasis on using fresh ingredients and flavoring them to provide zing. (Midwestern food is all of the above, minus the zing, which makes a big difference.) Southern food *is* often fried, that part is true, or simmered for hours with a flavor-rich piece of pork, but that's only because Southerners know that stuff tastes better that way.

Geographically, the southern region is ideally placed to provide the best, freshest ingredients: freshwater fish from abundant streams and rivers; an amazing variety of seafood from the Atlantic Ocean and the Gulf of Mexico; plump, tasty fruits and vegetables produced during the long, hot, humid growing season the region is blessed with. No place but the South has the delectable Louisiana crawfish, the light and refreshing Florida stone crab, the juicy Georgia peach, and the fat, red (and rarely mealy) southern tomato.

JUST TRY IT

Experimenting with southern cuisine (or any strange cuisine, for that matter) can give the newcomer insight into the region's history and way of life. It can help introduce you to a host of new foods to stimulate the palate and it can show that you are eager to cross cultural boundaries. In food-worshipping places like Asia, France, or the South, one of the most effective ways to make friends and to show that you are an open, adventurous person is to try all the new food offered to you, to ask questions about food and to learn to cook it yourself.

If you are lucky enough to be invited to the home of a traditional Southerner for Thanksgiving (where they often serve duck instead of turkey), for Christmas brunch or on New Year's Day (where you'll eat black-eyed peas for good luck in the coming year), you will be enveloped in southern hospitality at its best. You may be pleasantly shocked at the extent of the spread before you, your plate will be heaped with dishes that have family stories attached to them, you will be asked repeatedly if you would like more, and you will likely be made to feel a part of the family. To eat heartily at a southern table is a true entrée into southern culture.

A PASSION FOR FOOD

Most Asians and many Europeans are justifiably food obsessed, and although Americans in general are *not*, southern Americans *are*. Southern novels and memoirs are full of nostalgic descriptions of holiday tables or after-church Sunday "dinners" (which are really midday meals) and their accompanying succulent dishes. Mark Twain wrote about southern food, and Eudora Welty and Reynolds Price continue to. *Southern Living* magazine, with a circulation of two million, is more a collection of recipes than anything else. Southerners have concocted all types of rituals that center around food—family reunions, church suppers, crab and shrimp boils, pig pickings, catfish fries—and they talk about their food often and with a sense of pride.

Southerners treasure their family recipes and are willing to share them, as long as the dish is credited to the first cook who created it. Of course, lots of the best recipes were never written down; they were passed down from grandmother to mother to daughter (or son) by watching and helping out in the kitchen.

MULTICULTURAL CUISINE

Southern cuisine has had many different influences, each one contributing new ingredients, tastes, and cooking methods. The Native Americans of the South taught the early settlers from Europe how to tap maple trees for their sap, how to fish, and how to grow and use corn, a tremendously important ingredient in southern food. The colonists from England, Ireland, and Scotland brought their ingredients and cooking techniques with them when they migrated. In fact, early southern cuisine was really English cuisine with the exception of a few ingredients indigenous to America. The French, who came to Louisiana from both France and Canada, are primarily responsible for fine New Orleans cuisine as well as spicy Cajun cooking.

Most of what people today consider the most distinctively southern ingredients actually came from Africa with the slaves who labored on southern plantations. Every household had its share of black kitchen workers and cooks; their influence on southern cuisine was remarkable, and often went unrecognized. According to John Egerton, Africans were responsible for bringing such ingredients as okra, watermelon, yams, collard greens, and black-eyed peas to the South—each and every one still a favorite with Southerners of all races.

TOO MUCH AND TOO LITTLE

Southern food has been alternately characterized by tremendous abundance and terrible scarcity. During the height of the plantation era, before the Revolutionary War until the Civil War, the South was known for its great feasts and celebrations. Guests were treated like royalty, rich food and its display were meant to impress and delight. It was during this time, Egerton says, that Southerners got their reputation for being fine hosts and hostesses, when what the world calls "southern hospitality" was at its height.

From the Civil War until the early 1930s, most of the South knew want and hunger. The Civil War devastated the economy, which was primarily dependent on agriculture, and left most blacks and many whites without good nutrition for about 50 years. The poor ate mostly corn products and pork, prepared in many different ways, while the financially secure were able to feed their families better from their own gardens and farms. During hard times, the thrifty, creative southern woman, like her counterparts in other rural areas of the country, was able to get the most out of her garden and pantry. She pickled and preserved fruit, vegetables and meats, baked bread regularly and shared with friends and family when she could.

Perhaps Southerners are hospitable and food loving today because they either remember being hungry or have heard stories from their parents and grandparents about not having enough to eat. Southerners still appreciate and value abundance, whether during a family holiday celebration at home, or while eating out. The typical southern portion is huge and people like to eat until they feel satisfied. I don't think most Southerners would relish going to a nouvelle cuisine restaurant that serves pretty food arranged prettily on the plate. They wouldn't think much of paying for skinny little French beans tied up in a neat bundle with a limp green onion or a tiny round of beef filet in a narrow moat of some delicate sauce.

Southerners in fact, more than any other Americans, like to go to all-you-can-eat restaurants where you pay a fixed, low price (like $5.95 or thereabouts) and can visit the groaning buffet as many times as you like. They also go to cafeterias more than other Americans and their region boasts more cafeteria chains than anywhere else in the

Dishing up fried chicken at the local cafeteria.

country. (Some of the chains have thought about expanding into other areas of the country, but have hesitated, realizing that many non-Southerners tend to equate cafeterias with institutions like elementary schools and hospitals.)

After church on Sundays in the South, people flock to places like Luby's, Piccadilly, or Morrison's cafeterias. There, they eat turkey and dressing, black-eyed peas, mashed potatoes with gravy, meatloaf, beef stew, hot biscuits, and any or all of the cafeteria's six vegetable choices that day. For dessert, it's all types of pies, cakes, and cobblers with heavy sweet toppings and whipped cream. The food isn't fussy and pretentious; it's hearty and flavorful and served on a big plate that invites you to start eating. During and after the meal, everybody talks and visits with each other, thereby turning a meal at a so-called institution into a socializing event with fellow churchgoers.

FAST FOOD AND CHAINS

Of course the South has its share of McDonald's, Burger King, and Kentucky Fried Chicken outlets (which don't promote the art of slow, friendly eating), but it also has Krystal, a *southern* fast-food chain out of Chattanooga, Tennessee, with about 250 restaurants throughout the region. (KFC, by the way, was started by Harland Sanders, who was not even a real colonel or a real Southerner, as he was born in Indiana.) If you live in the Midwest you're probably familiar with White Castle, which is a lot like Krystal. They both sell minuscule hamburgers that you can buy by the box for real cheap—something like 43 cents a burger. The difference is that Krystal burgers don't have little holes cut out of them like White Castle burgers (called "sliders") do, and Krystals are seasoned with mustard and onions. Southerners love Krystals so much that they have them airflown when they are in White Castle country. They say that Krystals are as southern as Coke, and that even Elvis loved them.

Many small or medium-sized southern towns are filled with chains like Olive Garden, Shoney's, Bennigan's, T.G.I. Friday's, and

Sizzler, but don't have many small, intimate dining places where you feel the chef is cooking just for you. In the past, the best food in the South was always served at home—people had no money for eating out, so there were few restaurants. It probably still is.

THE WHISTLE STOP CAFE AND OTHERS

If you have come to the South in search of the Whistle Stop Cafe from the Fannie Flagg novel *Fried Green Tomatoes at the Whistle Stop Cafe*, you must know that there is no such place, but there are plenty of southern cafes that come close. The cafe that inspired Flagg to write her story is called the Irondale Cafe and you can find it in a town called Irondale, just outside Birmingham, Alabama. It was founded in the 1930s by Flagg's Aunt Bess and is still a popular place to eat.

Southern cafes in small towns are wonderful places to go to sample true southern homestyle cooking at a reasonable price. Cafes, Flagg tells us in her *Original Whistle Stop Cafe Cookbook*, were usually run by women who needed to make extra money for their families, so they cooked up the same food they made at home, only in bigger portions.

Cafes often open very early and serve filling breakfasts of grits, pancakes, eggs, and bacon and sausages. Their coffee is usually excellent. For lunch, they specialize in old-fashioned hot meals like fried chicken, chicken fried steak, and liver dishes. As usual in the vegetable-loving South, there is often a choice of three or four vegetables to accompany the main course. Cafes even have fried shrimp and fried catfish and hot biscuits made by hand, and all kinds of homemade southern pies. Everything gets washed down with Coke, Dr. Pepper, RC Cola, or iced tea. The portions are usually large, the waitresses friendly, the atmosphere homey, and the cooks fond of frying in bacon drippings.

HOW UNHEALTHY IS SOUTHERN FOOD?

If you ate at a southern cafe or in the home of a great southern cook every day you would probably get very fat. You would be happy, true, but you would be large. Many fat-rich southern dishes were cooked for people who labored in the fields all day. A daily breakfast of buttery grits, eggs, bacon, sausage, and hot biscuits was savored at the table every morning but quickly burned off during the next few hours of hard labor. Lunch was an equally heavy meal of fried chicken or pork, if times were good and such foods were available, with some kind of gravy, slow-cooked beans, three kinds of vegetables, more hot bread, and dessert.

Today of course, we don't work that way, and we have been told that it is unwise to eat that way. Whether it's a matter of pride or taste, many Southerners have been slower than other Americans to change their eating habits—even in the face of all kinds of doctors' warnings, and with the new, government required NUTRITION FACTS staring out at them from every product sold in America today. They still love mashed potatoes with little lakes of butter in the center, gravy (over chicken, tomatoes, even cantaloupe), and fatty cuts of pork.

And a meal wouldn't be southern unless *something* was fried. Frying supposedly became popular in the South during hard times when cuts of meat were below average and far from fresh. Frying was used to hide bad quality and to perk up taste. Catfish is often fried, to disguise faults in appearance and taste, and so is okra, to combat the accompanying slime. Fried green tomatoes are usually dipped in egg and buttermilk, dredged in cornmeal and then dropped in hot oil. Frying agents include various types of shortening, bottled oils, and bacon drippings. The latter, by the way, is so tasty that many Southerners simply cannot give it up. It is used as cooking oil, but it is also poured over things, like cornbread, as a flavor enhancer. (When I was a child, our housekeeper kept an empty mayonnaise jar in the fridge into which she poured off the fat left over after we had bacon. The fat would harden and get all white, and when the jar was full, she would take it home for her own use. She couldn't understand how my mother, who shunned fried foods, could consider throwing it away.)

Southerners love their food to taste the way it did when they were children, and their mothers and grandmothers were cooking. They want it to bring back memories and old times, and it won't if the chicken is lightly seasoned with a salt substitute and broiled, instead of soaked in buttermilk, dredged in flour, and fried; or if the vegetables are steamed, and the cakes made with margarine instead of butter. Eating traditional foods allows Southerners to reaffirm their southern identity and to feel a historical link with their ancestors. As writer Felicia Feaster said in a recent article for the *Atlanta Journal-Constitution*, "… this regional deep-fried decadence … is evidence that the South's never-say-die, rebellious spirit lives today, if only in the stomachs, intestines and arteries of its people."

Many Southerners of course do care very much for nutrition, otherwise they wouldn't look as trim as they do. Many transplants wonder how southern women especially have managed to achieve this miracle. They probably eat carefully and exercise regularly during most of the week, then indulge themselves in gustatory nostalgia on weekends, during holiday time, or at parties.

THE CUISINE OF LOUISIANA

The state of Louisiana is the culinary mecca of the southern region, and New Orleans is its core. The food of Louisiana is often spicier and the dishes more innovative than those found in other southern states (or anywhere in America). This is due to the influence of the French and Spanish colonists who settled in New Orleans in the 18th century and, with the Native Americans and Africans, created what is known as **Creole** cuisine, as well as the French Acadians exiled from Nova Scotia who made their homes west of the city and created what is called **Cajun** cuisine.

Many newcomers find it difficult to keep these two cuisines—and cultures—straight. It might be helpful to think of Creole food as rich, fancy food from the city, and Cajun food as spicy but simple, homestyle food from the country. The city food is made with lots of heavy creams and butter, while the country food is more *southern* because it is made with pork fat. Chef Paul Prudhomme, the most famous Cajun chef, says that Creole and Cajun foods also have much in common. They both make use of the freshest ingredients available, a variety of ground peppers, and what he calls the "holy trinity" of seasonings: onions, celery, and green bell peppers.

Louisiana food relies heavily on fresh seafood, especially shrimp, oysters, and that spectacular freshwater crustacean known as the crawfish. It's okay to call a crawfish a mudbug or a crawdad in Louisiana, but don't say "crayfish" (their real name), because that sounds funny to a native. May and June are the best months to eat fresh crawfish, but they are usually available from November to July. If you have never eaten them before, ask the waitress or waiter how to do it.

I admit that the first time I ordered crawfish at a Cajun restaurant, I was a bit wary. They really do look more like bugs than little lobsters and you have to be able to take the heads off and peel the shell around the tail to get at the meat without getting squeamish. They actually have just a small amount of meat inside them so it takes a whole basketful to fill you up—but their taste is so extraordinary that it is worth working for. After I finished my first portion, I ordered another (and another) and ate until my mouth was red (from both the color of the sauce and the heat of the spice) and neighboring diners began to stare at my tall pile of discarded shells. If you prefer not to labor for your supper, order a traditional soup like Crawfish Bisque.

If you want to cook crawfish at home, you can buy them whole, by the pound, or you can buy the meat already picked from the shell. (Avoid frozen crawfish if you can help it.) It takes from 50 to 100 crawfish to make up a pound of meat. A woman who was transferred to the South for a short period of time lived off the fresh crawfish she could buy on the way home from work at roadside stands. They were fresh, relatively cheap, easy to cook, and something she really couldn't get outside the South.

Dining out in New Orleans is an unforgettable experience—the city has more good restaurants than you can imagine. The really famous ones (and I won't name any names) are surprisingly expensive—like brunch for $35 per person! And some won't even take reservations, so you find yourself getting shuffled from waiting area to waiting area as you get hungrier and more frustrated. The smaller places often found off the beaten track can be just as tasty, less expensive, and friendlier.

If you want to learn more about the cuisine of Louisiana before you go restaurant hopping or try to experiment at home, here are some ingredients, dishes, and terms you should become familiar with:

beignets: hot fried dough triangles or rectangles sprinkled with confectioners' sugar and sold in New Orleans' French Quarter.

bread pudding: New Orleans' most loved dessert made with bread, cream, eggs, and sugar, and sometimes whiskey or other ingredients.

Eggs Hussarde: one of the famous egg dishes served for brunch in New Orleans restaurants; made with poached eggs, hollandaise sauce, ham, tomatoes, and a rich French wine-based broth.

Eggs Sardou: another of the above, made with poached eggs, spinach, artichoke bottoms, anchovies, hollandaise sauce, and ham; oh so rich.

etouffée: the French word for smothering, or cooking food in liquid, in a pot with a tight lid, until tender.

filé powder: made from sassafras leaves; an essential ingredient in any gumbo.

gumbo: an African word meaning okra; a stew made with okra, filé powder, roux (see below), and either chicken, sausage, seafood, or a mixture thereof.

jambalaya: a stew made with rice, tomatoes, onions, and either beef, smoked sausage, chicken, ham, shellfish, or a mixture thereof.

jazz brunch: a New Orleans Sunday restaurant experience characterized by rich food, strong cocktails, and lively music.

king cake: a crown- or oval-shaped cake baked for Mardi Gras and popularly served in schools and offices; a small plastic or china baby is baked inside the cake and the person who finds it inside his piece is responsible for bringing the king cake next year.

mirliton: an unusual green, pear-like vegetable (called "chayote" in the Spanish-speaking world) favored by Louisiana chefs who often hollow them out and stuff them with shrimp.

muffuletta: an Italian hero-like sandwich of Genoa salami, Italian ham, and olives; popular in New Orleans.

New Orleans coffee: very strong, very rich hot beverage made with dark roasted beans and chicory; often served café-au-lait style in large cups with hot milk.

oysters: a Louisiana obsession eaten raw or cooked, used in stuffings or dressings, and even deep fried and eaten on French bread sandwiches (called "oyster loafs").

pain perdu: New Orleans French toast made with old French bread.

poor boy: a large beef and gravy or shrimp sandwich served on French bread.

red beans and rice: a traditional dish served in New Orleans restaurants on Mondays.

remoulade: a sauce made in Louisiana from Creole mustard, chopped celery, and other ingredients and served with shrimp.

roux: flour that has been very slowly browned in oil until it reaches a certain shade; an important ingredient in Cajun dishes that lends taste and texture to the food.

smoked sausage: an essential ingredient in Louisiana cooking; popular types include andouille (say ahn-DOO-ee), Creole, or chaurice.

SOUTHERN COOKBOOKS

In the public library or a good bookstore, the shelves in the Regional American Cooking section are always heavy with southern cookbooks. The book by John Egerton mentioned above is an excellent one for information on the history of the cuisine, and anything by Nathalie Dupree, Edna Lewis, or Paul Prudhomme is worth buying and using. Sarah Belk's *Around the Southern Table* is another excellent choice for southern foods with a healthy or innovative twist.

Some of the oldest and best southern recipes can be found in cookbooks published by southern women's groups like the Junior League, which sells books to raise money for charity, or in community cookbooks compiled by church groups. Old copies of these books make fascinating reading, partly because the recipes are so unscientific ("Heat the oven" and "Add some flour" are common instructions), but also because they provide insight into the past. In many books, for instance, there are several recipes for the same dish, each named for someone else, so as not to wound the pride of any of the worthy lady contributors. The introductory sections of the older books often adopt a dramatic writing style to describe the organization that has worked so hard to do great works for the noble community. Current editions of Junior League or community cookbooks are not nearly as colorful, but they do offer tried and true (and sometimes even healthy) recipes that usually turn out nicely. These make great gifts to your non-southern friends who have no access to such local treasures.

Some southern cookbooks are more fun to read than to use. Fannie Flagg's Whistle Stop cookbook has all kinds of recipes that call for a can of mushroom soup or crushed Saltine crackers, not to mention gobs of shortening and jello, but her writing style is so amusing and comfortable that the book is hard to put down. An even funnier book is Ernest Matthew Mickler's *White Trash Cooking*, which includes recipes for Aunt Donnah's Roast Possum, Butt's Gator Tail, and Fried Squirrel, among others. Under the heading for Southern Fried Chicken is a poem that goes like this: "You take a chicken and ya kill it/And you put it in the skillet/And you fry to a golden brown/That's southern cookin'/And it's might fine." The book has wonderful photographs by the author (the cover shot is of a large, frizzy-haired woman who personifies the meaning of White Trash) and would also make a great gift to your friends back home.

Although southern cookbooks are a lot like other American cookbooks, they sometimes have differences in ingredients and instructions that can confuse the non-Southerner, so here are some guidelines for the adventurous chef:

- In general, southern cookbooks seem to be heavy in the poultry and dessert sections, so turn to them when you are searching for the best chicken and pie recipes to please your guests.
- Recipes are still called "receipts" in some South Carolina cookbooks.
- When a southern recipe calls for "sweet milk," that doesn't mean add sugar to your 2 percent; it means use regular milk as opposed to buttermilk.

- In New Orleans cookbooks, "shallots" are not those very expensive, powerfully flavored members of the onion family, but green onions. Green onions are never called scallions in the South.
- If you see "mayonnaise" on an ingredients list and you are trying to create a true southern salad, you should probably use Miracle Whip Salad Dressing, a sweeter version of true mayo.
- A "toe" of garlic means a clove of garlic.
- "Cooter" refers to red-eared, softshell turtle, a small variety that is legal to hunt and eat.
- In Louisiana cookbooks, when it says "mustard," use a good Creole mustard (like Zatarain's brand); never use American yellow mustard or French Dijon.
- "French dressing" in a New Orleans cookbook means a vinaigrette, not that thick, pinkish stuff Americans seem to love.
- The term "pilau" in a southern cookbook is the same as "pilaf," a rice dish.
- "Dressing," as in what you serve with turkey on Thanksgiving, is usually made with cornbread and cooked outside the bird in the South. "Stuffing," which is cooked in the turkey cavity, is a northern term.

SUPERMARKET SHOCK

Many city dwellers who move South to start new jobs are amazed by the supermarkets in the South. A friend who recently went from a life of hassle and bustle in New York City to the relatively pastoral Louisville, Kentucky, was pleased to find that her nearby supermarket was clean, enormous, and stocked with beautiful fruits and vegetables. The clerks and baggers are always pleasant and helpful, she says, and everyone stops to chat and ask how your day has been.

This can be a little annoying, though, if you're in a hurry, because the employees seem to know everyone in line, and feel it isn't polite if they don't really listen to the person when they've gone and asked them how they are. Perhaps it isn't wise to go to the supermarket (or any store in the South) when you are in a hurry. They aren't generally designed for busy people. The parking lots are large, and the aisles inside are long and numerous and filled with people you know.

One woman who moved from California to Montgomery, Alabama, was furious when a customer who had forgotten an item left her place in line and took almost 15 minutes to return. It turned out that she had seen someone she knew down an aisle and stopped to say hello. The former Californian was fuming when she saw the woman slowly walking back to her place, item in hand, chatting with the friend at her side, but nobody else in line was the least bit fazed, she said. They all would have stopped too.

The two largest supermarket chains in the South have silly names and long histories. There's the Piggly Wiggly, the mere mention of which used to make me crack up as a child, and the Jitney Jungle. The Piggly Wiggly was established in Memphis in 1916, and the Jitney Jungle in Jackson, Mississippi, in the 1920s. The latter store was supposed to be called the Jitney Jingle (jitney meaning nickel) but was referred to incorrectly in an advertisement for the store's opening and the alternate name stuck.

Many of the items in these megamarkets are just like those you'd see anywhere in the country. But there are exceptions. Consider:

- An awfully large amount of space is devoted to food made with **gelatin**. There's all kinds of canned and fresh fruits and vegetables suspended in brightly colored Jello; it's all edible, so don't let it frighten you.

- The **pork** section of the meat department has cuts of pork that you didn't know stores were allowed to sell, much less that people would buy. "It's like having a course in Pig Anatomy 101," said a woman who lived in Vicksburg, Mississippi, for six months in 1993. There are pig parts like snouts and feet and tails and ears, and there are cuts of pork called **streak o' lean** (which is like regular American-style bacon, also called "streaky bacon" in the United Kingdom) and **fatback**, which is cut from the back of the

pig and is used to flavor vegetables. **Salt pork** is salt-cured meat cut from the belly and sides of the pig and **ham hocks** are smoked pieces of the animal's hind leg. You also see packaged **cracklings** (a.k.a. cracklins), which are pieces of fat boiled then fried until they crisp up. **Chitterlings** (a.k.a. chitlins), the small intestines of pigs, are fried and served with hot sauce, vinegar, and chopped onions.

- Similarly, you might see chicken feet in the **poultry** section of the store. Chicken in the South should be especially fresh since most of the country's chicken farms are there.
- The **lard** and **shortening** choices are numerous. The former is rendered from pork fat, and the latter is made from vegetable oil.
- There are lots of **instant** foods like instant grits and instant cornbread mixes. Walk right on by these because they pale in comparison to the real thing, which isn't that tough to make.

- They sell fresh **rabbit** in the meat section. It's cut up and packaged in cellophane just like beef and chicken.
- In the **cornmeal** area, there are two choices: white and yellow. Southerners use the white, while the rest of the nation likes the yellow.
- The **greens** section in the fruit and vegetable area is as mystifying as the same section would be to a foreigner in a Chinese grocery. You'll see kale, collards, turnip greens, dandelion greens, and mustard greens. Get a good southern cookbook and experiment with these—they are very tasty and healthy. The **lettuce** choices are only the most basic, however, especially in small cities and towns: you get plenty of iceberg lettuce, but rarely see romaine or bibb, much less arugula, frisée, or mesclun mix.
- In the baking area, there are unfamiliar types of **flour**. White Lily brand, a soft durum wheat flour with a low gluten content, is considered the best flour for making the lightest cakes and biscuits; cooks who make their own swear by it. Martha White brand is also recommended.
- **Chewing tobacco** and **dry snuff** (used orally) are sold in individual packages near the checkout area just like cigarettes and bubble gum are in other areas of the country.
- In the frozen food case, you'll see a bag of mixed **frozen vegetables** called "Southern Medley." This consists of sugar snap peas, butter beans, field peas, butter peas, black-eyed peas, and turnip greens.
- The section that carries home and garden pesticides is full of all kinds of roach motels and roach bombs that you never heard of. Read labels before spraying.
- After you pay for your groceries in a southern supermarket and the bagger helps you to the car, you are usually expected to give him or her a tip; in other areas of the country, tipping is not allowed, but in many southern supermarkets, it is expected. A dollar is usually the right amount.

123

WHAT'S MISSING

If you're used to going to ethnic grocery stores or fancy food specialty shops for freshly grated Parmigiano-Reggiano cheese, hand-cut Nova Scotia smoked salmon or those delicious bitter Greek olives, you may have to do without when you move South, unless you are relocating to a place like Memphis or New Orleans or Miami, which have an established ethnic presence. If you are Asian or Mexican or from the Middle East, you will no doubt be sorely disappointed with the ethnic food sections of your local southern supermarket. In many towns, these may not even exist; in others, the ingredients on the shelves may only extend to taco shells, soy sauce, and canned Chinese noodles. One woman who often cooked with Italian ricotta cheese in her native New York was unable to find it anywhere in the Louisville, Kentucky, area, nor was she able to find her favorite canned tuna, Bumble Bee brand (white meat only, packed in water—not oil), not an ethnic food item, but an expensive, gourmet tuna.

Restaurants in many of the less crowded towns and cities of the South tend to be all-American. This may be frustrating to the ethnic food lover who used to be able to choose between Vietnamese, Korean, Burmese, Ethiopian, Polish, Indonesian, and Hungarian on any given night when he lived in Chicago, Washington, D.C., or Los Angeles. Even a nice-sized city like Montgomery, Alabama, can only boast of an Italian restaurant chain like the Olive Garden and a few fast food Mexican restaurants. In Vicksburg, Mississippi, Mexican consisted of heat-em-up-in-the-microwave tacos served on china.

Two New Yorkers who recently moved South were devastated to find no Jewish delicatessens to speak of and therefore no hot pastrami sandwiches, crispy kosher dill pickles, chocolate egg creams, or oozy Reuben sandwiches. They found bagels all right, but they were Lender's frozen, an okay substitute if you toast them and load them down with cream cheese. And the pizza in the South, to any average Chicagoan, is not worth eating, even if the kids love it.

In the South, the choices are not really there, not even in Atlanta, according to a restaurateur who moved there five years ago. However, things are bound to get better as many people of different backgrounds continue to relocate to warmer, friendlier climates. And there's always mail order if you really get desperate.

THE BARBECUE WARS

Dinner party conversations have stopped cold and friendships have been temporarily suspended over the topic of barbecue in the South. People from North Carolina swear that their state makes the best, but so do people from South Carolina, Georgia, Tennessee, and Texas. They argue over the kind of meat used, the cooking methods, the best barbecue restaurants, and most often, the sauce. (Chicagoans love to argue about barbecued foods too, but they mean barbecued *ribs*, not traditional southern barbecue.) Before we introduce the different types of barbecue, however, it is important to note that one of the grandest mistakes Northerners make when they move South is to use the word barbecue improperly. In the North, it is common to invite people over "for a barbecue" or to say, "Let's barbecue tonight." What Northerners mean is that they will be using a barbecue *grill* to cook the meat, chicken, fish or vegetables of their choice. Southerners don't *have* barbecues or say they *want to* barbecue—they *eat* barbecue, a specific food, usually pork, that is cooked in a specific way.

There are basically two types of barbecue: wet and dry. Wet barbecue is basted over and over with sauce as it cooks, while dry barbecue is marinated before cooking and brushed with sauce after it's done. In Memphis, dry barbecue is pork shoulder rubbed with dry spices that form a moisture-retaining crust over the meat. The sauce is served on the side and not always dipped into.

In Tennessee and North Carolina, barbecue is made from pork shoulder. In Georgia, it's chicken or pork (and, in small towns, sometimes even goat, possum, or squirrel). The meat is cooked and then either shredded, diced, or cut into slices. The best barbecue is

Making ribs in the barbecue pit of The Original Golden Rule Bar-B-Q, Irondale, Alabama, "The South's Most Famous Bar-B-Q Since 1891."

cooked very slowly, either rotisserie style or over an open pit. (Beware: many barbecue restaurants take short cuts on cooking methods and use phoney-tasting liquid smoke to add a smoky taste.)

The sauce is the crucial flavoring ingredient. In North Carolina it is vinegar-based, in Georgia it is ketchup-based, and in South Carolina it has some mustard in it. Memphis sauces tend to be tangy, while Kansas City sauces are sweeter. The vinegar-based sauces can take some getting used to because they are so sour; one person, upon trying her first southern barbecue, claimed that the meat was wonderful, but that the sauce gave you jaw cramps. Barbecue is generally served like a sandwich, on white bread or buns, and depending where you are, topped with sauce. You will *never* see it served on French bread, or wholewheat bread, or any type of fancy rolls. It is usually accompanied by coleslaw, pickles, and baked beans.

Barbecue is not something most Southerners cook at home, and some southern cookbook authors simply refuse to print recipes for it.

Barbecue is something you go out for, to a community event or more likely to a restaurant where the chef knows exactly what he or she is doing. Most barbecue restaurants are casual to the extreme in appearance, but packed with loving and loyal eaters who are more than willing to sit on benches and eat off paper plates resting on plastic tablecloths to get their favorite food. You are allowed to wear jeans when you go out for barbecue, and getting messy while eating is permitted.

Ask a good southern friend where to go to get the best barbecue (he or she will *probably* tell you) but don't ask people in large groups. You might start something.

GRITS LOVERS ALL

Sociologist John Shelton Reed says that while barbecue divides the South, grits glue it together. Everyone in the South loves grits, and hardly anybody in the North has ever eaten them. According to a recent study, people from New Orleans eat the most grits, followed by people from Birmingham and Montgomery, New York (transplanted Southerners, no doubt), Charleston and Savannah, Charlotte, Jacksonville and Tampa, Shreveport and Jackson.

Grits are actually made from white corn that has been removed from the cob, dried, degerminated (at which point it is called "hominy"), and finally, ground. They are rehydrated by adding water or other liquids and served as a sidedish at breakfast, lunch, and dinner in the South. In the supermarket, you'll see instant grits, quick grits, and regular grits. As mentioned previously, the first type is to be avoided, as it has been precooked and then dehydrated. Quick grits take about 5 minutes to cook, while regular grits take between 20 minutes and 2 hours. Some specialty shops carry fancy whole-ground or stone-ground grits, which also take a long time to cook but are delicious.

Even though grits are wonderful and filling just with butter and salt, Southerners cook them all kinds of ways: in a casserole with cheese, with red-eye gravy (see page 133), topped with shrimp (in

127

Georgia and Charleston), or in a highly seasoned steak, green pepper, and tomato dish (in New Orleans). Leftover grits are hardened in the fridge, sliced, and fried.

Fannie Flagg even claims that grits have all kinds of non-culinary uses: "I personally have used uncooked grits to put out kitchen fires, as emergency kitty litter (for a southern cat), killed fire ants with them, wrapped grits in cheesecloth and put them in my closets to absorb moisture, used them as little mounds of fake snow in Christmas mangers."

Like "barbecue," the proper usage of "grits" is under dispute. Northerners always refer to grits as plural, as in "Grits are yucky because they remind me of oatmeal," but many Southerners consider it to be singular, as in "Grits is my favorite food and I eat it every day."

MORE SOUTHERN STAPLES

Two more foods that are beloved by black and white Southerners alike are collard greens and black-eyed peas. Most non-southern white people have never indulged in these southern delicacies, although many blacks from all regions eat them regularly.

Collards are related to cabbage and kale; they are big green leafy things that grow just about anywhere, and they're cheap and available all year round, which is probably how they got to be so popular in the South. The traditional way to prepare them is to wash them thoroughly and simmer them with a ham hock, a piece of salt pork or slab bacon—for a long, long time—until they are free of vitamins but packed with rich flavor. (Turnip greens are also cooked this way in the South.) The greens like a little dash of hot sauce on them when they're done for extra zing. The green liquid left over after collards are cooked is called pot likker and, in the South, it is elevated to the status of a fine soup and served alongside the greens, the main course, and the freshly baked cornbread. Oh, and don't mind the smell the greens give off while they're cooking (many Northerners find it unbearable); once you've tried them, you'll think they smell as good as they taste.

Black-eyed peas, also known as cowpeas, are actually tender curvy little *beans* that have a dark spot (the so-called "eye") at the center. They come fresh or, more commonly, dried, and are also simmered with a tasty piece of pork. On New Year's Day, Southerners eat collards, which look like green dollar bills and therefore stand for prosperity, and Hoppin' John, a dish made with dried black-eyed peas, fatback, spicy red peppers, onions, and rice, which is supposed to bring good luck in the coming year. Some people say that each pea eaten on January 1st symbolizes one brave southern soldier killed during the Civil War. Some families hide a silver dollar in the peas, and the person who gets the serving with the money is the luckiest one at the table.

SOUTHERN BEVERAGES

If it seems to you that Southerners are always drinking something sweet and carbonated, you are right. They do drink more carbonated soft drinks, especially colas, than other Americans. Maybe it's because sodas cool you off in the southern heat, or because alcoholic beverages are shunned by southern Baptists, or because many of the famous colas were invented in the South and their consumption is a matter of regional pride. Coca-Cola, for example (often called "co-cola" by Southerners), was developed in 1886 in Atlanta, Pepsi in 1896 in North Carolina, and RC Cola in 1933 in Columbus, Georgia.

People in North Carolina have been fond of a locally made cherry-flavored soda called Cheerwine since the early decades of this century, while Kentuckians like Ale-8-One, a ginger ale-type concoction first made in 1926. Jumbo Orange is popular in Tennessee and Hoko Chocolate in Virginia.

The universally loved southern beverage isn't something fizzy, though—it's iced tea, made from real tea bags with lots of ice, served in a tall glass. Many Northerners have a problem with this when they first arrive in the South. When they stop in at the neighbor's house,

129

they get iced tea; it's the only beverage served at the church picnic and it's on the menu at McDonald's and Burger King.

More distressingly, newcomers find that the tea has *already been heavily sweetened* before it gets to them—even at McDonald's and full-service restaurants—even though nobody asked if they wanted sugar. One recent transplant to the South said that the only way around this in restaurants is to ask, politely but firmly, "Is it at all possible to have that tea without any sugar, please?" At someone's home, it is probably best to drink up and get used to it, or ask for a slice of fresh lemon to cut the sugary taste.

The South is associated with many alcoholic beverages, from moonshine to southern-made whiskey to fancy mixed drinks. Southerners feel strongly about their evening cocktail, and many couples set aside a certain time each night to sit, talk, and relax with one before dinner. For grand occasions, Southerners like to drink mint juleps, which are associated with plantation gentlemen who supposedly drank them on the porches of their mansions. They are made with bourbon, sugar, and the juice of fresh mint leaves. In keeping with tradition, they are consumed on the day of the Kentucky Derby.

In New Orleans, brunch at a restaurant is often accompanied by jazz and a Sazerac, a cocktail made with bitters, sugar, and Pernod, a very strong, licorice-flavored French liqueur, or a Ramos gin fizz, a frothy mixture of gin, sugar, egg white, orange flower water, cream, lemon and lime juice, and seltzer. Other mixed drinks are made with Jack Daniels sour mash whiskey, which has been made in the minuscule, dry town of Lynchburg, Tennessee, for more than 130 years, or with a famous Kentucky bourbon whiskey like Jim Beam.

GLOSSARY OF SOUTHERN FOOD TERMS
Dishes, Cooking Techniques, Interesting Information

alligator meat: this delicacy is getting more and more popular in Florida and Louisiana, and even in fancy restaurants in Manhattan.

The best meat comes from alligator farms, although it is legal to hunt the beasts in Florida and Louisiana during the month of September. Southerners prefer the tail to other parts. The meat is cubed, dredged, and fried, or made into a spicy gumbo or soup. Some people say that while alligator looks like pork, it tastes like chicken and frogs' legs; others claim the taste is barely there.

ambrosia: southern dessert made with orange segments, confectioners' sugar, and shredded coconut and chilled for several hours; a must at the Christmas dinner table.

beaten biscuits: biscuits that are especially light due to having been beaten with a rolling pin or mallet after being rolled out; these and all types of biscuits and breads must be served hot to please a Southerner.

benne wafers: thin wafers made with sesame seeds; primarily eaten in South Carolina.

Brunswick stew: a pre-Civil War dish originally made with squirrel meat, onions, and vegetables; today, most cooks substitute rabbit or chicken for the bushy-tailed beast and cook large pots of the stuff with potatoes, beans, tomatoes, corn, okra, and hot spices.

burgoo: a hearty stew made up of a variety of meats and southern vegetables served to large crowds; the signature dish of the Kentucky Derby.

buttermilk: Southerners love to drink buttermilk and they consume much more of it than any other Americans. True buttermilk is simply the sour liquid left over after butter is churned. Today, it is made with a bacteria culture, and it is often surprisingly low in cholesterol. Southerners drink it with cornbread, and use it in biscuit and cake recipes. If you consume it often, you might get what Southerners call "clabber" breath.

catfish: an ugly, whiskered, freshwater fish that is as beloved by Southerners as cornbread. Catfish filets should be dredged in corn-meal and deep-fried and served with, believe it or not, ketchup. It is usually accompanied by hush puppies, french fries, and coleslaw.

cheese straws: toasted cheese-sprinkled pastry sticks served as crunchy snacks at southern parties.

coke: the generic term used in the South for all carbonated soft drinks, not just that famous one from Atlanta.

cornbread: a southern favorite made simply with cornmeal, flour, sugar, baking powder and soda, salt, oil, and buttermilk in a proper black cast iron skillet. Devotees love to crumble it up in a glass of buttermilk and eat it with a spoon.

country ham: a salt-cured, smoked, and aged ham prized by Southerners, and sold *uncooked*. The ham should be washed thoroughly (the outside can be mouldy), sliced, and fried in a skillet before eating. It is usually topped with red-eye gravy (see below).

deviled eggs: hard-boiled eggs (sliced the long way) in which the hard yolk has been removed, whipped up with cream cheese, pickles, and mayo, and replaced in the white part. An absolute must for picnics, deviled eggs are so popular in the South that many households have special china plates with little recessed areas in which to hold them.

Goo-Goo Clusters: a yummy, gooey 80-year-old southern candy tradition from Nashville made with marshmallow, caramel, chocolate, and nuts.

hot sauce: found on tables in restaurants and homes throughout the South and used to liven up mildly flavored foods; the sauce can be prepared commercially (there are zillions of varieties), or made at home with tiny hot red or green peppers and vinegar; jars of sauce are even passed down from generation to generation in southern families.

hush puppies: deep-fried cornmeal batter that is probably the South's most popular main dish companion. Supposedly—although the stories differ—hush puppies got their name in the days when people used to eat by the campfire; when the dog barked, someone would throw him a fried cornmeal ball and say, "Hush, puppy!"

Lane cake: a white or yellow layer cake filled with coconut, dried fruit, and a dash of bourbon, and iced in white cream; named after 19th-century cookbook author Emma Rylander Lane of Alabama.

low country cooking: refers to the spicy cuisine of Georgia's and South Carolina's coastal areas. The best dishes are made with fresh crab, oysters, and shrimp.

Moon Pies: These 77-year-old southern treasures are not really pies, but two large cookies made like a sandwich with marshmallow in the center and then dipped in chocolate. Rural Southerners consume the most Moon Pies, but even people in Japan eat them these days. You're supposed to down them with an RC Cola for a quick meal.

pecan pie: the most famous southern dessert made with the most southern of nuts; sometimes called "Karo Nut Pie," because of the addition of Karo Syrup, a type of corn syrup; great with vanilla ice cream on top.

pimento cheese spread: a southern concoction of cheddar cheese, mayo, onion, and pimento used on sandwiches.

red-eye gravy: made by deglazing a skillet, in which slices of country ham have just been fried, using water or hot coffee (or sometimes even Coke!).

rice: the starch of choice in Louisiana, South Carolina, and Arkansas; red rice, a Savannah favorite, has tomatoes in it; Cajun dirty rice is made with chicken livers; and green rice gets its color from spinach.

rotel dip: a concoction of canned spicy tomatoes, called "Rotel Tomatoes," and melted Velveeta cheese eaten with crackers or chips; commonly found in Arkansas but originating in Texas.

shrimp boil: a box or bag of selected hot spices that you add to boiling water and drop unpeeled shrimp (or whole crab) into; also, a large, casual southern gathering at which you eat the spicy seafood.

smothering: a technique in which meat, chicken, and even vegetables are cooked slowly in anything ranging from a thin sauce to a thick gravy.

sweet potatoes: a much loved southern tuber that ought to be served next to a fancy cut of pork; also baked into pies that are not as sweet as most southern desserts.

Vidalia onions: large, sweet onions from Georgia.

watermelon: as much a southern staple as cornbread or greens, watermelon grown in the South is generally bigger, more flavorful, and less mealy than watermelon grown elsewhere. The watermelon rind is used to make a delicious, tart pickle that is sold commercially.

— *Chapter Six* —

A SOUTHERN LIFETIME

In this chapter, we will review the customs and rites that accompany the important stages and events in the lives of Southerners. Celebrations are sometimes unique to the region, but more often they are American or religious rites performed with a particularly southern flair. These include christenings, childhood birthday parties, summer camp, block parties, cotillion, high school sporting events, fall college football games, tailgating parties, going through sorority or fraternity rush, Freaknik, wedding rituals, joining genealogy clubs, and hunting clubs. Southern rituals reflect a regional love of partying and pageantry, as well as a respect and reverence for God, country, the past, and family traditions.

A SOUTHERN CHILDHOOD

There has been much written—and sometimes romanticized—about southern childhoods: growing up in small towns, going barefoot during the hot summers, eating watermelon, shelling peas, cooling off in streams, and being left unsupervised to run wild with other children (as Scout and Jem do in *To Kill a Mockingbird*). In the past, many southern children grew up in multi-generational homes and engaged mostly in family- and church-oriented activities. (Think of Opie in "The Andy Griffith Show" and the Walton kids as fictional, but partially realistic models, at least for white Southerners.) Both fictional and actual accounts of black southern childhoods describe lives of hardship and occasional family pleasures.

Lena, the central figure in Tina McElroy Ansa's *Baby of the Family,* which takes place in a small town in Georgia a few decades ago, lives with her parents, her brothers, and her grandmother, the matriarch of all matriarchs, who feeds, dresses, comforts, disciplines, and protects her. A rural southern childhood probably still retains some of that past innocence and feeling of safety and self-containment, but today since more than two-thirds of southern children live in metropolitan areas, most grow up in typical American fashion. The major forces in the lives of southern children are their parents, their friends, and the media, though church still remains an important factor.

A New Baby

In southern families, babies are adored and treasured. Before (and sometimes after) a baby is born, the friends and family of the mother-to-be will have a baby shower (or two) for her. The purpose of this ritual is to stock the nursery with all the items the infant needs: layette, bassinet, sheets, towels, washcloths, mobiles, stuffed animals, toys, books, and on and on. Baby showers are usually Girls Only affairs, held in the afternoon, often at lunchtime, with the present-opening as the highlight. Baby showers give invitees the chance to see all the adorable little clothes babies wear and to ooh and ahh and, in the South, say, "Isn't that just precious!?" over and over. The mother-to-be should always acknowledge each gift with a thank-you note, sent out well before the baby is due. (Afterwards, she will be otherwise occupied).

Once a baby is born (with *both* parents in the delivery room, as often is the American custom these days), relatives and friends will descend on the hospital room and the home immediately after the great event to coo over the wrinkled little wonder. Some new mothers hold all-day open houses in the South to show off a new baby; grandmothers do this too if the new grandchild lives out of town but is coming in for a visit. It is appropriate to bring a small gift for the baby at this time, but it is not necessary to do so if you've already given a gift at a shower. Some people in the South bring food to the house, knowing that the new parents will be too frazzled to take care of their own nutritional needs. Although mothers are still primarily responsible for taking care of the baby, some fathers feel strongly about doing their share.

A baby's first real social function is his or her christening. For this religious event, which marks the baby's introduction into the church, the infant will be dressed in his or her finest. In the South, a christening gown is often a treasured garment that has been passed from generation to generation. In some families, it is made of a fine fabric such as batiste or linen, cut so long that the hem touches the ground during the ceremony. As one Birmingham resident born in the Midwest said, "In Ohio, babies are christened in little smocked dresses. Here, those are what you wear to play in the dirt." One southern mother had a dilemma when her son was born because she had to choose between two gorgeous gowns, one worn by her grandmother when she was christened, the other newly purchased by her Italian mother-in-law. She solved the problem by dressing him in the new gown for the trip home from the hospital, an important event to many southern parents, and in the family heirloom for the church ceremony.

In New Orleans, a christening done in a Catholic church usually consists of a short, formal church service followed by a party at home. Only siblings, aunts, uncles, grandparents, and the chosen godmother and godfather of the child are invited to the church, but a sizable group of friends and family will gather afterwards for a large buffet lunch. Godparents are close friends or family members and they needn't be a married couple. Their official duties are to make sure the child receives an adequate Catholic education in the event of the death of the parents. Most godparents, fortunately, only have the job of remembering their godchildren at Christmas, Easter, and birthdays. Dress requirements for christenings in New Orleans are rather formal: "Wear what you would to a daytime wedding," said one mother.

Happy Birthday To You

A significant event in the life of a southern child, especially between the ages of 2 and about 10, is his or her birthday party. Most southern children invite 10 to 15 of their friends, cousins, and classmates for a 90-minute to 2-hour party held at home on a weekend day. During the party, they play traditional party games, sing "Happy Birthday," eat cake and ice cream (and sometimes lunch), and open the birthday gifts. Some children have their parties at indoor playgrounds, children's theaters, or children's museums.

Among some southern families in cities like New Orleans, where celebrations tend to be more elaborate than in other places, children's birthday parties can be grand events, with 20–30 little invitees as well as their parents, all of whom are expected to stay. Often an entertainer such as a clown who makes balloon animals, a magician, a storyteller, a face painter, or a person dressed up like a Disney character is hired to keep the children happy. There is special food for the children, like pizza and sandwiches, as well as salads and other choices for the adults. Some families even hire a bartender to serve the parents. Occasionally, the children come in costumes—an easy feat for children who live in New Orleans and participate annually in Mardi

Gras. If costumes are not required, nice clothes are: party dresses, party shoes, lacy socks, ribbons, and bows for girls, and nice pants and shirts for boys.

Presents for the birthday child are not always opened at children's birthday parties in the South because such activity often creates chaos; the mother cannot possibly keep track of who gave what for thank-you note accuracy, and the child, in the confusion, might blurt out something inappropriate like, "I already have *two* of these!" Gifts needn't be expensive for children's parties (spending $10–15 is about right) and it is fine to ask the mother of the child for a gift idea. Thank-you notes are expected in the South for children's party gifts; if the child is not old enough to hold a pencil, the mother takes charge.

School Years

In upper-middle and upper-class southern families, children are often sent to private schools where the educational pace is rigorous and performance expectations are high. Children are also encouraged to join lots of planned activities focused around school and sports, and to make lots of "play dates," in which they play at the homes of other children. This phenomenon is not particularly southern, but is common among Americans of a particular class, especially among families in which the mother does not work and is available to drive the child to his or her activities. Sometimes, a child will have a lesson or prearranged activity to attend every day after school. On Monday, for example, the child will have swimming lessons, Tuesday, it's piano, Wednesday, tennis, Thursday, play date, Friday, gymnastics, Saturday, soccer practice, and Sunday, Sunday school at church.

Parents within this social and economic class tend to push their children more than others, in the hope that the child will excel and will grow into a well-rounded, knowledgeable individual equipped to compete in society. Many southern children, whatever their social status, participate in activities associated with their church, like youth groups, Sunday school classes, or vacation Bible school. The latter activity, in which children learn Bible stories and Christian music, is usually held during school vacation but in recent years has expanded to nights and weekends.

Many southern children are raised to respect their elders and to defer to authority. As mentioned previously, good manners, saying please and thank you, yes ma'am and yes sir, are absolute requirements among southern children. Disrespectful behavior of any kind is not tolerated, at home or at school. Some schools in the South still allow corporal punishment for children who have misbehaved. (Spanking is currently banned only in Kentucky and Virginia.) According to the National PTA (Parent Teacher Association), the South is called the land of the "heavy hitters," although corporal punishment is only used occasionally. Those who condone the practice say they do so to prevent troubled kids from ending up in juvenile detention centers.

Sometimes, parents of children in southern schools are asked to sign a release form giving the school authority to use corporal punishment if an occasion arises in which the school finds it necessary. Newcomers to the region, especially people from other states, often find this disturbing and unacceptable. One smart mom simply wrote, "Contact me first" on the release form, so she could retain control over the situation if it arose.

The lines between church and state are sometimes blurred in the South within the walls of public and private schools. Each day in the states of Georgia, Virginia, Maryland, Mississippi, Tennessee, and Alabama, school children may have a 60-second moment of "silent meditation" or "silent reflection." Even though children are not required to pray during these times, those who don't bow their heads may be singled out and ridiculed, say some parents who are against school prayer. In some southern schools, prayers or moments of silence are allowed at pep rallies or before football games and graduation ceremonies. Again, this is an issue that often upsets newcomers, non-Christians, or those who are unaccustomed to open expressions of religious faith in a secular environment.

Newcomers to the region often relocate with the notion that education in the South is substandard, at least compared to schools elsewhere. Some newcomers say that the teaching methods in the South are old-fashioned: the teachers, as authority figures, dictate the lecture; the students take down the facts, ask no questions, and regurgitate them on the test.

Others claim that in southern schools there is little discussion about controversial topics, creative children are not offered outlets of expression, and multicultural education is not an option. Some complain that southern schools teach history only from a southern white perspective. One transplant said that her child came home one day saying that her teacher said the South didn't really lose the Civil War, just some major battles.

Although the South has some serious deficiencies within its public education system (so does Los Angeles, Chicago, New York, etc.), incoming parents should hold their judgement until they can assess the situation for themselves. Some newcomers are pleasantly surprised at how good the schools are; others simply opt out of the public school system in favor of private institutions (which tend to be cheaper in southern cities than elsewhere). One parent suggested that newcomers should spend as much time as they can assessing the schools in their area, visiting classrooms, interviewing principals, and talking to neighbors to ensure that their children enroll in the school that best suits their educational goals.

Summertime

During the summer, Southerners take family vacations together, often to escape the heat. Many southern children spend part of their summers away at camp, a particularly American phenomenon for kids from 9 or 10 and up. Some go to expensive camps in the mountains where they stay for 4–8 weeks and ride horses, go water skiing, do crafts, act out plays, sing camp songs, do archery, play volleyball, and go swimming in pools or lakes. Campers live in tents or cabins and sleep on bunk beds; bathrooms are usually more like outhouses, and are located down the hill. Others spend a week or two at YMCA or church camps doing much the same thing. The purpose of camp is really to teach kids about the outdoors and to foster a sense of community. In some southern cities, camp representatives come to schools each winter to give seminars about camp and get children to enroll.

Those children who stay home sometimes go to day camp, summer school, or sports camp or simply spend the summer playing with other neighborhood kids. In some neighborhoods, residents organize annual summer "block parties." Streets are blocked off, events, entertainment, and games planned, and cookouts organized. Tables are set up and the whole neighborhood comes out to enjoy the festivities. In the South, somebody usually roasts a pig or makes barbecue for such an event, and families bring homemade fried chicken, cakes, pies, and tubs of ice cream.

May I Have This Dance?

The cotillion, a formal series of dances held for children in sixth, seventh, and eighth grades, is an especially popular activity in the South. While the cotillion used to be exclusively for children of old, established southern families, it is now open in many instances to anyone who wants to go. In the past, you either had to be invited to the cotillion by an organization that sponsored it, or you had to submit an application and two references to join. (Needless to say, blacks and Jews did not apply.) These days, cotillions like the 35-year-old Town and Country Cotillion in Richmond, Virginia, send invitations to children from private and public schools and get hundreds of positive responses. Anyone who is interested in joining may call the directors to have their child's name added to the mailing list. In the 1994–95 season, which ran from September through February, the Town and Country Cotillion hosted nine dances for nearly 700 young people. The kids are not forced to attend; they think of cotillion as a party or

Margaret Mayo Williams, Grice Shelton McMullan, Lee Campbell Williams, and James K.M. Newton IV, members of the Town and Country Cotillion, Richmond, Virginia, Kay P. Williams and Nancy Z. Parrish, sponsors. Photo by Nancy-Pace Newton.

social event where they can be with their friends, says co-owner Kay Williams. It's only when the boys get to be in eighth grade, she says, that it gets difficult to sign them up—they'd rather do sports. What's more, the boys are not coerced into asking the girls to dance, an awkward misery for boys that age; the kids are simply matched up randomly.

Each dance in the cotillion season has a particular theme and dress code. On "Cruisin' into the Caribbean" night during the 1993–94 season, for instance, the dress code was "formal," which, the invitation says, means "short dresses, dressy skirts and blouses, and short white gloves" for "ladies" and "dress shirts, ties, dark socks and dress shoes, suits or sport jackets" for "gentlemen." But on "Hoe-Down" night, everybody was instructed to dress informally, and even jeans were allowed. Other themes, like "Halloween Spooks" and "Mexican

143

Fiesta," called for costumes. The fanciest night of the season is always the Christmas "Holly Ball" in which the kids wear their velvets and satins, girls carry "nosegays" or wear wrist corsages for a stylized piece called the "Christmas Figure," and parents and children share a special dance to the tune of "White Christmas."

Cotillion goers need not know how to dance to participate, but during the course of the season, they are instructed in such dances as the waltz, the tango, the two-step, and the jitterbug. Some programs have disco music; others have country and western or rap. The organization also gives instruction in manners, says Williams. "We teach social etiquette: how to behave in a receiving line, how to shake hands, introduce yourselves and look the other person in the eye while doing so. We believe that this helps children build confidence in social situations." The cost for the season is $165, Williams says, not including white gloves, nosegays, or party wear.

High School Highlights

The high school years are glorious times for many southern teenagers. Even though the purpose of going to high school is to gain knowledge, many teenagers see it as a four-year social event that revolves around school clubs and team sports. Cheerleading squad, marching band, pompom squad, football team, basketball team—if you're part of any of these in the South, you're in the thick of it, you're cool.

High school (and college) sports in the South were originally given major importance within the community because Southerners had few (or no) professional teams to root for. Even today, though, high school and college sports are a bigger deal in the South than elsewhere, and the fans are absolutely passionate. On a Friday afternoon before a game, entire high schools will be shut down—*during school hours*—for a pep rally. During this incredibly loud hour or so of cheering, players are put up on stage, cheerleaders give speeches, and coaches introduce that night's starters. On a typical Friday night fall football game, an entire community, babies and senior citizens alike, turn out at the high school field to sit in the bleachers and root for the guys on the field. Many know all the players and coaches by name and number. High school sports stars are treated like heroes as they walk through town.

In the South, if you can't play the sport, it's almost as good to be an official adjunct: a cheerleader or a band member. Cheerleading, in particular, has grown even more popular recently. Southern squads have won almost every national cheerleading competition in recent years at both the high school and college level. Cheerleaders, in case you are Not From Around Here, are responsible for getting the bleacher crowd into the proper go-get-'em spirit during the game. They dress in short skirts and sweaters in the traditional team colors and shout such things as "First and ten, let's do it again!" And, these days, they are gymnasts to boot, turning cartwheels, doing flip-flops, making human pyramids and impressing the crowd with their athletic ability. This new facet of what used to be solely a Pretty Girl thing has led some southern schools to insist on official varsity status for cheerleaders. They often practice daily after school, take gymnastics classes, work out with weights, and go to cheerleading camp during school vacations. And boys do it too, especially at the college level.

Cheerleaders should not be confused with pompom girls. The latter variety dress up in costumes that complement the band uniforms and march to the music, pompom movements synchronized, during halftime. Some schools have flag bearers who also do routines. Band members are usually a tight group of nonathletes who take their supporting roles very seriously. They too practice after school every day, and even in the summer before school starts. The band is led by a drum major or majorette and sometimes, though not as often as in the past, by high-tossing baton twirlers in tight, sequined suits and short boots.

The best bands are often asked to march in parades within the community or to travel to perform elsewhere. For these special occasions, band members may get new, glitzier costumes. When the

McGavock High School band from Nashville, Tennessee, was invited to march in the 1995 Orange Bowl Parade in Miami, the girls wore floorlength gold dresses, gold shoes, and "diamond" earrings. Their hair was done up in French twists, heavily sprayed to keep its shape. "We're the prettiest ones here," one female bandmember was quoted as saying in the *Miami Herald.*

Sobering Facts on Southern Children and Teenagers

According to a monumental study done by the *Atlanta Journal-Constitution* in 1993, which took into account census findings, university-sponsored studies, and various polls, southern children as a whole have it tougher than other American children. Consider the following statistics:

- More than 20% of southern children live below the poverty line— that's more than 3 million out of a total of 14.4 million.
- 45% of black children and 13% of white children live in poverty in the South.
- Southern children are more likely to be born out of wedlock, and to live in single-parent homes in which the parent works, than other American children.
- The divorce rate in the average southern state is higher than in states outside the region.
- More mothers of young and school-age children work in the South than elsewhere in the country.
- One in eight southern kids drops out of high school compared to one in 10 elsewhere in the United States.

The study also found that many southern children have little hope for making a better life for themselves when they grow up and enter the workforce. In addition, southern children, like other Americans, live with fear of violence, drugs, and AIDS.

According to another study of 3,000 Americans outlined in *The Janus Report on Sexual Behavior*, by Samuel S. Janus and Cynthia L. Janus, published in 1993, southern teenagers are more likely to have sex at an earlier age than teenagers from other regions. Sixteen percent of the Southerners questioned reported having sex for the first time between the ages of 11 and 14, compared to 12% in the Northeast, 11% in the West, and 7% in the Midwest; and 65% of Southerners began being sexually active between 15 and 18, compared to 51% in the Midwest and West, and 44% in the Northeast.

Southerners, however, were also more likely to think abortion, adultery, and one-night stands are immoral, according to the study. This rather inconsistent point of view, the authors say, can be attributed to the region's religious devotion: "They have sex and then they feel guilty about it," they said.

The Military Alternative

No, it is not your imagination that the military personnel you hear interviewed on television whenever the United States participates in military activity seem to all have southern accents. After high school, due to a love of country, high unemployment rates, and exorbitant college tuitions, many Southerners elect to join the military rather than pursue a traditional college education or enter the workforce. Despite the closing of military bases and defense department budget cuts, Southerners, especially those from northern Florida, Georgia, Alabama, Arkansas, and the Carolinas, continue to join the armed forces in high numbers.

In the June 1988 edition of *Mother Jones*, Molly Ivins speculates that Southerners join the military because they are fiercely patriotic as well as decidedly macho. "Conventional wisdom holds that the officer corps is still predominantly southern," Ivins reports, "and the ranks are full of working-class and rural southern kids, black and white. 'Has your boy done his service yet?' is a common question in the South. ..." A soldier in uniform walking around in the South garners a good deal of respect from those who pass him on the street; in other regions, the same sight might evoke catcalls from passersby who have little understanding of the southern military tradition.

A passion for the military first became evident in the region during the secessionist movement in the early decades of the 19th century. After World War II, the government built many military bases in the South, and Southerners made up about 50% of the officers who fought in the Korean War. In addition, a greater percentage of Southerners participated in Operation Desert Storm than soldiers from other regions. In 1992, Southerners participating in a Gallup Poll said that military spending was too *low*, an opinion not shared by most of those polled from the West and Northeast. Furthermore, presidential candidates seeking southern votes usually play up their military backgrounds when campaigning in the region.

THE COLLEGE YEARS

Not all southern teenagers go to college after high school graduation, but those who do often elect to stay in the South and attend large southern universities. Many southern kids know which college they will be going to from a very young age; they simply follow in their parents' footsteps. Alumni of southern colleges and universities tend to be very active, lending financial support and attending sporting events and class reunions with their children.

Each of the well-known southern schools has a reputation among students, alums, and other Southerners. Although this information is not hard and fast, it does contain some truth, and is worth knowing about:

University of North Carolina, Chapel Hill: one of the finest state universities in the country; difficult to get into if you are from out of state; students tend to be very bright.

Duke University, Durham, North Carolina: a top-rate private institution filled with non-Southerners, lots of whom are from New Jersey and New York.

University of Mississippi ("Ole Miss"), Oxford, Mississippi: a tradition-drenched, old-fashioned southern school filled with offspring of old southern families; female students are said to be beautiful, nice-talking belles-to-be.

Vanderbilt University, Nashville, Tennessee: a private school with a pretty brainy student body; thought of as one of the best private schools in the South; students come from the Midwest, Texas, and the East, not only the South; liberal arts education; preppy dressers.

Auburn University, Auburn, Alabama: a football-obsessed institution; lots of male and female jocks; girls said to be friendly, healthy-looking; students tend to major in technical areas; most students politically conservative and from Alabama; large Greek system.

University of Alabama ("Alabama"), Tuscaloosa, Alabama: students want to be doctors and lawyers; they dress fancier than the above, but are equally football- and Greek-obsessed.

University of Georgia, Athens, Georgia: another athlete-loving southern public institution; the Bulldogs' team mascot, a slobbering English bulldog named UGA, is so beloved that people gather before the game to dress him in his team jersey; former UGAs are buried at the stadium; rock music big on campus, due to town being the home of famous groups like REM and the Indigo Girls.

University of Virginia ("The University" to Virginians,**"UVA"** to others**), Charlottesville, Virginia**: founded and designed by *Mr.* Jefferson (not Thomas Jefferson); one of the nation's most beautiful campuses; rigorous academic standards.

Tulane University, New Orleans, Louisiana: huge party school; safety issues are a concern to students, given the New Orleans location.

University of Tennessee, Knoxville, Tennessee; the best public school in the state; famous for its "Rocky Top" fight song; very Greek.

Emory University, Atlanta, Georgia: very good school, also popular with New Yorkers and other Northerners; excellent graduate programs.

Clemson University, Clemson, South Carolina: huge, incredibly football-obsessed; known for its tailgate parties.

According to author Ann Barrett Batson, some southern girls chose small, private, all-girls' institutions (like Mary Baldwin, Converse, Hollins, Meredith, Mississippi University for Women, Sophie Newcombe, Queens, Randolph-Macon, St. Mary's, Salem, Agnes Scott, Sweet Briar, and Wesleyan), so they can stay close to home and receive a "quality education in a refined, close-knit environment." When parents want a "quality southern school with kids from quality southern families like ours" (which is code for an "exclusive country club school" attended by "prep school pals"), they choose Centre, Davidson, Duke, Hampden-Sydney, Millsaps, University of the South, Vanderbilt, Wake Forest, Washington and Lee, or William and Mary. State schools have no social stigma, Batson reports, if they are the best in the state, and don't have "ag-tech" (agricultural/technological) in their titles.

While each of these campuses has been integrated since the early 1960s, total black student population is often under 10 percent. It is often difficult for black students to be accepted on white campuses, leading many black high school students in the South to go to black colleges. The greatest concentration of private black colleges is found in Atlanta, where Spelman, Morehouse, Morris Brown, and Clark Atlanta all share the same neighborhood. Two of the oldest private black colleges in the South are Alabama's Tuskegee University (formerly Tuskegee Institute), founded in 1881 with Booker T. Washington as its first principal, and Fisk University, founded in 1866 in Nashville, Tennessee.

Most black students from the South go to public black universities like Tennessee State (in Nashville), Fayetteville State (in Arkansas), Florida A & M (in Tallahassee), Savannah State (in Georgia), South Carolina State (in Orangeburg), and Jackson State (in Mississippi). Recently, the public black universities have started enrolling large numbers of white students. In 1993, out of the country's 105 historically black colleges and universities, 13 percent of the student body was white, but Tennessee State and Fayetteville State were more than 30 percent white.

The South is also famous for its military schools, namely The Citadel and Virginia Military Institute. According to Batson, the military school option is often for the kid who, his parents say, "needs to grow up a little." This phrase is really code for a school "where they'll beat his rump if he misbehaves," Batson explains. In recent years, Southerners have been particularly vocal about their desire to keep The Citadel an all-male institution—a dream gone sour since the court-enforced admittance of Shannon Faulkner in the early 1990s. While driving in Citadel Country, in South Carolina, you might come across a bumper sticker that reads, "Save the Males."

Sorority Sisters and Fraternity Brothers

Social life at many southern schools revolves around sports and the Greek system, exclusive single-sex clubs with Greek names found on college campuses throughout the United States. Some colleges in the South have up to 70% Greek participation, others are under 10%, and some schools have no Greek system at all. The student peace movement in the 1960s and '70s, which led to the abolishment of some sororities and fraternities on college campuses in other regions of the country, did not generally have an effect on organizations in the South. Today, more and more students—both black and white—are joining sororities and fraternities in the South, although blacks stick mostly to black organizations and white to white. According to *The Encyclopedia of Southern Culture*, "The gregariousness, conviviality, and love of ritualistic pomp and hierarchical status usually associated with Southerners may account for the seemingly enduring popularity of Greek organizations in the region."

One's fraternity or sorority can have a major influence on one's college experience: members take their meals in the house dining room (which usually serves food superior to what you can get in the school cafeterias), participate regularly in house activities such as fundraising drives, go to formals and "date parties" with brother or sister organizations, and attend football games together en masse. Moreover, many members live in their fraternity or sorority house during their sophomore, junior, and senior years, and thereby form friendships mainly with other brothers and sisters.

In the South, certain organizations are thought to attract certain kinds of people, although types may differ from school to school. For women, the Kappa Kappa Gamma, Tri Delta, and Chi Omega sororities are said to be for belles-in-training. On the Auburn campus, Kappa Delta is the premiere sorority, filled with girls from the state of Alabama, most of whom are "legacies," i.e., daughters or even granddaughters of former Kappa Deltas. According to Maryln Schwartz in *A Southern Belle Primer,* in some years the competition for a place in these sororities is so tough that some girls will actually spend their freshman year at a school outside the South, join the sorority there, and then transfer to a southern school for the final three years of school. Their sorority affiliation transfers with them.

The rituals associated with joining a Greek organization are numerous. During the fall or winter term of the freshman year, the potential brothers and sisters go through a selection process called "rush." During this period, the sorority and fraternity houses schedule parties (also called "ice-water teas") in which they eyeball all the students who wish to join. Freshmen go from house to house, meeting people and trying to make a good impression. (Schwartz says that at Ole Miss prospective sisters even send baked goods and flowers to the house of their choice in an attempt to influence the members.) Sisters sing songs and put on skits about the sorority. Then, equipped with notes taken at the parties, the members analyze each interested girl or boy to decide if he or she is of their ilk. If a member of your family or a good friend was or is part of that organization, you have a better chance of getting in. During the analysis, members of a sorority say such things as, "Her mother was a Kappa and so was her sister," or "She's very cute and friendly," or "She's from my hometown, and I think she would be an asset to the house." Schwartz says that girls are judged by family position, clothes (should be designer), and parents' net worth, although this is not universal. Many sororities base their selections on personality and friendliness, and even let people from outside the South join. When selections are announced, there are tears of joy or sorrow. In some schools, the disappointed turn to previously designated "rush counselors" to help them deal with rejection.

During the first year of membership, both men and women are required to perform certain functions. Fraternity boys, in particular, are sometimes required to be at the beck and call of older members and to perform crazy stunts for their amusement.

Induction ceremonies often have secret rites associated with them that the new member is instructed not to reveal. Most fraternities and sororities have at least two formals a year, one in the spring and one in the fall, to which you must invite a date. Sometimes these are held at fancy hotels. Less formal parties, called date parties, are regular events, sometimes held at bars or clubs.

After spring break at Auburn University, sorority and fraternity members participate in an event known as House Party in which members go to Panama City for a weekend of partying on the beach. There is drinking associated with each of these rituals, although all colleges attempt to enforce the over-21 law. Drugs, however, appear to be much less popular among southern college students, in fraternities and sororities and in general.

Among members of sororities as well as other women on southern college campuses, there is an emphasis on appearance that is sometimes more pronounced than outside the region. According to one psychological counselor, a Northerner now employed at a large southern university, "I counsel a lot of insecure women, many of whom have low self-worth and worry that they are not pretty enough." Many of the women place boyfriends and social life before academics; they feel that if they can find the right guy, their lives will be set. The mood is reminiscent of that on the American college campus a generation ago. "They are looking for a male to rescue them, to take care of them, like a knight-in-shining-armor. When they get a boyfriend, their problems are over, until the guy breaks up with them. The guys here want to father or nurture the women," said the psychologist. "It's almost like the sixties never came down here. Women have a hard time asserting their rights. The women who do pull away or act aggressively, taking jobs after graduation in another city or going on trips to Europe, find that their boyfriends are frustrated with them," presumably because they are not keeping to their roles.

Football Freaks

When *American Demographics* magazine divided the country into regions based on sports choices, it called the southern region the "Pigskin Cult." In the South, football, especially at the high school and college levels, is akin to religion, players are gods, and coaches (especially the winningiest ones) are heroes. Basketball is also big in the South, especially in North Carolina, but football is king and rivalries between schools are legendary. Alabama and Auburn are probably the South's archest of rivals. Even preschoolers in Alabama are known to ask their fellow carpoolers, "So, who are you for ... Auburn or Alabama?"

Rooting for football teams gives Southerners a tremendous source of regional pride, of course, but some sociologists say that Southerners especially enjoy beating northern teams because it makes up for former losses on southern battlefields a long time ago. As writer Ed Hinton said in 1993, "Our football emotions stem from our stigma as the only American region ever to be thoroughly defeated, devastated, humiliated by war." The late Lewis Grizzard, writing in 1993 in the *Atlanta Journal-Constitution*, said that a South vs. North game is a case of "Us versus Them," that football is a matter of "our way of life against theirs." Since the majority of college football players in the South are black, the sport also cuts across racial boundaries. In other words, southern football is way, way more than just a game.

On an average Saturday game in the South, something like 75,000 or more fans will pack a stadium, although the University of Tennessee games often draw as many as 95,000. In 1993, out of the ten highest attendance records in the United States, six of the schools were southern: Tennessee, Florida, Georgia, Auburn, Alabama, and Clemson. And tickets are *hard* to get. The rituals associated with a Saturday game occupy the entire weekend. Some alumni travel many miles when their team is playing, staying in hotels or campers and getting together with old friends. Fans decorate their cars with team decals and fly flags from their cars and front porches. At the very least, friends gather together and watch games on television. Brides-to-be check team schedules before booking the church for a fall wedding. According to one Alabaman, "If you have your wedding the weekend of an Alabama or Auburn game, the groom is not likely to show up and his father definitely won't be there."

Fraternities, sororities, and alums are often responsible for organizing tailgate picnics before and after the game. These American mini-feasts are held in stadium parking lots; hosts bring homemade dishes, which they serve to their friends and families from the back of their station wagons, vans, recreational vehicles (RVs), even rented stretch limos. Some families use tablecloths, china, and crystal for tailgates and start feasting on gourmet or southern delicacies the Friday night before the game. Truly hospitable tailgaters hire caterers to feed 100 of their closest friends; a few hire bands to play team songs and cheers during the feast.

Some students go out to the stadium early to tailgate or have pre-game parties or picnics on the college or stadium lawn. Then they attend the game, and afterwards gather at the frat house for a more casual dance party. At many southern schools, fraternity and sorority members say dates and nice clothes are required for the game. (If you can't get a date yourself, friends fix you up.) Drinking often sets the tone for the day; people start at the tailgate, smuggle hard liquor into the stadium, and finish the day at the frat house awash in beer.

The support systems that surround college sports in the South are numerous. As in high school sports, there are cheerleaders, bands led by drum majors or majorettes, drill teams, etc., only at the college level, the competition to get into these groups is much tougher and the quality much better. Large southern universities also publish full-fledged magazines about their sports teams. And some southern schools choose what are called sports "hostesses" to represent each team. Hostess wanna-bes go through a tough selection process that includes several interviews by coaches and players. In 1994, at Auburn University, 400 women applied to be baseball hostesses (a.k.a. "Diamond Dolls") for a possible 20 spots. As one woman who was successful in her application said, "You are chosen based on appearance, your personality and how you come across, as well as your knowledge about the sport itself and your loyalty to the school. It's a lot like going through rush."

Freaknik in Atlanta

Many white American college students spend their spring breaks on beaches in Florida, Texas, even in Mexico, but black American college students have started a spring tradition of their own in Atlanta: Freaknik. Established in 1984, Freaknik, formerly known as the Atlanta Black College Spring Break, now draws more than 200,000 black college kids from all over the United States to Atlanta during the third weekend in April. The three-day event is mostly centered around cruising up and down the city's major boulevards in cars with music blasting. When the streets get too clogged to move, students jump out and dance and party in the streets. The city also plans Freaknik events such as concerts and food fests at parks and fairgrounds during the weekend.

Many Atlanta retailers look forward to Freaknik because the visiting students pump cash into local registers. Other Atlantans leave the city or close up shop during Freaknik because they see it as one wild, unruly, and sometimes dangerous event. The purpose of Freaknik—guys meeting girls, girls meeting guys—is not dissimilar from a typical spring break bacchanal on a Florida beach. There's just no sand, no salt water, no bikinis.

Coming Out, Southern Style

During the junior or senior years at college, some southern young ladies make their debuts into society. The debutante season used to herald the arrival of society girls who were now officially available for courting and, hopefully, marriage. Debutante parties, once an English custom, brought all the "right" young people together in the hope that they would marry one of their own kind. Today, the process is still selective, but it is no longer a symbol of availability and does not mark a girl's first exposure to members of the opposite sex. The deb season, which usually starts somewhere between Thanksgiving and the end of January, is still very much in place in cities such as Charleston, Atlanta, Little Rock, Birmingham, Memphis, Durham, Greenville, Columbia, Richmond, Mobile, New Orleans, and Savannah. In some southern cities, girls from prominent black families also "come out," as it is called, but black and white deb parties and seasons

157

are entirely separate. Some new Southerners get together and create their own deb seasons, but in the eyes of the oldest families, these "new money" affairs hardly count.

The debutante season used to come earlier, at age 18 or 19, but it is now planned after a girl's 21st birthday, in keeping with the legal drinking age. Debutantes are often chosen by the members of a prominent organization like an exclusive men's or women's club or, in New Orleans or Mobile, by a select Mardi Gras society. Some deb balls are sponsored by charity organizations that raise money for specific causes. Girls need not be gorgeous, but their parents need to be prominent and to have the wherewithal to afford all the clothes and catering bills it takes to look and host their best at all the season's events.

The highlight of the debutante season is the ball in which the girls are officially presented, all in white, full-length gowns, to an audience of other important Southerners. In Mobile, however, girls are presented in pink, at the Camellia Ball. Well-wishers send pink flower arrangements to complement the dresses, so the hall is filled with spring flowers. In Charleston, debutantes are presented at the famed, ultra-exclusive, and publicity-forbidden St. Cecilia's Society Ball (to which girls from divorced homes are not invited), founded in 1762. In Richmond, it's the German, sponsored by the Commonwealth Club. The men who run this organization handle all of the arrangements for the deb ball and attend in white tie and tails with short white gloves.

In most presentation balls, the names of the girl and her father are announced, then the girl walks by herself onto a spotlit platform or a space before the crowd and curtsies to the master of ceremonies. The first dance is usually reserved for the fathers, but later, debs dance with their escorts, prominent young men of a similar age (who, some say, are often conned into the event by the promise of good drink).

In the bestselling *Midnight in the Garden of Good and Evil*, an entertaining, nonfiction account of Savannah society, author John

Berendt describes a black debutante ball sponsored by the graduate division of the Alpha Phi Alpha fraternity. The women chosen as debutantes by this organization have to be enrolled in college and to be "of good moral character" to be approved. The sponsors also interview people in the community who know the girl and make sure she has a good reputation among members of her church, school, and neighborhood. The Alpha debs go through the same type of presentation as other debs do, but right afterwards they do a dance that they have been doing since the first debs were named in 1945:

> At the end of the presentations, the debs and escorts stood facing each other in two long rows that filled most of the dance floor. The hall was silent for a moment; then the string quartet struck up again. The escorts bowed in unison, and the debutantes curtsied, their gowns sweeping the floor in a foamy surf of white ruffles and lace. The couples then joined hands and moved forward in a graceful promenade, dancing a lilting minuet to the strains of *Don Giovanni*. ... A current of exhilaration coursed throughout the room. Women held their breath, men stared in wonder.

After the presentation ball, the family of the southern deb hosts a party of its own to which it will invite all the other debs, and for which each deb must have another formal dress. Friends and family also host teas, picnics, dinners, cocktail parties, and luncheons for debs. How does a girl going to Ole Miss get home to New Orleans for all the parties she is required to attend? She transfers to a local college like Sophie Newcombe, of course, just for the season, and re-enrolls when her dancing slippers are put away.

In the South, some families spend an enormous amount of money on deb parties and clothing. One Alabaman likened the expense of putting a daughter through a season to taking a second mortgage out on your home. Many debs travel to Atlanta or New York to buy designer dresses. Sometimes girls have their dresses made, choosing patterns that can be altered—sleeves shortened, trim changed—so they can be worn to another ball. According to one New Orleans resident, "It is impossible to get a dressmaker of any calibre here after Thanksgiving, because they are all busy making deb dresses, Mardi Gras ball gowns, or summer wedding dresses."

SOUTHERN WEDDINGS

A southern wedding is, in many respects, very much like any American wedding: there's the church and the bridesmaids and the ornate gown and the groom and the groomsmen and the family stresses and the spats, and the party afterwards. But southern weddings are often more elaborate than the typical wedding, and they have a different feeling to them, especially noticeable if you are a non-southern guest. Southern weddings represent the ultimate in hospitality in a region in which that talent is already in great abundance.

First of all, many southern weddings are not single events that start with a procession at 7 p.m. and end with a thrown bouquet at midnight. Southern wedding celebrations, among certain families, are 2-, 3- or 4-day affairs made up of showers, luncheons, rehearsal dinners, post-nuptial brunches, and more, not to mention that Here Comes the Bride thing. Out-of-town guests can expect to be invited to some or all of these parties, as can members of the wedding party and close friends and relatives.

Some southern brides (and their mothers) feel that their wedding is their real chance to be Queen for a Day and they put all their efforts into making the affair everything they (and their mothers) always dreamed it would be. The plans start being made the second the engagement rock (it better be big) is slipped onto the ring finger of the woman's left hand. In much of the South, the groom steps back from the picture at this stage, leaving the bride and her mother in their element. The groom may be allowed to write up a guest list, but the women are allowed to erase names, schedule showers, look for invitations, have thank-you notes printed up, and book the church, the country club, the caterer, the florist, and the hairdresser. According to author Sharon McKern, in *Redneck Mothers, Good Ol' Girls and Other Southern Belles*, the "ultimate full-scale southern wedding [has] twenty-four attendants, multiple matrons of honor, twin ring-bearers, quintuplet flower girls, and a reception to follow for 750 of the bride's closest friends."

After much deliberation, the bridesmaids are chosen (they can easily number more than 10), and then the search for the dresses begins. Southern brides often choose feminine dresses in pastel colors (and matching hats, if it is a day wedding) for their bridesmaids; Laura Ashley is a popular option. Some southern brides are intensely concerned that everything at the wedding *matches:* in other words, the bridesmaids' dresses must be accessorized with shoes, nail polish, and hair bows. Flowers, table linens, and napkins sometimes have to be figured in, and the exact peach color matched all around. All the girls have their hair done the exact same way and wear the same eyeshadow and lipstick. Some Southerners even claim that the bridesmaids' dresses should match the punch served at the reception.

The bride might choose to wear her mother's gown, or she may buy a costly new dress. Whatever her decision, she will certainly appear in a very feminine, full-length princess gown. Some southern brides break the rules with their bridesmaids, allowing them to appear in dark colors (if it is a night wedding), but rarely do you see a southern bride in anything other than white. Mothers-of-the-bride and mothers-of-the-groom also search long and hard for the right thing to wear.

Wedding Gifts

One or two months before the wedding invitations go out, southern brides (and sometimes grooms), especially those living in urban areas, register for gifts. This American custom entails spending hours at the china, crystal, and silver departments of fancy stores or specialty shops, choosing pieces that you would like to own. The store takes note of your choices and puts them on computer, so guests can order items over the phone and the store can send them out, keeping track of who gave what and how many. This form of technology-based generosity sounds cold and impersonal, but it gets the bride what she wants and saves guests the trouble of choosing something that the bride might have to return.

If a guest is uncertain where a bride and groom are registered, it is fine to ask the bride or her mother for the name of the store. Most brides register for a range of things, from baking trays, towels, sheets, and everyday china, glasses, and flatware to fine china, silver serving pieces, and entire sets of European cookware. Contemporaries of the couple are usually expected to buy the inexpensive items like the baking trays, while the friends of the bride and groom's parents usually take care of the $250 Wedgwood place settings.

Some southern brides are familiar with china and crystal patterns before they register. They not only were trained by their mothers to notice these things, but they grew up surrounded by fine pieces that were used regularly at home. Many a southern home is decorated with family treasures and heirlooms prominently displayed on antique furniture. Unlike many well-to-do brides in other parts of the country, brides in the South also know their silver patterns, and want to own complete settings for at least twelve. Some southern brides choose silver plate for their everyday flatware, and sterling for special occasions. According to Maryln Schwartz, the pattern a bride chooses says a good deal about her personality: "The belle who chooses Francis I (Reed and Barton) is a girl who wants it all. ... It's showy and opulent and so is she," she writes in *A Southern Belle Primer*.

In *Southern Ladies and Gentlemen*, writer Florence King claims that the reason Southerners are so silver-obsessed is because during the Civil War the Yankees specifically went after plantation silver sets: "It was their silver that Southerners took such pains to hide in the well or bury under the smokehouse. ... [Southerners] had to eat with

Wedding gifts on display at the bride's home for visitors to see.

wooden spoons or with their fingers for years, and such an existence hurt the Southerner's fierce pride and his enjoyment of nicety—for generations."

When all those gifts arrive, some southern mothers open the boxes (taking care to keep excellent track of who sent what) and arrange the offerings in a room so guests can come over and view them. In the South, this rite is sometimes called a "sip 'n see," an informal open-house invitation to friends, family, and neighbors to come over, *sip* an iced tea and *see* all the loot. (Some Southerners also follow this custom to show off a new baby or a load of graduation gifts.) Some brides even display the clothing purchased for their trousseau; the viewing of such things—including the undergarments—is called a "trousseau tea," says Schwartz. One woman from Arkansas said that when she received her wedding gifts, her mother removed her own china and such from the china cabinet and arranged the wedding gifts therein; she even made up the bed in the guestroom with the new set of linens for the bridal couple. Schwartz claims that some Southerners even hire professional gift displayers to lay out the loot.

Sip 'n sees often include gifts given to the bride for her shower(s). Often friends of the bride's mother, classmates of the bride, bridesmaids, the groom's mother, or aunts will give the bride a wedding shower. Like a baby shower, a wedding shower is a Girl Thing, and provides another opportunity for a couple to receive all the things they need to set up a household. Wedding showers usually have themes, such as kitchen, lingerie, bathroom, or bar. Sometimes, lingerie showers hosted by the bride's friends will be slightly racy, and she will receive skimpy, lacy items that cause members of the party to shriek and scream upon their opening. By the way, even if you give the bride a nice shower gift, you are still supposed to buy another gift for the wedding itself.

Wedding Festivities

A few days or a day before the wedding, one of the bride's mother's friends or an aunt might host what is known as a bridesmaid's luncheon for the female members of the wedding party as well as the out-of-town guests. The night before the wedding, the groom's parents become hosts for the rehearsal dinner, which usually starts with an actual rehearsal of the wedding processional and recessional, often held at the church, followed by a nice sit-down dinner at a restaurant or club for the wedding party and out-of-town guests. The friends of the groom still host a "stag party" for the groom either one or two nights before the wedding. This event always includes drinking and sometimes a visit to a topless bar (or worse), presumably so the groom can experience one last night of debauchery before he becomes a respectable married person. Brides, as you might imagine, rarely approve of this tasteless American ritual.

By the evening of the wedding, often held on a Saturday night, the mother-of-the-bride has checked and re-checked all the arrangements and appears calm and happy, despite the chaos around her. Somehow, she still has the ability to make her guests feel truly wanted, even though she is undoubtedly under a good deal of stress and is anxious to see everything go off as planned. This ability to make each person feel personally welcome—while managing the arrangements for hundreds of guests—is what makes the southern wedding different.

For a large wedding, the bride and her attendants often get together to dress, apply makeup, and have their hair done. When the limo arrives, the bride and family drive to the church, which has been decorated with flowers. After the guests have been seated by the groom's attendants, the processional begins. It is still common for the bride to forbid the groom to see her on the day of the wedding, until she walks down the aisle.

Many families hire organists or quartets to play music, or a soloist to sing before, during, and after the service. The first members of the wedding party to appear are the flower girls, dressed in miniature versions of the bridesmaids' gowns, followed by the ringbearer, dressed like a small prince. Then come the bridesmaids and some-times the mothers of the bride and groom. Finally, all rise as the bride and her father make their entrance, and make their way to the altar. The service is usually short and sweet, broken up by readings along the themes of love and commitment by selected friends or family of the couple. When the vows have been said, the rings exchanged, and the kiss planted, the bride and groom lead the recessional out of the church. Photographs are often taken at this time, and sometimes the entire event is videotaped. The happy couple then makes its way to the limo, which takes them to the party at the country club or the historic home that has been rented for the evening.

The parties that follow the wedding are distinctly different in one way from wedding parties outside the region. Southern parties tend to be drinking affairs (if the family are not strict Baptists, that is), while elsewhere the emphasis is placed on the food. Some families invite literally hundreds of their friends and family to the party, and often provide only a band, an open bar, and a small selection of hors d'oeuvres, served buffet style or passed by waiters. The flower arrangements are often large, gorgeous, and natural looking, and these days you'll see large carved ice sculptures at some weddings. Guests go through a receiving line, chat at cafe tables, dance, and gather round while the cake is cut and the bouquet thrown, but the party resembles a good dress-up party more than anything else.

In other regions of the country, the bride's family provides a sit-down dinner of several courses served by waiters. Often the main course is a costly meat dish (although chicken has become more and more acceptable.) Non-southern wedding parties are often filled with rituals that take place while the guests are seated; the new couple is introduced to the guests by the band leader and they make an entrance into the dining room accompanied by applause; people stand and make toasts; the photographer comes around and takes a shot of each table, etc. In the South, the toasts are made at the rehearsal dinner, and the photographer takes mostly candids of the guests. In addition, the southern wedding party usually lasts only for a few hours. Parties outside the South go on to at least the wee hours of the morning (although the older folk retire earlier). Perhaps the reason why southern affairs tend to be briefer, less ritualized, and without sub-stantial food is because there are so many *other* events held before the wedding to which many of the guests are invited. If a non-southern couple gave a quick party, with no dinner, the guests might ask themselves, "Is that all? We barely got to congratulate the happy couple before the band members put away their instruments." In the South, guests see each other at so many different pre-wedding celebrations that they don't feel cheated.

Southern families sometimes invite guests to one final event before the deed is done: a brunch the morning after the wedding. If the couple has not yet left for their honeymoon, they make an appearance.

In strict Baptist families in the South, weddings are also quite huge, but liquor is forbidden and dancing is not permitted. Hundreds of guests may come to these affairs, which tend to take place during the day, but only punch and cake are served. Sometimes, the family has one party for nondrinkers, and the bride and groom have a more casual get-together, with booze, for their friends. As one Southerner said, "Southerners tend to fall into two groups: the strict teetotalers, and the ones who have nightly cocktail hours." Some southern couples have small, elegant church weddings, followed by a southern buffet for 50 guests served under a tent in the garden of the bride's parents' home.

If a bride is not registered, it is appropriate to bring a gift to the reception and leave it on a table designated for gifts. In some weddings, guests bring a check or an envelope of cash for the newlyweds. Sometimes, the bride carries a drawstring bag on her arm for people to subtly stick envelopes into as she passes. For many new couples, cash or a gift certificate is the best gift; the amount varies according to the closeness of the relationship between the guest and the couple.

In many southern cities and towns, local papers send a society reporter to cover a wedding, and his or her detailed piece is found in the Sunday paper. Reporters tell their readers everything they want to know: how the bride looked, the color and style of the bridesmaids' gowns, what the mother-of-the bride wore, who came from out of town, which band played, what kind of cake they served and who caught the bouquet.

Do these fancy extravaganzas where the bride plays queen and the groom king guarantee a happy marriage for ever after? I'm afraid not. Divorce happens down South just like everywhere else in America. In fact, Arkansas, Alabama, and Tennessee had higher divorce rates in the early 1990s than other states. According to Maryln Schwartz, the scenario in which middle-aged men leave their wives for younger models is particularly painful in the name-conscious, tradition-bound southern region. What do the first wives, who are not always prepared to survive on their own, do? Some work in designer clothing stores and some start their own businesses. Many become flight attendants;

the salaries are good, there are travel benefits, and southern women already have all the skills to be excellent "hostesses."

ADULTHOOD: CLUBS AND AFFILIATIONS

According to Maryln Schwartz, in Mississippi there used to be a saying that went, "First there's Chi O [the sorority], then you get married, then there's the Junior League, then you die." While the choices for women are certainly broader in the South these days, there is still quite an emphasis among upper-class adults on joining clubs and being identified as members of a group.

Some clubs pride themselves on their exclusivity and do not readily admit newcomers, or for that matter, anyone who cannot document their southern roots back several generations. Although it is illegal for many clubs to turn away prospective members based on race, sex, or religion, there are some organizations that simply do not make outsiders feel welcome. Country clubs, where Southerners go to play golf or tennis, swim, have weddings or anniversary parties, brunch, lunch, dine, drink, and socialize, are sometimes very costly and out of reach for outsiders who do not know other members who can recommend them for membership. Many country clubs, dining clubs, or restricted societies were started in the days before there were good restaurants in town, so people of a certain class could meet, eat, and socialize with one another. Some of the oldest organizations in the South made it a policy to admit only Southerners in an effort to keep the Yankees out after the Civil War.

However, there are organizations throughout the South that are happy to accept new members. Garden clubs, book clubs, church clubs, bridge clubs, supper clubs, cooking organizations, guilds associated with the hospital, the ballet, the opera, the symphony or the museum, or other local groups are an excellent way for newcomers to meet people and/or to become involved in the community. In Charleston, many of the board members of the famous Spoleto Festival of music are not born and bred Southerners. While it is difficult to get into the Garden Club of Virginia in Richmond, newcomers are welcomed into the city's neighborhood garden clubs. In many instances, doors open to those who *behave* well, no matter where they come from and who their people were.

Junior League, which used to be highly selective in its membership, now has an open admissions policy, but still attracts a certain type of woman—one with means and a strong desire to use her time in charitable pursuits. The organization hosts balls, Christmas holiday markets, fashion shows and other fundraisers, in an effort to raise money for various charities concerned with social service or community arts. In addition, the group is quite famous in the South for publishing cookbooks composed of members' recipes.

In old southern cities, women and men of a certain class who share an interest in local history and architecture often become involved in local historic preservation societies. In places like Charleston, New Orleans, Natchez, Memphis, Montgomery, Richmond, Williamsburg, and Savannah, preservation societies ensure that renovations of historic homes, buildings, and gardens are kept to high standards and that the look and feel of historic districts are not compromised by redevelopment or the addition of modern or commercial structures. In many instances, members of history preservation societies live in historic homes or neighborhoods.

The Bony Hand

When Southerners begin to go gray, many develop an intense curiosity about past family members, something Florence King calls "tombstone twitch." That's when they start spending inordinate amounts of time in the local libraries, churches, archives, and courthouses searching for names, dates, and clues, and that's when they join genealogy clubs. Even if Southerners are not officially affiliated with a genealogy club, many spend their time in active pursuit of their family history; others hire professional genealogists who work on an hourly rate to do it for them. According to a Southerner living in Richmond,

Virginians in particular care very much about documenting and discussing their ancestors, especially if they were related to someone in the Confederate Army or someone with position and/or an aristocratic title. "Richmond society is very entrenched [in family history]. The FFVs [Order of the First Families of Virginia] can date their family trees back to the 1700s," she said.

In contrast, lots of Southerners begin their family tree with full knowledge that they came from humble beginnings or that their ancestors were slaves; they search simply because they want to know more about those who share their blood. One Arkansas native actually has a "Genealogy Room" in her house in which the family records are kept. "In the Genealogy Room," she says, "we do oral history, write letters to people who are in our family, and write to local librarians in various southern towns to find relatives. Then we travel to meet them, share stories, or to find their graves. At this point, we can go back 11 solid generations; one line goes back to King John and Eleanor of Aquitaine. My husband says that there is a bony hand on my shoulder guiding me to find my family." Pretty impressive for those of us who don't even know the name of the village our own grandparents came from in the Old Country.

At genealogy club meetings, members share stories about what they've found out, discuss new genealogy books, and strategize about various search methods. Southern women who can show physical, documented proof that their ancestors fought in the Revolutionary War often attempt to join the Daughters of the American Revolution (the DAR, first formed in the South in 1898). Similarly, southern women who can prove a relative's participation in the Civil War join the United Daughters of the Confederacy (the UDC, established in Nashville in 1894). Membership in the DAR in particular brings with it considerable status because the organization follows such strict admittance standards and documentation is more than two centuries old. DAR meetings take place on the local level about once every two months and are structured around a historical or patriotic theme.

Male Bastions: Hunting Clubs

Southern boys grow up going hunting with their daddies, uncles, and granddaddies. Along with fishing and going to football games, hunting is a regional male rite of passage. (In fact, there's a bumper sticker in the South that says, "Don't go hunting your kids. Go hunting *with* your kids.") There are more hunting licenses issued per capita in the South than anywhere else in the country, and if you are a southern white male with a good income, you are much more likely to keep one or more guns in the house than your northern counterpart, both for protection and sport. What one hunts is indicative of one's social status in the South. As one member of a hunting club said, "Duck hunting is a gentleman's sport, while deer hunting is a redneck sport. In other words, duck hunting is to deer hunting as golf is to bowling." (The same can be said about fishing for the noble trout and the lowly bass, by the way.)

Whether hunting deer or duck, squirrels or quail, southern men are comfortable with guns, the cleaning, handling, and firing of them, and with the idea of killing animals for sport. These talents and notions are not often shared by Americans living in urban areas who have never held a firearm (although they may have *seen* one, much to their dismay), or those concerned with the feelings and rights of animals. Southern hunters are very much opposed to gun control legislation, although some feel that curbs should be put on handguns as opposed to rifles or shotguns.

Although there are lots of independent hunters in the South, many men of a certain social class join or are periodically invited to hunting clubs—places they can go to shoot duck, eat duck, and talk duck with their male buddies, business associates, future clients, etc. (Let's make one thing clear: little girls, young ladies, and women almost never hunt in the South, although more and more of them are joining their husbands on fishing expeditions these days.)

At one such club in Arkansas, only about an hour from Memphis, a group of doctors gather during the duck hunting season, which starts

171

the day after Thanksgiving and goes through mid-January. The group leases the land from a farmer who, in the winter months, floods his soybean fields to attract ducks flying south on the Mississippi flyover, a migration route that takes them from Canada to as far south as Mexico or Central America. The farmer also puts hunting pits (that have been camouflaged to blend in with the crops) in the fields and duck decoys in the water to encourage the ducks above to come down for a rest.

According to one of the members of the club, "In the morning, the farmer will come and fix us coffee and breakfast, then he'll hitch up something with benches in it to his John Deere tractor and haul us to the pits. We'll hunt until about noon, and then call him on our cellular phone to come pick us up." Hunters usually stay overnight, so the clubhouse is equipped with single bedrooms, a large dormitory room, and a giant socializing room with a fireplace. At another hunting club in Louisiana, members are awakened at 3:30 a.m. by an oldtimer pushing a cart of cups of steamy, muddy coffee. "G'mornin'," he says, "Thirty-nine and rainin'. ... Good for the ducks and bad for you. ..."

As one of the doctor/hunters puts it, "Killing ducks is only about 5% of the experience. The rest is the anticipation of it, the preparation, the camaraderie, the philosophizing we do there, the swapping of information, the eating, the being together. Sometimes, after we stop hunting at midday, we take out our duck calls and attract the ducks so we can just watch them or take still photos or videos of them."

For many hunters who join expeditions, the eating is absolutely the highlight of the event. Some clubs have enormous kitchens complete with multiple gas stoves, ovens, smokers, and giant freezers in which to store game of all kinds: quail, goose, grouse, elk, deer, etc. The cooks at these places are experts in cleaning and preparing many varieties of game. Sometimes a member will be appointed resident wine connoisseur and be given a budget for the purpose of buying wine. At the hunting club in Arkansas, each season members pay about $500 each for wine and about $2200 each for everything else.

Some of the larger hunting clubs are owned by large corporations like Coca-Cola and Tyson Foods and used primarily to entertain clients. If as a newcomer, you get invited to one and have no experience with guns or hunting, don't panic—members are usually more than willing to initiate you. To find out more about ducks and duck hunting, look into joining Ducks Unlimited (known as DU), a national organization with a large southern following dedicated to conserving duck habitats and wetlands in an effort to ensure the proliferation of the species. Call 901-758-DUCK for information.

OLD AGE, DEATH, AND DYING

In the South, the elderly are often treated with reverence, their wisdom and knowledge admired, their eccentricities accepted, their desire to remain independent respected. As one Southerner said, "Old people in the South are the keepers of tradition and the past, and the South has more past than other regions of the United States." When Southerners get sick or have to go to the hospital to have surgery, often members of the community gather round to help feed the spouse left at home, or to coordinate daily visits to the hospital to keep company with the sick, or to see if he or she needs anything. This is especially true in smaller, tight rural communities in which families have known each other for many years.

Southern Funerals

Funerals in the South take many different forms, depending on the class, race, and economic standing of the deceased. In general, however, Southerners tend to be very comfortable with the idea of death, with making funeral arrangements, and in coming in contact with the dead person during the funeral home visitation and the ceremony itself. Much of this ease stems from the typical Southerner's religious devotion, and his or her certainty of the existence of heaven as a paradisiacal hereafter. Funerals of black Baptists in particular emphasize the belief that life on earth is a trial that often brings suffering and that, for the good Christian, death brings great joy and a release from pain.

In *The Encyclopedia of Southern Culture*, Charles Reagan Wilson says that a southern funeral during the colonial era was "an occasion for the display of both grief and hospitality" and that Virginians in particular "made their death ceremonies into elaborate events." Within the plantation household, memorial services were held for both white owners and black slaves and they were buried communally in the family graveyard. According to Wilson, in the late 19th and early 20th centuries, funerals for important figures included the displaying of "symbols of Dixie," and eulogies tended to emphasize the deceased's contribution to the southern region.

Formerly, Wilson says, family members and people in the community handled the preparation of the body and the building of the coffin, and wakes, ceremonies, and post-funeral gatherings were held at home, or sometimes in church. "Sitting up" ceremonies, in which family members stayed awake all night with the body, were common, and it was standard for families to shovel dirt into the grave themselves. As Wilson states, "The most trying time was likely at the burial itself, as everyone stayed until neighbors, friends, and family had shoveled the last spade of dirt into the grave. Hysterical behavior was not uncommon at this point." Today, bodies are laid out at funeral homes and funeral directors arrange visitations, ceremonies, and interment, although some families still sit up with the body. The social aspect of post-funeral get-togethers is still strong.

Today, black funerals in the South (and elsewhere in America) are often emotional, heart-rending, elaborate, and expensive events. As congregants take their seats in the pews, ushers, sometimes dressed in white, hand out programs, handkerchiefs, and fans. In many instances, the casket is left open at the front of the church, and each attendee is instructed to file past, offering his or her final goodbyes. Close friends or family members of the deceased often cry openly for the dead, reaching in the casket to touch the body or to kiss the cheek, and to express their grief. As is the custom in the black church, when everybody is seated, the preacher gives a dramatic speech during which congregants shout out, "Amen!" or "Yes!" to show their agreement. Gospel singers often sing hymns.

The idea that the deceased is on his or her way "home" is emphasized during the eulogy, as the preacher, friends, and family go to the pulpit to recount the deceased's good deeds. In some black churches, at the end of the funeral ushers hold up the flower arrangements sent to the church and call out who gave what. The spouse of the deceased is sometimes asked to pull the veil over the face of the dead as a final act before the coffin is closed. After the service, funeralgoers travel to the cemetery to see the coffin interred, and then gather back at the church or in someone's home for a feast. For a jazz funeral, a New Orleans custom done on a grand scale for musicians, a Dixieland jazz band accompanies the mourners to the gravesite playing somber music befitting the occasion; on the way home, though, they pick up the pace with lively music. Due to the composition of the soil in New Orleans, the dead are buried above ground in stone tombs that sometimes hold two caskets, one on top of the other.

Black Southerners sometimes bury the deceased with important items or place household necessities on top of the grave. Some blacks believe that the dead are capable of remaining in the earthly world and doing damage to the living if not made comfortable and/or placated when they die. (Read John Berendt's *Midnight in the Garden of Good and Evil* for insight into the life of a black woman in Georgia whose profession is handling harmful ghosts or "haints.") These ideas stem primarily from African spiritual beliefs.

White funerals in the South tend to be less outwardly emotional in tone than black funerals, although this is not a hard and fast rule. Among many upper class families, grief tends to be hidden or saved for a more private setting. Some Southerners interpret this stoicism as a trait inherited from English ancestors and sustained by suffering and economic hardship. As one lifetime Southerner explained it, "I was

175

brought up to endure pain. … I don't remember ever being told not to cry when hurt, but I just knew that it was expected of me."

Sometimes a measure of grief is displayed at the visitation or viewing, which is held at the funeral parlor for one or two evenings before the funeral. The family of the deceased spends the evenings there, usually from 5 p.m. on, greeting and socializing and reminiscing with those who wish to pay their respects. (Some Southerners simply receive guests at home.) The funeral home usually provides food and coffee, but close friends and family send food to the home of the deceased to feed the spouse, who is presumably too upset to bother with such things. People send flowers to the funeral home, and these are displayed all around the casket. In some families, photographs are taken of people next to the open casket and saved as precious mementos.

The casket is often closed just before the service. Before this takes place, people gather around, as one Southerner tells it, to assess the appearance of the dead and take a final look. "We'll say, 'Don't Aunt Aggie look pretty? Ain't her hair nice?' It's a way of saying goodbye, a closure." The funeral service itself is often short and dignified.

It is not mandatory to attend the funeral if you have visited the family during the viewing, nor is it necessary to follow the procession to the cemetery if you have attended the service. (Sometimes, a simple sympathy card is all it takes to let the bereaved know that you are thinking about him or her.) After the interment, friends and family will meet at the home of the deceased, bringing bowls and platters of southern food in quantity enough to feed the multitudes.

— Chapter Seven —

HOLIDAYS, ANNUAL RITES, AND EVENTS

Southern celebrations have a good deal in common with American customs in general, but there are definite differences and subtle touches that are particular to the region. The southern values of family togetherness and community spirit, a heritage of hospitality, a passion for good, homemade food to share with family and friends, and a veneration for history make holidays, festivals, celebrations, and annual events especially important in the region. Some of the yearly occurrences that shape southern lives include: holidays such as Christmas, Easter, New Year's, and Memorial Day; family reunions, spring pilgrimages, the hunting and fishing seasons, Civil War battle re-enactments in which men, women, and children perform in period costumes, and the frenzy of Mardi Gras, which annually transforms areas of the South into enormous masked balls.

CHRISTMAS

Southerners celebrate Christmas with a vengeance, just like many other Americans. Some neighborhoods are known for their extravagant holiday house decorations, including door wreaths, colored lights, lawn ornaments of Santa and friends, and crèche scenes. Annual competitions are held to determine which house is the best lit up. Southerners also decorate themselves with Christmas cheer, donning theme sweatshirts, earrings, and necklaces. Interiors of homes are Christmas wonderlands, complete with huge heavily decorated and tinselled trees, 'snow' sprayed from a can onto the windows, and Christmas knickknacks on every surface. Many newcomers are amazed at how committed Southerners are to showing their Christmas spirit. In older communities, like Charleston, houses are decorated on the exterior either in an understated manner—a single, elegant door wreath, for instance—or not at all. Inside, however, the residents take out their tasteful family Christmas treasures—the handmade stockings, the carved angels, the special holiday candlesticks—and decorate their trees with beautiful ornaments.

Before the holiday, children put on Christmas plays at school, towns and cities decorate streetlamps and trees with lights, and Santa Claus can be seen around town, sometimes perspiring in the December heat, dressed in full red regalia. On Christmas morning, the present-opening frenzy sometimes prevents families with little ones from going to church, but other Southerners attend. That night, families join forces for Christmas feasts. Southerners eat turkey with oyster dressing, and a sherry and milk concoction called syllabub, as well as the usual rum-spiked eggnog and rich baked ham.

In Louisiana, Christmas traditions differ to some extent. Children say "Papa Noel" instead of Santa Claus and shout "Joyeux Noel!"

instead of "Merry Christmas." After Catholic Mass on Christmas Eve, some residents indulge in a Cajun "reveillon" or post-Mass feast (complete with wild game and five or six other courses), a custom dating back to the 17th century. The most spectacular Christmas events in Cajun country are the bonfires held on the banks of the Mississippi River. For 200 years, Cajuns have followed the custom of burning wooden cabins and tepees so that Papa Noel would know how to find his way through the swamps to the homes of Cajun children. Sometimes onlookers set off quantities of firecrackers to accompany the burnings, which last up to five hours. And these days non-Cajuns seeking tourist dollars organize bonfire events in which they burn huge structures resembling plantations and boom boxes.

Throughout the South, people believe that it is bad luck to leave Christmas decorations up past December 31. As journalist Frances Cawthon said in an article for the *Atlanta Journal-Constitution*, "This is an old southern superstition, origins unknown. But diehards consider it stems from God himself. We don't dare let Jan. 1 dawn with any Yuletide decor around. ... As a southern friend said somberly to me once when we both were in Manhattan, still ablaze with Christmas in late January, 'No wonder New York has so many problems.'"

THANKSGIVING

Although many southern families celebrate this annual feast of thanks, generally the holiday does not carry the same weight as it does in the North. To many Southerners, Thanksgiving is a Yankee holiday celebrated with distinctly Yankee foods, like cranberries and pumpkin pie. Southerners often get together for dinner on Thanksgiving, but they serve southern foods like pecan pie, corn dumplings, corn puddings, and greens. The main course is often fresh wild fowl (duck, quail, pheasant) shot by the hunter in the family. The Thanksgiving meal is begun by a special blessing given by the host or head of the family. To many Southerners, however, Thanksgiving primarily represents the start of the duck hunting season and a lineup of football

179

games rather than a time to call the family home from the corners of the country, eat stuffed turkey, and discuss the pilgrims.

EASTER

Churchgoing reaches its peak in the South during Easter, the region's most religious holiday. In New Orleans, in particular, from Palm Sunday through Easter Sunday the holiday is observed with reverence and fanfare. Catholic children have their first communions during the Easter season. After church, families have elaborate Easter parties, which sometimes resemble family reunions. Guests wear lovely springtime dresses or light-colored suits and children don little suits or lacy pastel frocks, hats, and party shoes to participate in Easter egg hunts and stuff themselves with candy. New Orleans also hosts an annual Easter parade complete with floats, throws, and an Easter bonnet contest.

All over the region, Easter is a celebration of springtime and its colorful flora. In some parts of the South, celebrants gather Confederate violets and other spring blooms to decorate their churches. On the Saturday before Easter in Winston-Salem, North Carolina, members of the Home Moravian Church clean and decorate the headstones of their ancestors with spring flowers—daffodils, tulips, azaleas, and hyacinths. Some years up to 60,000 people from Moravian churches in the area attend the Easter morning service held in the graveyard.

NEW YEAR'S DAY

Unlike most other Americans who only have parties on New Year's *Eve*, Southerners also get together on New Year's *Day* to eat special southern foods associated with the holiday and, of course, to settle in and watch several college football championship "Bowl" games in a row. Eating black-eyed peas with rice and green leafy vegetables is a southern New Year's Day tradition; these foods are said to ensure a lucky, prosperous year. According to Sibley Fleming, columnist for the *Atlanta Journal-Constitution*, other superstitions associated with New Year's Day include:

- If a black cat crosses your path that day, you will have especially bad luck in the coming year.
- The first man to come into your house on January 1 will be an important figure in your life in the year to come.
- If your left eye quivers, someone you know well will be dead in two months.
- If you see your shadow with your head missing, you will lose your own head (literally, not figuratively) in the coming year.
- You shouldn't clip your nails or cut your hair on the first day of the year or you will be "snip[ping] off good fortune.

Some black Southerners attend a special New Year's Eve midnight service at church to pray in the new year and to hope for faith in the coming year.

MEMORIAL DAY

In the South, Memorial Day, which falls on the last Monday in May, is a serious holiday that marks more than the first day in which it is acceptable to wear white shoes. Many other Americans have little knowledge of the meaning of Memorial Day—they simply think of it as a Monday off from work or the perfect occasion to have the first outdoor cookout of the season. In much of the South, especially in more rural areas, Memorial Day is the time to remember and honor the dead, those who died in war or other deceased family members.

Descendants visit the graveyard in which family members are buried to clip the grass, scrub the headstones, and place fresh flowers or a wreath on the graves. This event is done en masse in some southern communities. One or two days later, a church "homecoming" will be held with preaching and singing and what is called a "dinner-on-the-ground" in which congregants bring a covered dish to share with fellow churchgoers. The food is placed on a long table and people help themselves.

Some Southerners gather to do this not on Memorial Day in May, but on Decoration Day, which falls on the second Sunday in June. In *Womenfolks*, author Shirley Abbott relates the events of a typical Decoration Day in her family's Arkansas community.

> The survivors and descendants come to weed the graves and sweep them clean, just as the front yards used to be weeded and swept around the houses that the dead once occupied. … We who come on Decoration Day read the names and dates [on the tombstones] and try to remember all that we can. On these mounds, as austere and primitive as any in the annals of anthropology, we firmly plant plastic nosegays.

Memorial Day and Decoration Day give Southerners a chance to gather and remember their past, and to show respect for their ancestors by caring for their graves. According to one Southerner, you can always tell how entrenched a town is in community spirit by the way its graveyards are kept.

AFRICAN-AMERICAN HOLIDAYS

African-Americans in the South celebrate several annual holidays that have to do with issues of freedom and self-expression. January 15, the anniversary of the birth of Martin Luther King, Jr., is now a national holiday on which schools, banks, and government offices are closed. Kwanzaa, developed by Dr. Maulana Karenga in 1965 as an alternative to traditional Christmas celebrations, takes place from December 26 through January 1. Kwanzaa is a time to sing, share gifts, and to ponder Dr. Karenga's seven hopes for African-Americans: unity, self-determination, collective work and responsibility, cooperative economics, purpose, creativity, and faith.

Black Southerners also celebrate Juneteenth, which falls on June 19th, the day in 1865 when the slaves of Texas finally learned of their emancipation. According to one story, news of the emancipation was kept from the slaves until 1865 by their owners, who wanted them to work through the harvest. Although Juneteenth is an official state holiday only in Texas, it is celebrated less formally in Louisiana, Arkansas, South Carolina, Georgia, North Carolina, Mississippi, Alabama, and parts of Florida. Typical Juneteenth festivities include parades, games, or contests, feasting (usually on Texas-style barbecue and chili), dancing, praying, and speechmaking.

MARDI GRAS CHAOS

Mardi Gras is a spring carnival that is devoted to pleasure, partying, and playing dress-up. It is more opulent, dramatic, and frenzied than any other festival that takes place in America. As a former king of carnival once said, Mardi Gras is the time to let "melancholy be put to rout, and joy unconfined seize our subjects, young and old of all genders and degrees ... that the spirit of make-believe descend upon the realm and banish from the land the dull and the humdrum and the commonplace of daily existence."

For those of you who are unfamiliar with the elaborate rituals of Mardi Gras, here are a few facts about this extravagant, no-holds-barred southern ritual:

- Mardi Gras is French for "Fat Tuesday," the most important day of the holiday celebration. Fat Tuesday occurs on a different *date* every year, but it's always exactly 46 days before Easter, on a Tuesday between February 23 and March 9. The day after Fat Tuesday is Ash Wednesday, the beginning of Lent.
- The 12-day Mardi Gras festival marks the last chance for people to indulge in rich food and drink (and untamed behavior) before the coming of Lent, in which such indulgences are given up.
- Although pre-Lenten masked balls were held in New Orleans in the 1700s, Mardi Gras officially started in Mobile, Alabama, in 1830, when a group of revelers calling themselves the Cowbellion de Rankin Society paraded in the streets ringing cowbells and waving hoes on New Year's Eve. This was the first "mystic society." Offshoots from this group later went to New Orleans to establish the ritual there in 1857. Mardi Gras is celebrated in Mobile, throughout the New Orleans area, in Shreveport and Bossier City, Louisiana, Pensacola, Florida, and on the Mississippi Gulf Coast.
- Today, a Mardi Gras season consists of parades of floats and riders from various mystic societies, as well as parties and masked balls. Some societies do not parade, but have masked balls, and some balls include debutante presentations. Close to 40,000 people *participate* in Mardi Gras in New Orleans, and that does not include the millions of people who *watch*. (Many New Orleans residents, by the way, understandably escape the city during Mardi Gras, and head for a clean, quiet ski slope somewhere.) The celebration annually brings half a billion dollars into the community.

- Organizations parade on the same day every year, using the same route through the city; the societies that parade closest to Fat Tuesday are the most famous and their floats and costumes the most spectacular. Similarly, the balls held on the evenings closest to Fat Tuesday are the most exclusive, and the nights and venues are the same every year.
- Each organization adopts one theme that is carried out in floats, costumes, and balls each year; typical themes include Greek mythology, astronomy, astrology, historical events, fairy tales, sports, or any subject that insures opulence and provides dramatic opportunities.
- In Mobile, there are black mystic societies and white societies, but the races remain separate; in New Orleans, there are black, white, and mixed societies. Many organizations, especially the older ones, are single sex; most are all-male.

Mardi Gras has its own vocabulary of strange words. Here are a few:

krewe—a carnival organization or "mystic" society that participates in Mardi Gras; some societies are very old and exclusive,
but others encourage new members to apply and to buy tickets

185

for masked balls. Members pay annual dues, but many krewes give part of their proceeds to charitable causes. Membership ranges from 60 to 1,500.

throws—highly desirable items that float riders throw to the crowd during the parade when street revelers scream, "Throw me somethin' mister!" Throws include cups printed with Mardi Gras or krewe motifs, coasters, frisbees, stuffed animals, posters, dolls, t-shirts, candy, cards, flags, earrings, hats, pearls, beads, and **doubloons**, coins imprinted with krewe insignia. Three of the largest krewes alone throw 2 million cups, 3.5 million doubloons and 350,000 gross of beads from 110 floats in a single season.

flambeaux—torches traditionally carried by black men in white robes during parades to light the way for floats at night.

tableau—the story or theme upon which the masked ball is based.

To the uninitiated, the names of the mystic societies sound awfully unusual. Consider this sampling: Aphrodite, Gladiators, Argus, Isis, Ashanti, Napoleon, Babylon, Orpheus, Bacchus, Pegasus, Caesar, Pontchartrain, Centurions, Rex, Diana, Zeus, Elks Jeffersonian, Zulu.

As you can see, many of the names have to do with Greek, Roman, or Egyptian mythology, African tribes, historical figures, even a local lake. The Rex organization, founded in 1872, started the ritual of daytime parades, and gave the festival its official colors of purple (for justice), green (for faith), and gold (for power). Zulu, a popular black organization, was founded in 1916. The Elks Jeffersonians participate in what is called a "truck" parade, in which members simply ride atop a flatbed truck rather than an elaborate float. Bacchus was the first krewe to hire a celebrity as its representative (Danny Kaye in 1969). This is now a common feature among some krewes, and stars such as Dolly Parton, Bob Hope, and Dan Ackroyd have appeared as krewe representatives in recent years. Bacchus sponsors a huge BYOB (bring your own booze) party in the New Orleans Superdome each year. Members buy tables of 10 and invite guests, and you can wear just about anything. A woman with a tall beehive hairdo complete with blinking lights, wearing a mink coat, was spotted there one year.

- Seventy parades are held each year in four "parishes" or Louisiana counties. Each parade starts with the appearance of the captain of the krewe, followed by the officers, the king and queen, the maids and dukes, the title float, the floats filled with riders, and accompanying dancers, motorcyclists, and clowns.

- Even kids have their own krewe, the Little Rascals, which sponsors a parade and a formal party for children 5 to 16. Luckily, the schools are closed for three days during the Mardi Gras season.

- Spectators are so intent on getting their share of throws, that riders must now be harnessed to floats to prevent accidents. Riders are responsible for buying their own throws and costumes, which annually cost about $500 and $200, respectively. In New Orleans and environs, riders buy throws in huge stores and warehouses devoted to carnival merchandise. Krewe members also pay dues to help finance the floats.

- There are float and costume designers who work year round in New Orleans planning, building, and sewing for Mardi Gras. Most krewes rent rather than build their own floats, and many floats are used over and over again. (In Mobile, however, no float is ever used twice.) The most famous float designer is Blain Kern, who owns Mardi Gras World, a theme park devoted to the carnival.

- In the organizations that do not parade, the masked ball is the central event of the season. In a traditional organization, the male members choose a tableau or story to act on a stage, in full costume, wearing masks, while an orchestra plays. The women, dressed in their very finest silks, taffetas, and sequined gowns with gloves, sit in the auditorium watching the men (who are sometimes intoxicated). Then the debutantes of the season, the current royal court, and the former royal court are presented.

Afterwards, the "call outs" begin, in which an announcer calls out the name of a woman who has been asked to dance by one of the men, whose identity is often a secret to the woman. After the dance, the man gives the woman a favor, a trinket inscribed with the name of the organization and the year. Some trinkets are nicer than others, and what you receive depends on your status within the organization. After the dances are finished, the King and Queen's Supper is served at a hotel. Some organizations take over suites of hotel rooms every year and have multiple parties that span a three-day period.

- Gay and lesbian organizations take over the French Quarter, which is no longer a parade route, for a wild masquerade party every year.
- Krewes disband every year due to financial pressures, and new ones form regularly to take their place. In recent years, three of the oldest organizations, Comus, Momus, and Proteus, disbanded to protest a new rule that forces all krewes to adopt anti-discrimination policies.
- *Arthur Hardy's Mardi Gras Guide*, a $2.99 magazine that covers every detail about carnival (including times, dates, parade routes, descriptions of throws, historical information, etc.) is an essential annual publication for every carnival goer.

A Safe Carnival

A Mardi Gras parade can be a dangerous event. Sidewalks can be 50-people deep, floats weigh many tons, and drunken people do stupid things. The New Orleans police force, although famous throughout the country for its expertise in crowd control, cannot keep accidents from happening during the madness. If you have never attended a Mardi Gras celebration before, here are some safety tips and other practical recommendations:

- Watch your children extremely carefully; don't let them run out into the street or reach out toward the floats, and don't perch them in trees for a better view. If you bring a ladder for them to sit on, as many locals do, make sure you don't walk away from it.

- Don't wear a mask that obscures your vision in any way, and don't let children wear such masks.
- Arrange a meeting spot with your children in case they get separated from you.
- Plan on visiting the bathroom before you get to the parade route; you won't find a clean portable toilet anywhere.
- Leave valuables at home or in the hotel, and don't wear nice jewelry.
- Don't arrive by car, if you can help it; you may inadvertently leave your car in a tow zone and be forced to find your way to the towing company lot during the wee hours of the morning to reclaim it. (What's worse, lots of towing companies accept cash only.)
- If you are not in good health, don't come to the parade; it is next to impossible for an ambulance to make its way to you through the crowd. One New Orleans resident said that you should have access to a motorcycle if you are pregnant during Mardi Gras; the bike can traverse sidewalks to get you to the hospital if need be.
- Don't bring glass bottles or heavy food containers to the parade.

Real Southern Royalty

The selection of kings and queens of each New Orleans krewe differs from organization to organization. Some are chosen randomly; others are deliberated upon by a select group of members, and some kings choose their own queens. For the Mardi Gras celebration in Mobile, there is only one queen, chosen from among the debutante pool by a small group of Mobile Carnival Association members. The identity of the queen is kept a secret from the community (the chosen family is told a year in advance) and announced on the Saturday night before Mardi Gras. She is crowned by King Felix and reigns for four days. Black organizations in Mobile choose their own queen, and she is presented in a ceremony all her own.

In *Queens of Mobile Mardi Gras 1893–1986* (subtitled *She Walks in Beauty*), by Emily Staples Hearin and Kathryn Taylor deCelle, the authors tell us that to be selected as queen in Mobile, the young lady "must be a Mobilan—usually third or fourth generation—and someone in her family has usually been a former King or Queen or has been in some Mardi Gras Courts of the past years. Her family must have worked closely with and contributed time and money to the Carnival Association," the authors say, yet "the honor cannot be bought for love nor money."

However, the parents of the deb selected must be able to shell out close to $25,000 for the elaborate gown it takes two expert seamstresses more than six months to design, sew, and bead. According to the book, the royal couple must also pay for the "jeweled crowns they wear ... [but] this is just the beginning ... because there are favors,

Gowns of former Mardi Gras queens on display at the Museum of the City of Mobile, Alabama. Photograph courtesy of the Museum and Ocean Springs Distributors, Gulfport, Mississippi.

flowers for the ladies of the Court, clothes, and the cost of dinner dances and luncheons. It has become more elaborate and more costly each year. ..."

Queens gives a fascinating account of the past century's royal personages, complete with photographs of the queens with their court. The queens of the last 26 years in particular are featured with full-page photographs and full-page descriptions of royal robes. The queens wear relatively simple floor-length gowns, but their robes are unbelievably ornate, with huge Medici-style, stand-up collars (often resembling wings) and six-yard-long trains that are ornamented with beads, sequins, fur, jewels, metallic threads, velvet, and pearls. The king wears a long-haired wig and a weighty crown, as well as satin knickers, white stockings, and buckle shoes. The royals are accompanied by little boys called pages, who wear wigs and feathered hats and white satin outfits.

Each of the queen's trains is designed according to a theme chosen by the queen. In 1983, Queen Mary Louise DeMouy chose a peacock theme for her train. The book describes it as follows:

> The Queen's mantle of deep teal blue velvet is lined with pale blue silk and descends over six yards in length. Rhinestones, large crystal jewels and bugle beads form a glittering sunburst at the rounded shoulder. Queen Louise's monogram may be seen among the glittering feathers of a gracefully resting peacock, which sets the basic theme for her robes. ... Five delicate peacock feathers swirl up the back and are created of amethysts, royal blue and aurora borealis stones. ...

The Queen of the Mobile Mardi Gras, formally called the Queen of Love and Beauty, is presented on the Saturday night before Mardi Gras at the Civic Center. Members of the public are welcome for the price of a ticket.

FAMILY REUNIONS

Southern family reunions are representative of aspects of the southern character: the desire to be social, the strong notion of family, and the wish to eat well and to share good, homecooked food. Reunions are often held during the summer, especially on the Fourth of July. They are usually organized by the family matriarch—the one with the best organizational skills, the sharpest memory, and the greatest desire to see her family all in one place, if only for a day or two.

Some reunions include only immediate family and first cousins; others stretch out their arms to take in anybody with the slightest connection as well as good friends. Some are loosely structured get-togethers planned a week in advance; others involve months of planning, with family members across the country receiving regular updates or newsletters about the event's activities. Some revolve around an activity, such as putting together a family reunion cook-book, or reading the poetry or letters of a deceased family member. Some are held on the back porch at Grandma's house or in the family church; others are held at resorts where blocks of rooms are booked a year in advance. Some are held annually, others every other year or more. All revolve around food and eating those specialty dishes for which certain family members are famous. All are primarily occupied by talk, reminiscing, and figuring out whose nose Aunt Lillian's baby granddaughter got.

Both black and white southern families cherish their family reunions. In 1991, 250 members of the Overton family—the white Overtons and the black Overtons, the latter being descendants of slaves from the family plantation—joined forces to attend a family reunion in Tennessee.

In *A Book of Feasts: Recipes and Stories from American Celebrations*, authors Kay Goldstein and Liza Nelson describe a family reunion in Upson County, Georgia. Attended by 200 family members, many of whom came from far away, this family reunion was sched-uled to coincide with the 200th anniversary of the birth of the family patriarch. Guests ranging in age from 3 months to 94 years gathered on the family farm (which has its own family graveyard) to catch up on news, eat, even meet for the first time. In the "genealogy tent," hand-lettered family trees were on display. Somebody stayed up all night to roast a pig, while somebody else tended a homemade stew cooked in a 150-year-old pot in which a child was once hidden from the Yankees during the Civil War. Everybody donated $3 for expenses and brought a covered dish. Offerings included: fried chicken and cornbread in many versions, homemade pickles, myriad salads, countless casseroles, 35 different pies and, hold your hats, *296* different cakes!

Many southern families do not have official family reunions of any sort because most of the family members still live near one another and see each other at family functions year around.

IT'S OPEN HOUSE IN THE SOUTH

When spring comes to old southern towns and cities like Natchez, Richmond, Holly Springs (Mississippi), Mobile, Talladega (Alabama), Charleston, and Savannah, it's spring hour tour or "pilgrimage" season. This southern ritual, in which designated antebellum mansions or other historic buildings open their doors to the public, helps raise money for historic preservation groups and garden clubs, and sometimes for the mansion dwellers themselves, who are faced with the high cost of annual upkeep. For antique collectors, history buffs, or nosy folks who love to drive by old homes at night and wonder just what goes on through those lighted windows, spring house tours are a delight.

The homes are often on the National Register of Historic Places, so they are American architectural masterpieces and usually decorated with antiques made by notable craftsmen and portraits of family members painted by important artists. Those who lead the tours, members of the preservation group or the owners themselves, sometimes dress in antebellum garb such as hoop skirts, so while visitors are listening to the mini-lecture about why the curtains "puddle" onto the floor, or the reason for "petticoat mirrors," they can fantasize about what the original owners might have worn back in the 19th century.

Some tours are accompanied by other events, such as ribbon-cutting ceremonies, parades in which marchers wear Confederate costumes, dances, dinners, and the coronation of the Pilgrimage Queen. In addition, some tours include important churches, cemeteries, art galleries, governor's homes, and smaller period dwellings. If you cannot make it to the spring pilgrimages, there are others held in Natchez and Charleston in the fall.

CIVIL WAR BATTLE RE-ENACTMENTS

Most outsiders believe that Southerners have never fully accepted their defeat in the Civil War, that they are obsessed with the Civil War, or even that they are still *fighting* the Civil War. The Confederate flag still flies over the state capitol building in South Carolina and is part of the Georgia state flag; some people in Charleston continue to celebrate the day the state seceded from the Union; Confederate monuments and plaques can be found in town squares all over the region.

For 65 years, the Kappa Alpha fraternity on the campus of Jacksonville State University in Alabama celebrated the beginning of Old South Week by marching in Confederate uniforms to meet their hoop-skirted dates; the practice was abandoned in 1992. Kids in southern playgrounds play Yanks and Rebels; portraits of Robert E. Lee hang in important places. As one Southerner said, "I've heard my relatives talk about General Sherman like he just died. They say things like, "He didn't have to go and burn Atlanta. That was so rude!"

It is true that many Southerners have strong feelings about the Civil War that are not matched in the North. (As a Northerner who lived for a time in the South once said, "You don't hear us going around screaming, "We won! We won!"") To understand the southern point of view on the subject, a Northerner would have to place himself in southern shoes. The war was, after all, mostly fought on southern soil. The South lost many fine men in the war, and those who survived came home to find their land destroyed, their homes and even their cities burned. What followed was a period of confusion, poverty, hunger, and displacement—for both blacks and whites—that marked southern life for several generations. Most Northerners are as removed from the Civil War as they are from a war that took place on foreign soil. It is intangible to them, neither part of what they see nor mentioned in family stories.

Many white Southerners go through a period in which they become fascinated by the Civil War: *my* ancestors fought in it, they think; *my* ancestors died in it; it happened right here, on *this* soil. This fascination leads them to visit Civil War battlefields, many of which have been turned into historic sites, and to attend battle re-enactments held annually. National battlefield parks such as Kennesaw Mountain, Vicksburg, Manassas, Chicakmauga and Chattanooga, Richmond, Petersburg, Fredericksburg, and Antietam are all popular sites for Southerners to visit in Tennessee, Virginia, and Maryland, as well as Gettysburg in Pennsylvania.

In a typical battle re-enactment, hundreds of men dress in both Confederate and Union uniforms and act out the event. They build encampments, fire mock bullets, scream out and fall down "dead" when "hit." Women and children also dress up in period costume to make the vision complete. When a Northerner called for tickets to such an event in Alabama, the woman who helped her asked which re-enactment she wanted to see: "the one on Saturday, in which the South wins, or the one on Sunday, in which the outcome is *historically correct*?" (italics mine).

OTHER SOUTHERN FESTIVALS AND EVENTS

The South is full of county fairs, festivals, and events that celebrate agriculture, flora and fauna, crafts, food, and historical occurrences.

In Kentucky and North Carolina, there are several tobacco festivals (although these are slightly on the wane of late due to the harmful nature of the product). Kudzu is feted in both South Carolina and Georgia. The Swine Time festival, complete with Greased Pig, Chitlin Eatin', and Best Dressed Pig contests, is held annually in Climax, Georgia, while other Georgia towns annually celebrate the catfish, the mule, and the rattlesnake. In Dayton, Tennessee, the Scopes trial is annually re-enacted; in Spivey's Corner, North Carolina, they have the National Hollerin' Contest. In Thomasville, Georgia, April is Rose Festival time, and in St. Martinville, Louisiana, in March there's the hog butchering celebration, complete with cockfighting. The seed-spitting contest is the highlight of the Watermelon Festival held in Mize, Mississippi, as is the sweet potato-pie eating contest of the National Sweet Potato Festival in Vardaman, Mississippi. Some of these celebrations include parades, clogging contests, community feasts, and the coronation of the queen or the princess.

Chapter Eight

RELIGION

The South is a land where passages from scripture are painted on the sides of barns, where God is thanked before a bountiful meal, where college kids actually get up on Sunday mornings to go to church, where preachers interrupt primetime network television with important messages, where people end their answering machine message tapes with "Have a nice day and God bless." The South is truly the "Bible Belt," a phrase coined in the 1920s by H.L. Mencken (who also called the region "The Sahara of the Bozart," referring to its absence of high culture, and "The Hookworm Belt").

In the South, you might see a Bible study group having their weekly meeting at the IHOP (International House of Pancakes) or a church group dressed in matching t-shirts getting ready to take a vacation together at the airport. The best compliment one Southerner can give another is to say that he or she is "a good Christian." Most millionaire preachers you see on television—the so-called "televangelists" or "electronic preachers"—are from the South, most Christian television broadcasts come out of the South, and about half the national viewing audience is from the southern region.

When school prayer was disallowed before a football game recently in a southern town, students banded together in protest to blast transistor radios, in unison, when the Lord's Prayer was read on the air by a radio announcer. In 1983, in Hawkins County, Tennessee, parents of children attending a public school protested the use of a general reader that contained a tale about Martians because it implied the use of mental telepathy, which they equated with the voice of the Devil.

This is not to imply that all Southerners are religious fanatics, but to say that devotion to religion and church are the South's most defining characteristics, that religion and southern identity are inextricably linked. According to a comprehensive nationwide survey done in 1991 by the Graduate School of the City University of New York, more than 90% of Southerners claim a religious affiliation, with a majority calling themselves Baptist. Black Southerners have been found to be the most religious, the most likely to attend church regularly, and to say grace before a meal.

In the 1993 Southern Life poll conducted by the *Atlanta Journal-Constitution*, 96% of all Southerners had Bibles at home, compared to 90% of non-Southerners. Of black Southerners, 99% owned a Bible.

Out of the region's 15 million Baptists, about half attend church regularly. In addition, about 86% of white southern Protestants believe in the Devil compared to about 52% of non-southern white

Protestants, according to a Gallup Poll mentioned by John Shelton Reed in his 1993 book, *My Tears Spoiled My Aim.*

NEWCOMER DISCOMFORT

"Are you in the military?"

"Who do you root for: Auburn or Alabama?"

"What church do you go to?"

—the three things Southerners most often ask newcomers, according to a Californian transplanted to Alabama

The expatriate recently transferred to Southeast Asia probably experiences culture shock when dining on a chili-laden dish; the transplant to Paris has to learn to deal with incessant cigarette smoke being blown into his face and his food, while the newcomer to New York has to remember to look inconspicuous and to wear a purse that doesn't invite stranger's hands. In the South, though, a stranger goes through culture shock when his new neighbors pay a visit, cookies in hand and the all-important question on their lips: "What church will you be attending?" Sometimes people from various churches will phone you at night to invite you to their church, in the way those annoying fundraising types do. "Within ten minutes of meeting me," one newcomer said, "a man asked me what church I belonged to. I felt like I was the newest prize in town."

In the South, one's faith—as a Christian, usually a Protestant—is assumed. The majority of Southerners are Baptists or Methodists, so they have little experience with religious otherness. Most Southerners rarely speculate about God's existence—they *know.* Southerners speak about religion and God as something personal, something they have experienced and therefore know to be a real and powerful force. As novelist Bebe Moore Campbell said, in an interview done by *The New York Times Magazine* in December of 1994,

> My grandmother in the South, my father's mother, her friends, would sit on the porch and they would talk about

199

Jesus like they knew Him. What He had done for them. I
mean, they would have a whole conversation about Jesus.
I'd sit there and listen to them and I'd wonder, Who are we
talking about? Who came to see you? Who did that?

In the North and West, one's religious affiliation is private, and
one's faith can take many (or no) forms. A Northerner would no
sooner ask another person his religious affiliation upon first meeting
than inquire into his sexual preference. Outside the South, you might
know somebody for a year without ever knowing that he meditated
every morning at 4 a.m. with other members of his particular sect of
Eastern religion, that the lady in the next office was an atheist, or the
guy down the hall a Catholic.

When newcomers hear the church question, they often stiffen,
clam up, and begin to stutter an evasive response, especially if they are
not Christian or if they come from a background in which religion is

DOES EVERYONE UP HERE
HAVE A SOUTHERN ACCENT?

not worn on one's sleeve. The wrong answer is, of course, "None of your business, thank you very much." A nicer response is something like, "We haven't quite decided yet," or "We practice a different faith, but thank you anyway for asking."

There are many newcomers to the South who do not find the church question offensive or the talk of God discomforting. They see it as a welcoming gesture, an opportunity for a quick entrée into what might be an otherwise closed community. Some newcomers take all their different neighbors and coworkers up on their invitations to church—that way they get a sampling of what's out there and can choose the congregation that best suits their needs. Visitors to both black and white churches in the South are welcomed wholeheartedly by members, often being asked to stand up and introduce themselves and say where they're from. Members will come over to them during this time and shake their hands. (It doesn't hurt to put a few dollars in the collection basket when it comes around by the way, as a show of gratitude.)

HISTORY AND PRACTICE

Southerners were not originally so religious. The early settlers were Anglicans, but as they moved west to populate the frontier, their faith weakened. In the mid-18th century came the Great Awakening, a revival movement that brought many southern colonials to evangelical Protestantism. The Second Awakening or Great Revival came to the frontier in the late 18th and early 19th centuries to further spread evangelical religion. During the Civil War, poor white Southerners were evangelized to fight for the South and slavery, a system, preachers said, that had been sanctioned by God. Today the South is the most religious region in what is considered a very religious country.

Although the Protestant religion in the South today takes many different forms, there are some basic tenets and practices that are commonly found in the southern evangelical church:

- An emphasis on conversion. In the southern churches, one is never ·too old to be "saved" or "born again," which is synonymous with establishing a direct and personal connection with God. Even if someone has spent an entire lifetime sinning, being saved wipes that person's spiritual slate clean and gives him or her a place in heaven. Human beings are seen as essentially sinful, but they can be made clean by accepting God. The Lord is always willing to forgive any individual, as long as he or she personally seeks salvation. The act of being baptized is essential and can take the form of a sprinkling at infancy or a full dunking at adulthood. Baptism is seen as the most essential rite of passage in a Christian life.

- Dramatic preaching. Evangelical preachers are often great orators, with the ability to persuade audiences to accept God, to admit and renounce sin, and to be reborn. A magnetic preacher is the center of the church. He or she expects congregants to open their hearts and souls to God as a way to achieve salvation. During the service, the preacher appeals directly to the congregants to agree with or echo his statements, a technique known as "call and response." He tells stories of sinners who were reformed after accepting God, people whose health, jobs, and family lives were changed markedly after their conversions. The informal and openly religious nature of the southern church is a far cry from the placid, formal, tiptoe-in-if-you're-late atmosphere of other Christian denominations.

- Moving music. Music, especially in the black church, is emotional and powerful. It invites congregants to participate by singing, shouting, clapping, getting up and swaying or dancing. Good gospel singing often starts out slow and builds up to an intensity that encourages dramatic displays of religious feeling from the congregants. Choirs in the South usually face the audience—they are not hidden up in the balcony or behind a curtain so their voices serve only as a backdrop to the service.

- The idea that the Bible is the Book, to be read and reread and to be taken literally.
- A lifetime commitment. Although the Sunday service is the essential event in the southern church, members often attend several other church-related activities each week or each month. The church sponsors events such as Bible study classes, youth groups, lectures, Superbowl parties, excursions and trips, and social service activities, such as feeding the homeless or helping build housing for the needy. Many Southerners give 10% of their annual family income to the church, an act known as "tithing." Children go to church camp during the summer or attend vacation Bible school; at the very least, they go to Sunday school and then to the church service with their parents. Many churches still sponsor a Wednesday night service, which serves as a kind of midweek morality reminder and ends with a communal meal. The larger churches publish weekly newsletters to let congregants know the schedule of events and community news, such as who had a baby, who became a grandma, who is in the hospital (and which room he or she can be found in), who turned 100, who got baptized, and whose baby was formally dedicated in the church. All these newsy bits keep members in touch with each other, encourage contact between members, and reinforce the sense of community. Many black Southerners, in particular, credit the church for directing their lives, welcoming them in like family, giving them hope for the future.

CHURCH CUSTOMS

After church, congregants gather outside the church to meet and greet and share news. For many, church is the major social event in their lives, their weekly chance to dress nicely and see and be seen by other members of the community. After sitting in church for many hours (services in the black church can last for four hours or more), churchgoers are understandably starving. Some congregants head right out to the nearest cafeteria after church to partake of an enormous buffet. In the old days, the extended family would regularly meet at the home of the head of the family to share a Sunday dinner, served in the early afternoon. (Some southern families still do this weekly.) Sunday dinner is a major feast complete with turkey, roast chicken, baked ham, green beans, fried corn, okra, squash, sweet potatoes, and cornbread, washed down with iced tea and followed by those incredible cakes and pies. These days, each family usually contributes a dish (usually the one for which the mother or wife is famous) so that one person does not need to do all the cooking. Some churches host the big Sunday meal right on the grounds, with scores of members participating.

Southern churches have annual homecomings, in which congregants gather from far and near to celebrate an important event such as a preacher's anniversary, or to clean and re-flower graves in the church cemetery. Homecomings usually include a communal feed such as a dinner-on-the-grounds, in which members offer a covered dish to be shared by fellow picnickers.

Black churches regularly sponsor revival meetings, singing and preaching events that bring in new members as well as encourage old members to renew their faith. According to one newcomer to the South who attended a revival at her Atlanta church, "You go to church every day for three or four days or even a week. You hear different choirs, listen to guest ministers and speakers. People stand up and testify or make statements about the existence of God in their lives. Someone will tell a story about how he was ill or lost his job and that he prayed and God answered his prayers. People shout out 'Amen!' as people tell their stories."

RELIGION AND RACE

Sunday has often been called the most segregated day of the week in the South (and in most of America). According to an article that appeared in the April 1995 edition of *Town and Country* magazine, a newcomer was told that in Charleston, "We do not drink with nor pray with blacks." For the most part, churches in the South do tend to be segregated, although today this is due more to the differences between the two styles of the church than to policy. The black church service is often more joyous and boisterous than the white, more music-focused and more outwardly emotional (although both are considerably more demonstrative than services outside the region). Black churches frequently reflect black culture, focusing on the black experience, while white churches focus on white issues and culture.

The black church has also traditionally taken a more dominant role in the lives of its worshippers. Many southern blacks see the church as their family, the place that kept them going, even kept them alive. From the antebellum era, through lynching, Jim Crow, and Civil Rights, and up to the present, the black church has often been the brightest spot in lives filled with toil and humiliation. As Bebe Moore Campbell explained in *The New York Times Magazine* interview:

> The black church was the one place where, even if Mandy Sue had been scrubbing Miss Ann's floor all week, she was *Mrs.* Mandy Sue Brown in church and she was the head of the usher board, and so you could go there and get respect. It was where, traditionally, people courted and where you could dress up, because you didn't dress up to go to work. … Church was a good social time and there were no white people there to oppress you.

The church obviously did not play the same role in the lives of white Southerners, although to some it was undoubtedly their salvation.

Politically, black churchgoers tend to be Democrats, while for the most part, religious white Southerners tend to be Republican. Black and white Baptists, then, have traditionally taken different positions on political issues, although the two groups are similar in terms of religious conservatism. White religious Southerners have aligned

The birthplace and childhood home of Martin Luther King, Jr., Atlanta, Georgia.

themselves with conservative causes that are considered by many to be extreme. They are generally fiercely opposed to abortion, adamantly intolerant of homosexuality, pro-military and anti-gun control, pro-school prayer and anti-welfare, tough on crime; and many have been slow to accept racial equality and women's rights. Many of these far right-wing views are preached within church walls or on Christian radio and television programs in the South. The black church, in contrast, has historically been more broad-minded and devoted to change. The black church was the center of the Civil Rights Movement and its ministry gave us Martin Luther King, Jr.

There are some churches in the South with racially mixed congregations, particularly in Atlanta. A few United Methodist Churches in Birmingham, Charlotte, Columbus and Augusta (Georgia), and Clemson and Greenville (South Carolina) have black pastors leading primarily white congregations. At the Plaza United Methodist Church in Charlotte, a white church that hired a black pastor in the summer of 1994, the transition has not been completely smooth, according to an article published in 1995 in *The New York Times*. Some white members of the church left in protest upon the new pastor's arrival, while other new black members joined the congregation. One elderly white male member of the congregation took it upon himself to maintain the old ways of the church: "If the preacher went on past noon, a standard practice at black churches, [he] would get up and open the church doors. If the sermon got too loud, he would hold his hand up to his ear as a signal to tone things down."

Although integration in churches is probably not going to happen in our lifetimes, some progress is being made by religious Southerners. In early 1994, 150 black and white Southerners joined hands to help rebuild two churches that were destroyed by three white southern boys who, while intoxicated, had entered the buildings, set hymnals aflame, and watched the structures burn while screaming racial slurs.

NOT ALL BAPTISTS

As previously mentioned, there are many different religions represented in the South, and many different sects within the Christian religion. The Church of Christ, a type of restorationist Christianity that came to Tennessee and Kentucky in the early 19th century, is particularly strong in the South today, especially in Nashville. The church, which models itself on the earliest Christian faith, does not allow drinking, smoking, dancing, or music (members sing without musical accompaniment), not to mention other forms of sin, and adherents see themselves as the only true Christians.

Most of the Catholics in the South live in Louisiana (which is about 40% Catholic) but the region as a whole is considered the least Catholic in the United States. Southern Catholics are known to have less formal relationships with priests than northern Catholics, possibly due to the warm and friendly aspect of their personalities. Jews in the South also appear to have more southern than ethnic characteristics, including the accent, the hospitality, and the love of company and entertaining. Neither group has historically suffered from organized discrimination like blacks did, probably because in the South, what mattered was whether you were white or black, not what religion you practiced. Jews especially found themselves respected by Christian Southerners because of their knowledge of and importance in the Old Testament.

Jews have lived in the South in small numbers for many generations while retaining their religious identity, even if they could not get kosher food, had to travel to larger towns or cities to worship on the high holidays and had trouble meeting potential Jewish spouses. According to one Jewish woman whose mother grew up in Greenville, Mississippi, in the early 20th century:

> When my mother was young and it was time to look for a fellow, her family took her "visiting" all over the South to meet Jewish boys. They went to parties and dances in Birmingham, Montgomery, Atlanta, and Memphis. The women would write letters to each other saying, "My daughter is 16 years old. ..." Once one girl got married, then she would try to find someone for her sister or best friend. That's how all the Jews in the South got to be related back in the early 20th century.

Although many of the smaller synagogues of the South have been torn down or are currently being used for other purposes, the buildings, temple documents, and Judaica of the South are being preserved through the efforts of the Museum of the Southern Jewish Experience in Utica, Mississippi. (Call 601-362-6357 for more information.)

Today, there are many Jews in the South's larger cities, especially in Georgia, Virginia, and Florida (although most Jews in the Sunshine State are concentrated in the southernmost cities—not part of the true South). Congregations tend to be reformed or conservative, with the smaller sects unrepresented. Although the Jewish high holidays are not officially recognized as public holidays in the South the way they are in the North, Jews in the South today have little trouble getting matzo at Passover or gathering the requisite number of Jews to pray. Still, said one Jewish woman who moved from Chicago to a suburb of Atlanta, "It is unnerving to hear a rabbi say 'Shalom, ya'll' from the pulpit."

Chapter Nine

SAY IT SOUTHERN

The southern accent is the South's strongest identifying characteristic. It defies geography: people living as far north as Cairo, Illinois, have an accent, so they are considered southern; those as far south as Miami don't, so they are not. In the media, it walks hand-in-hand with stereotype: the sheriff with the crew-cut and dark aviator sunglasses who pulls over the speeding car has an accent, as does the guy with the tattoo swigging a beer in his pickup truck, the lug who keeps saying "Huh?" and the pretty lady who asks if there's anything she can get you. When you hear a southern accent on film, it evokes a certain response: fear, anticipation of a wicked or violent act, disdain for the slow and the dumb, or even a sense of comfort, of being taken care of. Other American accents rarely have that power. According to Molly Ivins writing in the June 1988 edition of *Mother Jones* magazine:

> The extent to which a southern accent is associated with low IQ in American popular culture is hard to exaggerate. Look at all those World War II movies: three guys wind up in the Army together from basic training to heroic death. The hero is always a handsome, brave, blond kid from the Midwest. His pals are a smart, wisecracking New Yorker ... and a southern slope-headed ridge-runner too dumb to tell c'mon from sic 'em.

Newcomers to the South initially react to the accent with uncertainty and awkwardness. They often cannot help but associate it with what they've seen on the screen. In some instances, newcomers can't *understand* it, especially on the telephone. It's like going to see a performance of Shakespeare's *Macbeth* in which they get the general gist of things, but miss the fine detail—it's English all right, they think, but it's not *my* kind of English. Some newcomers make a conscious effort not to let easy southernisms (like "y'all") or the melodic quality of southern speech slip into their vocabulary. ("If I ever start sounding like *them*," they say, "shoot me.") And Southerners also dislike it when one of their own begins sounding too "Yankeefied." After being immersed in southern society for a while, however, newcomers sometimes realize how stiff and plain *they* sound compared with Southerners. Consciously or unconsciously, they soon begin sounding like Southerners.

GETTING RID OF IT

For Southerners themselves, the accent can be a source of shame. "I worked at getting rid of my accent," said one Southerner. "I wasn't proud of being southern because Southerners are thought of as stupid and racist. Losing my accent was one way I rejected my culture."

211

In the late 1980s and early 1990s, Southerners who wanted to "get ahead in business" and "make a good first impression" took classes in How to Lose Your Accent, and paid good money for them. With the Olympics on its way in the summer of 1996, some Atlantans wanted to make sure they wouldn't appear dumb and unprofessional. Some enrollees in an "accent reduction" course in Chattanooga and other southern cities were tired of hearing themselves imitated by newcomers or being told that they sounded "cute," "sexy," or "funny." They worked at turning "y'all" into "you guys," replacing "I'm fixin' to …" with "I'm going to …," shortening those drawling vowel sounds, literally training their tongues to speed it up in there.

Of course, classes like these, when publicized, brought with them a backlash of criticism from Southerners, especially since they were often taught by Northerners. "Traitors," Lewis Grizzard called the suckers who handed over big bucks to destroy what came naturally. "I personally think everybody [who] has a southern accent and wants to change it should be flogged," he said. Maybe people took his threat seriously, as these classes have petered out of late, or maybe they are being held at secret locations to protect the identity of the turncoats.

THE AMERICANIZATION OF LANGUAGE

Some Southerners are of the opinion that the southern accent is being flattened, washed out, Americanized by accent-free people on television, radio, and the movies, and by all those incoming Northerners. Even air-conditioning has been blamed—for bringing Southerners inside from the porch (and all the good talk it generated) and onto the couch to stare blankly at the screen. Some people think that southern youngsters sound more like those non-accented Midwesterners they hear on the news every day or those awesome-sounding kids on "Melrose Place" or "Beverly Hills 90210" than like their parents or grandparents.

Linguists sometimes discount the media theory; they believe that "the principal forces of change in contemporary American English are social ones—mobility (especially the upward kind), mass education, and urbanization ...," according to Michael Montgomery of the University of South Carolina writing in *The Encyclopedia of Southern Culture*. In other words, upwardly mobile, urban Southerners speak more like their northern and western counterparts than like other Southerners who live outside their social circles and beyond the metropolitan area. In addition, linguists believe that southern children, like all children, learn language and speech patterns from their parents, family members, and peers, not from a talking box. As long as Southerners continue to see themselves as different and to take pride in their speech patterns, experts say, the accent will persist.

Southerners who adopt speech patterns from outside their own culture often have the ability, like the children of immigrants, to switch back and forth from one "language" to the other, depending on their audience. Black Southerners, in particular, often speak one way when in a professional setting (especially when whites are present) and another way when at home or with other blacks. Southern businessmen who regularly deal with outsiders can be good-old-boy-like with their southern clients and employees, and more formal and clipped with their northern clients. Similarly, southern teenagers can sound as cool and flippant as any kid from the Valley when hanging out with friends, and as humble and respectful as the situation demands when at home or in church. As one Southerner from Arkansas living in Illinois said, "I don't think I have much of an accent anymore, but as soon as I get on a Delta plane and I hear those stewardesses say 'hey' [hi], 'nahce' [nice], and 'ahce' [ice], my accent comes back."

A VARIETY OF ACCENTS

Southern speech, of course, is not made up of one accent shared across the board by all residents below the Mason-Dixon line. The southern accent takes many different forms, which vary according to social class, age, gender, ethnic background, education level, race, and region. Those from mountainous regions speak differently than those from the lowlands, as do those from the islands versus those from the mainland. These speech patterns are different enough to keep linguistic scholars busy charting tones, word usage, inflections, etc., and they have published the technical tomes to prove it.

To the outsider, all Southerners probably sound the same. But the native Southerner with a good ear can place another Southerner by his accent, as Henry Higgins did when he first met Eliza Dolittle selling flowers in Covent Garden in "My Fair Lady." Dr. Charles Hadley, a professor at Charlotte's Queen's College, is often called upon to coach actors in southern speech so they will sound convincing in the roles they play; he even coached Vivien Leigh for her role as Blanche DuBois in "A Streetcar Named Desire." According to an article on Hadley that appeared in the February 1995 issue of *Southern Living*, once when a director commanded him to "do the [South Carolina] accent" he said, "Which one? ... Would you like the islands off the coast, the Gullah? Would you like the Charleston or the Lowcountry around Charleston? ... Would you like the Piedmont section or would you like the Appalachian? ... Do you want urban, rural, redneck, what?" The director was totally stumped.

According to the *Encyclopedia*, linguists divide the southern region into two major subregions when classifying accents: Coastal Southern, which stretches from Virginia all the way to Texas, and South Midland, which includes the Piedmont area and the southern Appalachian mountains from Virginia through South Carolina as well as the hilly areas in Georgia and Alabama. The early settlers in the lowlands spoke like their former countrymen in London and the south of Britain, while those in the uplands spoke like their relatives in north Britain, Scotland, and Northern Ireland, says the *Encyclopedia*. But southern speech developed and changed with the influx of African slaves and as it came in contact with Native American languages as well as the Spanish and French of other colonizers. Today, black and white Southerners share many speech patterns,

although the exact relationship between the two has long been a politically charged and highly controversial topic among linguists.

These two subregions do not include the unique speech patterns found on the islands off the coast of South Carolina and Georgia, or the creole dialects of Cajuns and Creoles found in southern Louisiana. The former dialect, called Gullah, is a mixture of English and various African languages, and resembles the creole dialects found on islands in the Caribbean. Gullah, unlike other southern dialects, is difficult for the outsider to understand, even though it incorporates more English than African words. The Louisiana dialects are mixtures of French and English.

Many older Southerners of a certain class, especially people in Charleston, Richmond, Savannah, and Mobile, speak with a particularly gentle, melodic accent that outsiders sometimes find mesmerizing. According to one Northerner in her late thirties living in Birmingham and married to a native, "The generation before ours, especially the educated ones, have beautiful and cultivated southern accents. They sound like FDR would have sounded if he had been from the South. Here, if we hear someone with a refined accent we say she has 'lotsa magnolia.'"

Whatever their class or age, according to the *Encyclopedia*, Southerners sound different from the rest of us because they do the following with language:

- Use the "ah" sound for "i," as in "time," which sounds like "tahm," and "think," which sounds like "thahnk."
- Drop the "r" sound after a vowel, as in "beer," which comes out like "beeyah," or "mother" and "sister," which come out like "mothah" and "sistah."
- Draw out their vowel sounds, or drawl, as in saying "ba-yed" for "bed."
- Pronounce short "e" vowels as "i," as in saying "pin" for "pen" and "tin" for "ten."

Southerners also seem universally to drop that hard "t" sound when pronouncing words like "Atlanta," which comes out "Adlanna," or "center," which in the South becomes "sinner." They often raise their pitch at the end of a sentence that is not a question, but which then comes out sounding like one, and place the accent on a different syllable in certain words (e.g., *cre*-ate instead of cre-*ate*, and *ho*-tel instead of ho-*tel*). Mountain people or members of the lower classes in the South are often accused of speaking with a nasal sound, which is said to be responsible for the southern twang.

SOME SOUTHERN WORDS, PHRASES, AND EXPRESSIONS TO KNOW

It is common knowledge that Southerners love to talk and that they would much rather give a long explanation than a short, to-the-point one, to tell a story rather than skip it, to preach a long sermon rather than a short one. Southerners have a strong oral tradition, and enjoy telling ghost stories, folktales, or simply illustrating a point with a vivid anecdote. Their vocabulary is often thought to be the most colorful, expressive, dramatic, and folksy in America. According to Maryln Schwartz, Southern belles still call the fridge the "icebox," the couch the "sofa," and a purse a "pocketbook." There are volumes and volumes of words, pronunciations, and phrases that are unique to the South. Here are a few that often puzzle the newcomer:

aim to: plan to, as in "I aim to make it out to see you sometime soon."

big: the polite way to say fat, as in "Look how Martha's let herself go—she's gone gray and gotten big."

bless out: to yell at someone relentlessly, as in "After I broke the window she really blessed me out."

bless your heart: used to show concern or thanks, as a response to the mention of a headache, or to receiving an unexpected gift.

carry: drive, as in "Can you carry me to town?"

cattywampus: off kilter, crooked, as in "That frame's catty-wampus."

cher: Louisiana talk for "sweetie," "honey," or "dear."

coming up: growing up, as in "When I was coming up, we did things differently."

commencin' to: beginning to, as in "I'm commencin' to be on my way."

directly: soon, as in "I'm aimin' to deliver that directly."

favor: to look like, as in "Your new grandbaby really favors your side of the family."

fix: to prepare, as in "I'll fix lunch for you if you like."

fixin' to: going to do something, as in "I'm fixin to go to the market."

get in the bed: go to bed

go mad and bite yourself: to be really thrilled about something, as in "She's so happy about her new grandbaby, she's gonna go mad and bite herself!"

"Gol dawg it!": a curse alternative, used interchangeably with "Gol dang it!"

hey: the Southern form of "hi"; a friendly greeting used in such phrases as "Hey, how you?"

hissy fit: a temper tantrum, a fit you have when you're really upset; sometimes shortened to hissy, as in "If you don't buy the child what she wants, she's gonna have a hissy."

ink pen: a regular pen, like a ballpoint.

jump the broom: to get married.

like to: nearly, almost, as in "I like to cried when I heard that song."

make good grades: the same as to *get* good grades.

meet up with: get to know, as in an advertisement for chewing tobacco that said, "Meet up with a cleaner chew."

mess of: a large portion of, as in "I'm fixin' to make a mess of greens."

might could: may be able to, as in "I might could look that up for you if you can hold on a second."

over yonder: over there in that direction, as in "The dog's over yonder past that fence."

pour the tea: to have a good gossip, share some choice news, as in "I can't wait to sit and pour the tea with my old friends."

precious: a compliment, an expression of something beautiful or extremely cute, as in "That little girl of yours is so precious;" used interchangeably with "lovely" and "darling," but not really synonymous with "sweet" or "nice," which are less complimentary.

reckon: think or believe, as in "I reckon I can do that for you."

stories: soap operas, as in "I'm fixin' to watch my stories now."

swanny: used instead of swear, as in "I swanny, if she ever does that to me again, I'm gonna …"

tacky: not in good taste, without class, cheap; the worst insult you can give someone in the South; you might get called tacky if you wear a print dress to a deb party; synonyms include **trashy**, **crass,** and **cheesy**, which means tacky-slimy, as in the guy in disco clothes who sits next to you at a bar.

And, Southerners **don't** say:

Civil War: it's the War Between the States, the War of Northern Aggression, the Unfortunate Incident, even That Late Unpleasantness. Certain battles are called by different names in the South as well: Antietam is called the Battle of Sharpsburg, and Bull Run is called Manassas. General Sherman is usually called by his full name, William Tecumseh Sherman, in the South.

curse words: the one that starts with 's' and the one that starts with 'f' are terribly impolite when released in good company in the South; see "Gol dawg it" or "I swanny," above, for alternatives. (Similarly, mentioning sex or using sexual terms in public is also not done.)

dying or **dead**: in the South, it's proper to say someone has "passed," "passed over," "gone home," "departed this life for the next," or "passed on."

Jesus Christ or God: these sacred names are only to be spoken in church; they are not used flippantly or to begin a curse.

nigger: the "n" word, an absolutely forbidden word for whites to use about blacks, although blacks say it about each other; old-fashioned white Southerners sometimes use "Negro" or the offensive "nigra," and many still say "colored." **African-American** or **black** are the best choices.

pop: in the South it's soda, coke (a generic word for anything fizzy), or co-cola.

sack: bag is the word of choice.

washroom: in the South, it's bathroom or restroom or, better yet, ladies' room.

yeah: it's "yes" in the South, and usually followed by "sir" or "ma'am."

AND THEN THERE'S Y'ALL

Unlike some other regional words, y'all is used throughout the South by all types of people. Moreover, it is one of the first southernisms newcomers pick up, and the first thing their friends back in Chicago tease them about when they come home for a visit. (Use of the northern equivalent of y'all—"you guys"—in the South is usually a dead giveaway to one's outsider status.) Y'all, which is a contraction of the awkward "you all," is so useful a pronoun that even people outside the region are supposedly starting to use it.

The most important rule about using y'all is to remember that it refers to two or more people, not to a single person. Sometimes Southerners say "y'all's," which indicates the possessive form as in "Y'all's new house sure is nice."

SOUTHERN CITIES AND TOWNS

One way to really stick out in the South is to pronounce the name of a southern city or town incorrectly. Outsiders usually make this mistake because they place the accent on the wrong syllable, or because they have the habit of pronouncing every single sound in every word. Hence, Summerville rolls off the northern tongue as SOME-er-vill, when it should be SUM-vull.

As one person from Tennessee put it, Southerners have a way of swallowing sounds at will. Mobile, that fair city in Alabama, is not pronounced MO-bile with a long "i" sound, but mo-BEALE, with the accent on the second syllable. Marietta, Georgia is not pronounced MARE-ee-et-ta, but May-RET-ta, by the natives. Blytheville, Arkansas is not BLYTHE-ville with a full "th" sound, but BLY-vull. (As you can see, the ending "ville" in the South comes out "vull," said ever so quickly.) And New Orleans isn't always pronounced the Cajun way, as N'Awlins; some natives prefer to say it the French way, pronouncing each syllable as in New OR-lee-ans. When traveling in or to the South, it might be wise to ask a southern friend how to pronounce the name of a town, just so when you get there you won't embarrass yourself.

SOUTHERN NAMES, TITLES, AND NICKNAMES

Southern names seem to fall into three categories: the historically derived, the double name, and what can be called southern unusual.

Those who name their children according to the first category are attempting to honor relatives, both past and present, to uphold family naming traditions, or to pay tribute to biblical or historic figures. (Not too many Southerners run out to buy those baby name books when they find themselves with child because there is too much family to name after.) Many names in the South have a story behind them, and it is typical for people to ask, "Where did that name come from?" Certain names in the region carry a good deal of weight, and having them can provide the extra edge someone needs to get a dinner reservation when all the tables are already booked or even to beat out someone with equal qualifications for a job.

In the South, boys are commonly named after their fathers, grandfathers, and those beyond, resulting in those familiar designations of Junior, III, IV, etc. Both boys and girls are often given their mother's (or grandmother's) maiden name as a first or a middle name, which is why you meet people of both sexes in the South who are named Gray, Tyler, or Porter. Having a last name as a first name is one way to keep the past alive and to remember previous generations, and it sound so classy. Girls are also given old-fashioned names such as Alma, Lily, or Hannah, not because they are currently in vogue, but because they are being named after a dear old great aunt or a great grandmother.

The double name is still commonly used in the South for members of both sexes. Some Southerners say that this is because there are so many relatives to name after, that it's easier to narrow it down to two than to choose just one. Others say the tradition comes from Ireland and Scotland, where because there were so many Marys, Josephs, and Bobs, the middle name had to be used so people would know who was being spoken to. Some popular double names for girls today include anything starting with Mary, as in Mary Jane, Mary Gretchen, Mary Evelyn, Mary Louise, Mary Elizabeth, Mary Virginia, Mary Beth, or anything starting with Sue, as in Sue Ellen. For boys or men, it's Billy Bob, Billy Don, Joe Frank, etc., with the first name often made into the diminutive by adding "y" or "ie." If there are two cousins named James in the South, then their families will call them by their first and middle names, as in Jim Buck and Jim Clark, so as not to get them mixed up.

The Southern Unusual category consists of names that you don't hear much outside the region: Opalene, Wilma, Lamar, Wyladene, Vern, Pearl, Ruby, Maybelle, Louella, Raynell, Clovis, etc. These names sound rural and old-fashioned, and some were no doubt made up by families as an artistic gesture.

In a close family in which the grandmother is part of the household, she might be called Big Mama, and the mother Little Mama or just Mama. A close older relative might even be called "Ma," and the true mother called "Real Ma." Similarly, in a family in which father and son have the same name, the father may be Big Bob and the son Little Bob. In some two-child southern families, the son might simply be called "Brother" (which can be shortened to "Bubba") and the daughter "Sister," as in "Brother, go tell Sister it's time for supper." Sometimes, the husband and wife in a southern family call each other Momma and Daddy instead of their first names. In the old days, they would even call each other Mr. and Mrs. whenever addressing each other in front of others, even the children. And, even today a daughter calls her father Daddy in the South until he departs this life, even if she's 60 and he's over 80. (In the North, Daddy is almost invariably shortened to plain old Dad once the child reaches adulthood.) Grandparents are called Grandmama and Granddaddy, and grandchildren are called grandbabies.

It is polite in the South to call adults by Mr. and Mrs. until told not to. When a newcomer to the South addressed her colleagues in a memo by only their first and last names, her supervisor marked up her draft, adding "Mr.," "Mrs.," and "Miss" before each name. Both Mrs. and Miss, by the way, are simply pronounced as "Miz."

Although many women in the South are starting to keep their maiden names when they get married, most do not. Many women compromise by keeping their maiden names as middle names, but few hyphenate their maiden names and married names, a common practice in northern urban areas. Even Jane Fonda is called Jane Turner in Atlanta, although she is known the world over by her famous family name. Elderly women, especially the genteel kind, are sometimes called Miz Lillian or Miz Blanche, but some consider this condescending.

If somebody has served in the military, people will address him by his military title rather than use the generic Mr.

A few decades ago, before integration, it was common in the South for whites to drop titles when addressing blacks, as a way of keeping the racial hierarchy in place. Although whites demanded to be called Mr. and Mrs., blacks were spoken to like children, using only their first names. In newspapers, whites were always referred to using titles, while only the first and last names of blacks were used.

When addressing invitations, in the South, it is still most common to use the formal Mr. and Mrs. Steven G. Harrison III, for example, as opposed to Martha and Jim Harrison, especially for a fancy occasion. If the invitation is for the woman only, it is most proper to say Mrs. Steven G. Harrison III. In a club or school directory, women are sometimes still listed by their husband's names, with their names in parentheses, e.g., Mrs. Steven G. Harrison III (Martha). Sometimes directories use the woman's full name, maiden name included, as in Martha Digby Harrison.

Chapter Ten

SOUTHERN MUSIC AND LITERATURE: A RESOURCE GUIDE

Two of the South's greatest contributions to America and the world are its music and its literature. Listening to the lyrics of country music songs and reading the fiction of authors such as Eudora Welty, William Faulkner, Dorothy Allison, and Carson McCullers, to name only a few, are excellent ways to access southern culture, to learn how Southerners think and how they live. Although southern music is now beloved across America, and classics such as Faulkner's *The Sound and the Fury* are required reading in many freshman American literature classes, many music lovers still quickly mash that radio button when country music or jazz comes on, and readers forgo southern fiction because they think it's difficult to understand.

For those newcomers who have little or no experience with regional music and fiction, who don't know the difference between Cajun and zydeco, and don't know which southern novel to try first, here are some basic definitions of southern forms of music, complete with lists of musicians, as well as a quick explanation of southern fiction and a list of recommended authors.

SOUTHERN MUSIC

The first thing to understand about southern music is that all the different forms share a good many characteristics, that they have all borrowed from each other, and that none remains completely "pure." Many musical forms started in the South and many of the most famous musicians and singers have southern origins, but southern music moved north and west with migrating Southerners and is now considered mainstream American music.

Much of southern music grew out of oppression. Black southern music, in particular, developed from a combination of African rhythms and musical styles that were mixed with lyrics sung by black slaves (or later, hard laborers) as they worked the fields. White music, too, was the music of hill people who took the English, Irish, and Scottish ballads of their heritage and over time changed or added simple lyrics to reflect their lives of toil, poverty, and heartbreak. Church hymns and prayers also provided fodder for southern music, both black and white.

Here are some short descriptions of the major types of southern music, complete with historical information as well as names of important figures. As you will see, each form evolved through the influence of other forms, and each continues to evolve.

Folk Music

In the late 18th and early 19th centuries, settlers in the South sang the ballads of their British homeland. Over time, lyrics and melodies were developed to reflect their simple lives. Songs were often about poverty, lost love, the nature around them, and religious themes, and were sung to the accompaniment of a fiddle. In those times, singing and dancing were two of the few forms of communal recreation.

Hillbilly Music

This type of music, born in isolated Appalachia out of folk music, was the precursor to country music. It was not commercially known until the early 20th century but served as a local form of entertainment at fiddling contests, barnraisings, quilting parties, and other events, even casual get-togethers held on the porch. Instruments were often homemade and lyrics were dramatic—emotional stories of family troubles, religious devotion, disappointed lovers, even dogs, trains, and mommas. Hardly any hillbilly musicians could read music or write down their own pieces, but they learned the fiddle, the banjo, and the harmonica from other family members. In the early 1920s, when a radio station in Atlanta played hillbilly music to a wide audience, the genre began to catch on. Popular early hillbilly musicians included John Carson, Jimmie Rodgers, and the Carter Family (A.P., Maybelle, and Sara).

Country Music

In the early 1920s, with the establishment of the WSM radio station (which stood for "We Shield Millions," the slogan of its sponsor, the National Life and Accident Company) in Nashville, Tennessee, mountain music got its first major exposure. Hillbilly musicians were asked to appear on a weekly program called Barn Dance, which in 1927 became known as the Grand Ole Opry. After World War II, hillbilly music, which made a significant impact on the way non-Southerners viewed the South, began to be called by a more dignified name—"country music." Stars included Charlie Pride, one of the few black country music singers, Minnie Pearl, Grandpa Jones, Tennessee Ernie Ford, Loretta Lynn, Hank Williams, Jimmie Dickens, Jim Reeves, Chet Atkins, Hank Snow, Patsy Cline, and Kitty Wells. In the early 1960s, the basic country music style was polished, or made more processed; backup singers were added, voices were encouraged to be less twangy, and bands were equipped with electric guitars, drums, saxophones, and pianos. This supposedly new-and-improved form of country music came to be known as the "Nashville Sound."

Today country music is beloved nationwide, with more than 2,200 all-country radio stations and millions of fans who annually purchase more than $1.5 billion in records, tapes, and CDs. Nashville is still Country Music U.S.A., and tickets are still hard to come by for the Saturday night live broadcast at the Grand Ole Opry, which sits comfortably amidst a huge country music theme park outside the city. The Nashville Network, a cable television channel, is flourishing, and the annual broadcast of the Country Music Awards is a three-hour primetime event.

Branson, Missouri, located in the Ozark Mountains and nick-named the "Hillbilly Las Vegas," with its 20-odd live country music theaters and more than 4 million tourists annually, is giving Nashville a run for its money. Branson, which is supposedly for lovers of old-time country music without all the frills, has hosted such stars as Johnny and June Carter Cash, Mel Tillis, Roy Clark, Mickey Gilley, and Ray Price, all of whom hang around after the show to sign autographs for fans. The town caters to families and babies are seen regularly at all venues, most of which have a no-liquor policy.

One reason why country music is so appealing is because the melodies are simple, and the lyrics tell true stories of universal feelings: broken hearts and rejection, love and devotion, hard times and drinking nights. Country music artists are often from lower- or working-class families and have suffered themselves but risen out of the depths through music. People can really relate to country music, especially when feeling sad, when the country is at war or the economy is going to hell. Even if, on principle, you reject country music as being sappy and silly, if you're in the right mood, it can really affect you (or make you smile, so you forget your troubles). Paula Schwed, a New Yorker living in the South, collected her favorite lines from country music songs into a book called *I've Got Tears in My Ears From Lyin' on My Back in My Bed While I Cry Over You ... Country Music's Best [and Funniest] Lines.* Here are some of her collected treasures:

> "I wouldn't take her to a dog fight even if I thought she
> could win"
> "If I say I love you, consider me drunk"
> "Hello, Mexico, and adios, baby, to you"
> "You're the reason our kids are ugly (but I love you anyway)"
> "If I don't love you, grits ain't groceries"

Some of today's biggest country music stars include Garth Brooks, Alan Jackson, John Berry, Clint Black, Tracey Byrd, Mary Chapin-Carpenter, Wade Hayes, Ty Hernoon, Toby Keith, Alison Krauss, Dwight Yoakum, Tracey Lawrence, Patty Loveless, Reba McEntire, Tim McGraw, John Michael Montgomery, George Strait, Travis Tritt, Tanya Tucker, Kenny Chesney, Joe Diffie, Wade Hayos, Hal Ketchum, Neal McCoy, Shania Twain, Emmylou Harris, Suzy Bogguss, Trisha Yearwood, Tammy Wynette, Wynonna (formerly of The Judds), Lorrie Morgan, George Jones, Bobby Bare, and Dolly Parton, as well as Brooks & Dunn, Alabama, 4 Runner, and The Mavericks.

Bluegrass

Bluegrass, which originated in the South but became commercially successful in the North, is an instrumental type of old-time Appalachian music played on non-electric guitars, five-string banjos, fiddles, and mandolins. First made popular at the Grand Ole Opry by

Kentuckian Bill Monroe in 1939, bluegrass, like jazz, is known for its improvisational style and its emphasis on virtuosity. (Remember "Duelling Banjos" from way back in '73? That's bluegrass.) Bluegrass greats include the Stanley Brothers, the Osborne Brothers, the Country Gentlemen, Jimmy Martin, Jim & Jesse, Mac Wiseman, Cumberland Express, Sam Bush, Don Reno, Lester Flatt, and Earl Scruggs.

Ragtime

Ragtime, named and developed in the Mississippi Valley in the 1890s, is a highly developed musical style centered around the piano. Influenced by black folk music and used in minstrel shows, ragtime was long associated with the plantation myth. Ragtime made a profound impact on jazz and dance music in the first quarter of the 20th century, and later on pop music. Scott Joplin is thought of as the master of ragtime.

Jazz

Jazz was born in the first years of the 20th century in a neighborhood of New Orleans called Storyville that was filled with clubs, gambling joints, and brothels. Most of its originators and participants were freed black slaves who had come to New Orleans after emancipation. Jazz, which is a major element of blues, ragtime, pop, and even rock music, is highly improvisational and relies on the voice to be used as another instrument to accompany the strong rhythms created by the piano, the drums, the saxophone, the horns, and the clarinet. Traditional jazz took its form from European music, its beat from African music, and its brass instruments from America. Jazz has evolved in myriad ways since its birth in New Orleans, but jazz in its original form (known as "Dixieland Jazz") can still be heard in New Orleans at Preservation Hall. The unrefuted king of Dixieland jazz was Louis Armstrong; other greats included Sidney Bechet, Jelly Roll Morton, and King Oliver.

Blues

Blues originated in the Mississippi Delta at about the same time as jazz but was less sophisticated musically and did not borrow from classical European musical forms. Work songs and field hollers, church music, and folk drumming, as well as the black slave and fieldworker experience are at the root of blues. Lyrics have to do with toil, love, nature, and hopelessness, and songs have a slow, repetitive sadness to them. The guitar was the only instrument used in the early days of the blues. The Father of the Blues was Alabama-born W.C. Handy who composed blues based on the music and stories he heard from ex-slaves on and around the Mississippi River. Handy wrote the three blues classics "St. Louis Blues," "Beale Street Blues," and "Memphis Blues." B.B. King, Leadbelly, Muddy Waters, Howlin' Wolf, Ma Rainey, and Bessie Smith are known as blues greats.

Gospel

Gospel music is essentially a combination of hymns, spirituals, and Biblical texts with elements of the blues and/or ragtime music. Gospel music is said to be strongest in Chicago, but many of the great gospel singers were born in the South. The Father of Gospel Music was Thomas A. Dorsey, a composer and publisher from rural Georgia, who developed gospel music in the 1930s. (See the documentary film, "Say Amen, Somebody," for an excellent account of gospel's origins.) Gospel music has both black and white varieties. White gospel tends to edge toward the Christian contemporary genre of music that has become more and more popular in recent years. In the black church in particular, gospel singing is very moving and emotional, and is meant to cause the audience to have a religious experience or simply to participate by clapping or singing along. It helps people forget their troubles by asking them to open themselves up to Jesus Christ, to be moral individuals, and to have hope for the future. Live gospel music is performed every Sunday in any city, South or North, in which there is a strong religious black population. It is available to

Mose Vinson, Memphis blues singer. Photograph by George McDaniel, courtesy of the Center for Southern Folklore Archive.

all who wish to hear it, but it might be wise to call a church ahead of time to make sure visitors are welcome. (They usually are.)

Some notable gospel singers and groups include Mahalia Jackson, The Golden Gospel Singers, The Silvertones, Jake Hess of the Statesmen Quartet, Clarence Fountain and the Five Blind Boys, Rev. F.C. Barnes, The Gospel Gents, Gold City, Gaither Vocal Band, The Nelsons, The National Travelers, The Kingsmen, the Dixie Hummingbirds, The Cathedrals, Heirloom, The Greenes, Heaven Bound, Jeff & Sheri Easter, Voices of Light, and The Spirit of Memphis.

Cajun

Cajun music is a musical stew of different types of music: African-American, African-Caribbean, Native American, Spanish, Scotch-Irish, and primarily French folk music. It is the music of the Acadians, the French who were forced to flee Nova Scotia in the mid-18th century and came to settle in southern Louisiana. The defining instruments in Cajun music are the accordion and the fiddle, and the lyrics are usually sung in Cajun, a Louisiana French/English patois. It is primarily played in dance halls and at music festivals in the region. Some of the best Cajun artists include Michael Doucet, Steve Riley, the Mamou Playboys, Beausoleil, Dewey Balfa, Filé, Hector & Octa Clark, and D.L. Menard.

Zydeco

Zydeco, the music of Louisiana's black Creoles, has a good deal in common with Cajun music. Zydeco consists of a mixture of rhythm and blues, Cajun, and soul, with strong African-Caribbean influences. The piano accordion is used rather than the traditional accordion and the saxophone takes the place of the fiddle. The washboard, a metal vest that is scraped with a spoon or other metal objects, drums, and the electric bass are all used. Zydeco is primarily fast dance music, while Cajun music is ideal for Cajun waltzes. Some important zydeco artists and groups include Buckwheat Zydeco, Boozoo Chavis, Beau

Jockques, Queen Ida, the Zydeco High Rollers, Clifton Chenier, and C.J. Chenier.

Rockabilly

The rock sound that came out of the South in the 1950s was essentially a mixture of rhythm and blues and country music, while northern rock was influenced mostly by jazz and blues. Rockabilly's first hit was "Blue Suede Shoes," by Tennessee native Carl Perkins in 1956, but once Elvis Presley (born in 1935 in Tupelo, Mississippi) came on the scene, everything changed forever. Elvis's appeal came from the fact that he could sing and move the way black musicians did at the time. (The disc jockey at the radio station that first played his songs, in fact, rather than identifying him directly as white, mentioned only his high school, which clued listeners in immediately.) He was handsome, he was sexy, his voice was throaty and emotional, and he had tremendous swoon appeal. Like his first listeners, Elvis came from a lower-class background; he was raised in a shotgun house, and his musical education came from listening to music at church and imitating country music and black blues singers on the radio.

As he grew more and more popular and then began to go downhill before his death in 1977, his fans grew more and more obsessive and he became one of the 20th century's strongest cult figures. Strangely enough, Southerners today as a whole are not the nation's most devoted Elvis worshippers, perhaps because they saw him as one of themselves, not as an immortal godlike figure. Blacks, in particular, never took to him, because they associated his and other white southern music with "redneck" culture and its underlying racism. According to a survey conducted by the *Atlanta Journal-Constitution* in 1993, white Southerners own slightly fewer records and pieces of Elvis memorabilia than other Americans.

Elvis' rock and rockabilly brothers from the South include Jerry Lee Lewis, Roy Orbison, Ronnie Hawkins, Gene Vincent, and Little Richard. Southern rock, as a genre, was a '70s phenomenon and was

clearly linked to southern culture and values. Famous southern rockers include the Allman Brothers Band, the Charlie Daniels Band, Lynyrd Skynyrd, and the Marshall Tucker Band.

Other Info

The following record companies produce southern music:

Rounder (folk), Flying Fish (folk), Rhino Records (good for collections), Alligator (specializes in blues), Light Records (gospel), A.I.R. Records (gospel), Benson Music Group (gospel), Black Top (blues and folk), and High Tone (rockabilly). For excellent, up-to-date information on southern music, including schedules of bluegrass and Cajun music festivals, check out *Dirty Linen* magazine, a bimonthly.

In addition, the Center for Southern Folklore (152 Beale Street, Memphis, TN, 38103) is a wonderful source of information on Memphis blues and other southern music. The Center regularly puts out music collections from their archives and the gift shop carries various publications and books on the subject. "A Slice of Southern Music" is an excellent beginner's collection featuring one or two examples of various southern musical forms, including Delta blues, gospel, country, and rockabilly.

For current information on jazz concerts, many states (including Alabama, North Carolina, Louisiana, and Georgia) have a Jazz Foundation Hotline or information line featuring a recorded message of dates, venues, and times.

SOUTHERN LITERATURE

Southerners, with their strong oral tradition, unique forms of speech, collective pride and/or shame about the past, and love of region, have made a tremendous contribution to the body of American literature. Sure there are urban New York stories, tales of the Old West, fiction about Boston society, and Midwestern farm novels, but none of these regional genres is as distinctive and enduring as southern fiction.

There is really no such thing as The Southern Novel, but southern fiction does have some general themes and methods of characterization that are evident in many examples of regional fiction:

- Nineteenth-century fiction from the South is often set on the plantation, which provided material for creating idealized and romantic characters such as the belle, the gentleman, the rogue, the loyal slave, and the mammy. In the "moonlight and magnolias" novel, the hierarchical nature of southern society and the system of slavery are sometimes glorified.
- The land, its beauty and purity, and the morality and independence of those who tend it are major themes in antebellum, Reconstruction, and modern southern novels.

- After The War, fiction came to deal with the theme of the Lost Cause (although few works dealt with the actual battles themselves). Writers made much of the idea of a society changed forever, the loss of independence and the southern way of life.
- The North, in southern fiction, is often representative of the evils of industrialization and its accompanying materialism. Northerners are portrayed as being corrupt, money-focused, disrespectful of history and the land. In contrast, the South is seen as a people- and community-oriented place with firmly rooted traditions.
- Characters in the historical novel and popular fiction are often from either the upper class or the lowest classes. At either extreme, characters are stereotyped. They have a decided place in society and are made to act accordingly. Landowners are alternately seen as gracious and good or cruel and abusive. Mothers are all

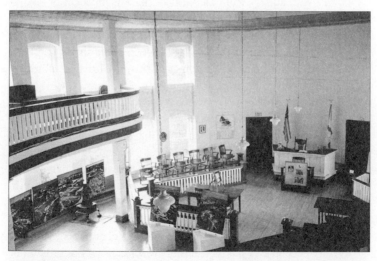

Interior of the courthouse in Monroeville, Alabama, the hometown of Harper Lee. The courtroom was replicated exactly for the film of To Kill a Mockingbird. *Notice what used to be called the "colored" section on the upper level.*

goodness and light, belles are beautiful; slaves are either ever-present helpers, simple and agreeable, or violent and sexually loose. Lower class white people are portrayed as hard-drinking, violent, unpolished, racist, and sex-crazed.

- Many southern stories and elements in southern fiction are derived from African folktales, ghost stories, anecdotes, and tall tales passed from generation to generation.

- An attachment to people, a community, and/or a town features largely in the southern novel. This quality is what writers and critics call a "sense of place." As novelist Eudora Welty wrote, writers from the South care "passionately about Place. Not simply in the historical or philosophical connotation of the word, but in the sensory thing, the experienced world of sight and sound and smell, in its earth and water and sky and in its seasons."

- Twentieth-century fiction often deals with the individual or the family who suffers from alcoholism, incest, physical or sexual abuse, slavery, racism, divorce, sexual confusion, or fear of sexuality. These figures are especially tragic in the regional novel because they are held against the backdrop of the strong southern values of home, family, church, patriotism, Christian morality, and the myths of the aristocratic family.

- Most southern fiction differs from other American fiction because of its feel for southern language and forms of speech. Many authors have the ability to capture the melody and idioms of southern speech by writing in dialect or through the use of dialogue that beautifully and realistically captures metaphors, puns, and sayings. The narrative voice in novels is usually strong.

- Southern novels are character- and plot-centered as opposed to being grandly philosophic or abstract. In short, they are good *stories* about interesting people. Southern characters are often terribly eccentric (what Northerners would classify as crazy) but fully accepted members of society; they are lovably humorous, wise without being worldly or well educated. Southern characters often feel the weight of the past and struggle for a way to interpret it in the modern world.

- Southern black fiction shares much with white fiction, in terms of narrative voice, characterization, and the themes of family, religion, the land, and community. However, the black novel or poem is often also concerned with struggle and oppression, the black slave experience, poverty, sharecropping, and the Civil Rights experience, and the tone is one of anger and/or hope.

Recommended Reading

Here is a list of important writers and recommended titles from the 19th century to the present. Most of the following books either take place in the South or feature a main character who is a confirmed (and often displaced) Southerner. (Authors John Grisham and Anne Rice usually set their books in the South, but the stories are not particularly southern, in the literary sense, so they are not included.) Nearly all these books are readily available at bookstores, although a few of the older ones might be more easily found at public or university libraries. Bookstores in the South have unusually large Regional Fiction sections with many contemporary titles autographed by the author.

Notable 19th- and Early 20th-century Writers

Thomas Nelson Page—tales of plantation life; *Marse Chan: A Tale of Old Virginia*

John Pendelton Kennedy—plantation novelist; *Swallow Barn*

Ellen Glascow—historical novelist from Virginia; *The Deliverance, Barren Ground, The Sheltered Life*

Joel Chandler Harris—folklorist, creator of Uncle Remus and Brer Rabbit tales

Mark Twain—frontier author; *The Adventures of Huckleberry Finn*

Kate Chopin—*The Awakening*

20th Century Writers and Playwrights of the "Literary Renaissance": First Generation

William Faulkner—premier novelist from Mississippi, created mythical southern Yoknapatawpha County, wrote of broken families, race, the land, in an experimental style; start with *The Sound and the Fury* or "The Bear," a short story

Thomas Wolfe—a writer from Asheville, North Carolina; *You Can't Go Home Again, Look Homeward, Angel*

Richard Wright—black novelist from Mississippi; *Black Boy, Native Son*

Zora Neale Hurston—black folklorist, novelist; *Their Eyes were Watching God, Jonah's Gourd Vine, Dust Tracks on the Road*

Marjorie Kinnan Rawlings—Florida writer; *The Yearling, Cross Creek*

Lillian Hellman—playwright; "The Little Foxes"

Erskine Caldwell—wrote about poor whites; *Tobacco Road, God's Little Acre*

Robert Penn Warren—poet, promoted agrarian philosophy in manifesto called *I'll Take My Stand*, and novelist, *All the King's Men*

Carson McCullers—writer from Georgia; *The Heart is a Lonely Hunter*

Eudora Welty—Mississippi novelist of southern family life and customs; *Delta Wedding, Losing Battles, The Optimist's Daughter*

Second Generation Writers of the "Literary Renaissance"

Flannery O'Connor—Georgia novelist and short story writer; collections include "Everything that Rises Must Converge," "A Good Man is Hard to Find"

William Styron—*Lie Down in Darkness, Sophie's Choice*

Truman Capote—*Other Voices, Other Rooms; Music for Chameleons* (short stories)

Harper Lee—wrote a brilliant book about growing up in a small southern town, *To Kill a Mockingbird*

Ralph Ellison—black writer from Oklahoma; *Invisible Man*

Walker Percy—*The Moviegoer, The Last Gentleman*

James Agee—Tennessee writer; *A Death in the Family* (novel), *Let Us Now Praise Famous Men* (nonfiction, about tenant farmers)

Tennessee Williams—playwright; "A Streetcar Named Desire," "The Glass Menagerie," and "Cat on a Hot Tin Roof"

Notable Authors of Contemporary Literature

Reynolds Price—North Carolina writer; *Kate Vaiden*

Olive Ann Burns—*Cold Sassy Tree*

Kaye Gibbons— *Ellen Foster, A Virtuous Woman, A Cure for Dreams, Charms for the Easy Life*

Dorothy Allison—*Bastard Out of Carolina*

Lisa Alther—*Kinflicks*

Pat Conroy—South Carolina writer; *Prince of Tides*

Bobbie Ann Mason—Kentucky writer; *In Country, Shiloh and Other Stories*

Barry Hannah—Mississippi writer; *Airships*

Josephine Humphreys—South Carolina writer; *Rich in Love, The Fireman's Fair*

Clyde Edgerton—North Carolina writer; *Raney, Walking Across Egypt, The Floatplane Notebooks, Killer Diller*

Jill McCorkle—*Tending to Virginia, The Cheer Leader, July 7th*

Florence King—nonfiction, humor; *The Florence King Reader*

Bailey White—nonfiction, humor; *Mama Makes Up Her Mind*

John Kennedy Toole—deceased New Orleans author of a great and funny novel, *A Confederacy of Dunces*

Madison Smartt Bell—*The Washington Square Ensemble, Waiting for the End of the World*

Rita Mae Brown—*Bingo, Rubyfruit Jungle*

Padgett Powell—*Edisto*

Mary Hood—*And Venus is Blue, How Far She Went* (short stories)

Anne River Siddons—*Peachtree Road*

Lee Smith—*Oral History, Family Linen*

Harry Crews—*Also Going to War*

Jim Grimsley—*Winter Birds, Dream Boy*

Lewis Nordan—*Wolf Whistle, Music of the Swamp, The Sharpshooter Blues*

Ellen Gilchrist—*Victory Over Japan, The Annunciation, In the Land of Dreamy Dreams*

Willie Morris—*Last of the Southern Girls*

Dori Sanders—African-American writer; *Clover, Her Own Place*

Alex Haley—saga of a black slave family, *Roots*

Tina McElroy Ansa—African-American writer; *Baby in the Family*

Alice Walker—story of sisters in rural Georgia, *The Color Purple*; *Meridian*

Nikki Giovanni—poet

Maya Angelou—poet; *Why the Caged Bird Sings*

Carol Dixon—*Going Home*

Doris Jean Austin—*After the Garden*

Ernest Gaines—*The Autobiography of Miss Jane Pittman, Bloodline*

Other Info

One of the best ways to get a taste of southern fiction is to read one of the many anthologies of short stories or collections of writing available in bookstores and libraries. Some of the more recent anthologies include:

The Art of Fiction in the Heart of Dixie: An Anthology of Alabama Writers, edited by Philip D. Beidler (The University of Alabama Press, Tuscaloosa, Alabama, 1986).

Black Southern Voices: An Anthology of Fiction, Poetry, Drama, Nonfiction, and Critical Essays, edited by John Oliver Killens and Jerry W. Ward, Jr. (Penguin Books, New York, New York, 1992).

A Collection of Classic Southern Humor: Fiction and Occasional Fact by Some of the South's Best Storytellers, edited by George William Koon (Peachtree Publishers, Atlanta, Georgia, 1984, book II published in 1986).

Florida Stories: Tales from the Tropics, edited by John and Kirsten Miller (Chronicle Books, San Francisco, California, 1993).

A Modern Southern Reader, edited by Ben Forkner and Patrick Samway S.J. (Peachtree Publishers, Atlanta, Georgia, 1986).

New Orleans Stories: Great Writers on the City, edited by John Miller and Genevieve Anderson (Chronicle Books, San Francisco, California, 1992).

New Stories from the South, The Year's Best, edited by Shannon Ravenel (Algonquin Books of Chapel Hill, New York, New York, published annually since 1986).

Roy Blount's Book of Southern Humor, edited by Roy Blount, Jr. (W.W. Norton, New York, New York, 1994).

The Signet Classic Book of Southern Short Stories, edited by Dorothy Abbott and Susan Koppelman (Signet Classics, New York, New York, 1991).

Stories: Contemporary Southern Short Fiction, edited by Donald Hays (The University of Arkansas Press, Fayetteville, Arkansas, 1989).

That's What I Like (About the South), and Other New Southern Stories for the Nineties, edited by George Garrett and Paul Ruffin (University of South Carolina Press, Columbia, South Carolina, 1993).

The university presses of major southern universities often publish new work by up-and-coming authors, as do academic journals and periodicals. Algonquin Books of Chapel Hill (now owned by Workman) is responsible for introducing the rest of the country to many new southern writers.

PRACTICAL TIPS
FOR NEWCOMERS

Newcomer guides, like the other ones in the *Culture Shock!* series, often focus on specific, practical information for newcomers, such as: "Do not bring American appliances to New Delhi" or "Rental prices on expatriate flats in Singapore range between $2,000 and $4,000 a month." This book, you may have noticed, deals with none of that (see *Culture Shock! United States* by Esther Wanning if you seek such information). The southern region is simply too vast and too varied—climatically, topographically, economically, housing wise—to give such detailed, precise advice. However, there are some practical tips about life in the South that may prove useful, however general they may be.

1. Be prepared to live in an air-conditioned environment for at least half the year. Although North Carolinians living in the mountains experience delightfully pleasant summers, most Southerners sweat through at least five months of the year. South Floridians begin getting 90-degree days in April and the heat often doesn't let up until about November (even with the benefit of those so-called "cool" ocean breezes). Even if you've never liked air-conditioning and resisted using it up north or in your new home down South, you'll become dependent on it in no time. Many newer homes in the South have central air-conditioning systems, while other homes and apartments have individual window units. Central air tends to be more efficient, less noisy, and less expensive. Whatever the system, be prepared to pay very high electricity bills in the South if you use air-conditioning regularly. Some electric companies have payment plans that allow customers to overpay their bills during the cooler months, so that the bills during the hot season are not astronomical.

Those who have never spent time in climatically-controlled environments might find themselves with stiff necks, sniffles, or creaky joints when they wake up in the morning. There are some Southerners who believe that using the air-conditioner for long periods of time or going back and forth between artificially cooled indoor environments and the warm and sticky outdoors can cause people to be more susceptible to colds or to contract arthritis. Ceiling fans are an excellent alternative to air-conditioning because they keep air circulating and they help cut down on humidity. A good compromise is to run your ceiling fans *and* keep your air-conditioner on at about 80 degrees.

Despite air-conditioning, the humidity will affect food in the kitchen if you are not careful. For instance, a regular bag of sugar, if not placed in an airtight container or ziploc bag, will quickly turn into a sticky, lumpy mess. Crackers will become moist and tasteless, as will pretzels, chips, or anything crunchy. Be careful not to leave food out in the sun at picnics because it will spoil more quickly down south than it would up north. As one Southerner recommended, be doubly cautious about food handling and safety in the South.

Humidity can also mildew the clothes in your closet. Never use plastic in the South to protect or cover your clothes—a good alternative is cotton sheets. Some Southerners place a bar of soap in the closet to absorb humidity; others leave a closet light burning continuously.

2. You never saw such a big bug. Late at night in the subtropical South, strange creatures come out of their daytime hiding places to search for tidbits in your kitchen. If you happen to surprise these fellows by turning on the light on your way to the fridge, you will get the shock of your life. There, munching their way through the bananas you left on the counter, crunching their way through the tin foil you covered the leftover bread with, will be the biggest, ugliest insect creatures that ever lived—cockroaches, two inches long, **THAT CAN FLY**. These lovelies are really called palmetto bugs, because they live in palm trees and palmetto shrubs (when they're not swimming in your sugar bowl, that is) and they are much more difficult to kill than most other bugs. You can try Raid and you can try traps, but the only way to really do it is to be quick with the heel of your foot (and hold your ears for the crunch).

The best way to avoid these unwanted visitors is to be obsessively clean, keep all snacks in jars or plastic containers with tops, and never leave food out. (An excellent way to keep bugs out of your flour bin is to place a bay laurel leaf in the container.) However, if you live in an older house or one in which the foundation is weakening, you will get roaches no matter how hard you try to keep them away. They even like to eat book bindings, clothing, and glossy paper! People in the North and West generally need only a twice yearly visit from the exterminator, but in the hot South, you may need him (it's usually a him, only hims kill bugs) every month. These days extermination companies make chemicals that not only kill the bugs but make them sterile, so they cannot lay thousands of little eggs under the fridge, all of which will hatch and dance around your kitchen at 2 a.m. Hire these guys—they're worth every dime they charge.

Exterminators also, by the way, kill other southern friends like wasps, bees, ants, and silverfish, and they know how to set traps for giant water rats that may seek cozy shelter in your garage during the winter months if you live near the coast. (Spare the lizards you see in and around your house—they eat bugs and harm nobody.) Companies provide thrice-yearly lawn-spraying service to keep ticks, fire ants (aggressive, larger reddish-black ants), and fleas at bay. Ants also get into your car in the South if you don't keep it free of crumbs, and they are difficult to get rid of.

If your kids find their way into an anthill, mix baking soda, meat tenderizer, or aspirin with water until it forms a paste and apply to the sting. In New Orleans, locals use a product called Dr. Tishner's for the same purpose.

3. Learn how to equip your house for a southern natural disaster: a hurricane. The official hurricane season lasts from June through November. The National Hurricane Center, located in Miami, publishes lots of brochures on the subject, so get yourself some *before* the storm surge causes that 20-foot wave to soak your condo, the wind gets up to 150 miles an hour, and the electricity goes off for a week. (Call 305-229-4470 for more information.) When buying a house, make sure the shutters are in good condition and learn how to use them. (Some need special tools.) If you don't have shutters, go into savings to have them made or you will be sorry. These days, some companies make shutters that are permanently attached to the sides of your windows, but fold up inconspicuously when not in use. (After Hurricane Andrew, which devastated south Florida in the summer of 1992, there was a two-year waiting list for these.)

Some of the things you'll need to stock your home during the blast from above include: candles, flashlights, extra batteries, a transistor radio, and a few days' worth of canned or other nonperishable foods.

You should fill your bathtubs and sinks with water and buy water purifying tablets. Also, go the extra yard and buy hurricane or "wind damage" insurance; some of those who didn't have it in south Florida in 1992 are still without proper shelter. Homeowners' insurance in hurricane-damaged areas can be difficult to acquire, so make sure you read your policies very carefully.

Foul weather of any degree can be dangerous in the South. According to one lifetime Southerner, don't take a simple rainstorm lightly. Lightning can strike even in the most benign-looking storms.

4. When buying a home in the South, here are some points to consider: If you're looking in Louisiana, Arkansas, Florida, Alabama, or Mississippi, you may have periodic flooding to contend with. Despite those tremendous southern dikes called "levees," much of the South is subject to floods, even after tropical storms. Major storms will damage or destroy homes, but minor ones might not, if your home is built on a good piece of land. (This can change from house to house even within a single neighborhood.) Make sure you hire a competent inspector before you close the deal; in some areas of the South, you are required by law to buy flood insurance, just in case.

Have the inspector you hire check thoroughly for termites, a common southern house-eating problem. If you have them, you will have to tent the house (better done before you move in). Tenting costs are based on the square footage of your house, and the process takes about 24 hours. In some areas of the South, burglars look specifically for tented houses to break into; some people even hire security to watch the property during the process. The chemicals are harmful to plants even on the outside of the house, and cleanup indoors after a tenting can be extensive. Some banks in the South require tenting and a roof inspection before they will finance the purchase of a new home. For those newcomers who are wondering what a tented house is, they're those huge structures that appear to be wrapped up like large, brightly colored packages.

You often get a lot more house for your money in the South, although this may not be true in the Atlanta area or in the most upscale neighborhoods in other cities. Someone from a nice part of suburban New York who moved to a beautiful area near Louisville, Kentucky, was amazed at what her money could buy: thousands of square feet of new house on nearly an acre of land with a large backyard pool looking out onto a private golf course for considerably less than what she sold her three-bedroom home for. Beware of newly constructed housing developments that have been put up quickly just to accommodate transients like yourselves; these may look good and new, and the price may be right, but workmanship, some newcomers say, can be shoddy, and things start falling apart after a year or so.

Old southern houses can be distinguished from newer ones by their kitchens, bathrooms, closets, and garages. Kitchens of older homes are just places to eat in, bathrooms just places to you-know-what in, and closets and garages may be small or nonexistent. In *New Times in the Old South*, Maryln Schwartz says you can tell New Southerners from Old by their huge, orderly closets and their enormous, Jacuzzi-equipped bathrooms. In Arkansas, lots of people have carports rather than garages because it keeps the rain off just as well.

In New Orleans, old houses were built without closets because owners paid taxes by the room, and a closet was considered as such; today, residents still use heavy antique armoires for their clothes. Stairwells were also taxed, so sometimes you see staircases on the outside of the homes. Older homes in New Orleans and throughout the South have raised first floors, transoms (small, rectangular "windows" that open over the doors throughout the house), large windows (needing large drapes), high ceilings, and lots of connected rooms, to keep the air circulating and to encourage cross ventilation. Some have screened-in "sleeping porches" used in the summer months b.a.c. (before air-conditioning). Most have large porches in the front and sometimes the back, where people used to sit to relax, chat with neighbors, even shell peas.

Many larger old houses were equipped to accommodate servants, so you'll see both front and back staircases, butler's pantries, and servants' living quarters out in the back. (Today, these are often advertised as "mother-in-law cottages.") Some homes even have little windows cut into the doors of the rooms so servants and mistresses could peek back and forth.

In parts of Florida, since most early residents came only for the winter season, closets in older homes are particularly small, and many are cedar-lined to keep the varmints away. Some Florida homes have screened-in patio rooms called "Florida rooms," which were constructed as places to sit and enjoy the outdoors without getting bitten by bugs. They were often furnished with rattan, wicker, or cast-iron porch furniture, the floors were made of colorful tiles set into patterns, and the walls were decorated with sea horses made out of shells or Florida wildlife motifs. Lots of homeowners these days convert Florida rooms into family rooms.

Throughout the South, you'll see smaller old homes called **shotgun** houses and **dogtrot** houses. The former type, built during the 19th century, is a long, narrow cottage (Elvis was born in one, in Tupelo, Mississippi), while the latter consists of two rooms separated by an interior passageway or a breezeway. Throughout the South you'll also see homes built in the Greek Revival style, with long white columns that have become associated with the plantation era and lifestyle. In Florida, Louisiana, and Alabama, you'll find Spanish-style homes, with red tiled roofs and white stucco exteriors. The Georgian Revival style, which is the style of Colonial Williamsburg, is common in North Carolina, South Carolina, and Virginia, while the French style, with French doors and windows, can be seen in New Orleans.

One New Orleans resident recommends that those interested in buying an old house in the city should hire a different real estate agent for each neighborhood under consideration, because each agent is an expert in only his or her area.

Shotgun houses in Atlanta's Sweet Auburn neighborhood.

If you formerly lived in an integrated neighborhood and wish to repeat the experience when you move South, you may have trouble finding such a place (except maybe in the parts of New Orleans called "salt and pepper" neighborhoods). Although black and white Southerners often work or go to school together, they do not often live side by side. When a family moving from an integrated suburb of Chicago to the Atlanta area asked their real estate agent to show them integrated neighborhoods, the agent showed them white/Asian—not white/black—areas.

251

Many Southerners use housekeepers or maid services to clean their homes. All the newcomers I spoke to said that such helpers are readily available, mostly through word of mouth. Often, two or more women (sisters, sometimes) will join forces so they can clean several houses per day. Some families in the South have had the same housekeeper for years, and she is treated as part of the family. When the children of the household grow up and start families of their own, sometimes the housekeeper goes with one of them. When the house-keeper retires, the family feels responsible for her and often continues to support her in some way until her death. The traditional house-keeper in the South cleans, cooks, and watches the children, a rarity these days. More people in the South have separate babysitters and housecleaners.

Similarly, some Southerners use gardeners or lawnservices to keep their lawns and gardens looking neat year around. In the summer you'll need weekly lawnservice, while in the winter you can have it once every two weeks. One woman who has lived in Charleston for several years said that you can always tell when a non-southern family has moved onto the block because you'll see the man of the house sweating profusely over the mower every Saturday, determined to cut that grass himself. Many Southerners love to garden in the spring and fall, but nobody gardens in the steamy summers. Again, word of mouth is the best way to find a good lawnservice.

The growing season in the South ranges from 200 days in northern parts of the region to 300 days in the southern parts. Some of the most popular flowering plants and trees you see in southern gardens include hydrangeas, magnolias, dogwoods, azaleas, camellias, gardenias, and crape myrtles. Magnolias (picture them by moonlight) and oak (strung with Spanish moss) are found throughout the southern landscape and, thanks to filmmakers and novelists, are commonly associated with southern culture and the Old South myth.

If you are unfamiliar with southern soil and flora, it might be wise to hire a landscape architect to give advice about planting. You could also read the new *Greenthumb* magazine, back issues of *Southern Living* magazine (at your local library), *Southern Gardens, Southern Gardening* by William Lanier Hunt (Duke University Press), *The Mid-South Garden Guide* (Memphis Garden Club), *Enchanted Ground: Gardening with Nature in the Subtropics* by Georgia B. Tasker (Andrews and McMeel), or *The Peachtree Garden Book: A Month-by-Month Guide for Lawn & Garden Care in the Southeast* edited by Edith Henderson (Peachtree Publishers of Atlanta). Some excellent gardening titles are available through the Center for Southern Folklore, 130 Beale Street, Memphis, Tennessee, 38103, (901) 525-FOLK.

It is not absolutely essential to install a sophisticated burglar alarm system in most southern homes (although this may not be true for long). In many southern cities and towns, people are not constantly worried about crime the way they are in much of the urban or suburban United States. In some places, mothers still feel safe leaving their kids in the car while they run quickly into a store, and many people leave their cars and homes unlocked. In south Florida, however, even the most modest homes have some form of security system, like iron grates over the windows and doors, or large canine creatures.

You can expect to find many homes in the South with outdoor, inground pools, which are considered an important selling point (after central air-conditioning). Plan to pay someone to clean your pool and chlorinate the water every two weeks or so if your swimming hole is situated near lots of trees. Some southern states are trying to pass laws requiring homeowners to install fences around pools for safety reasons. Some fences are quite reasonably priced, especially nylon mesh and chain link varieties. Tragically, many children drown in their own backyard pools. At the very least, buy a floating pool alarm that sounds if anything falls into the water.

If you choose to buy a mobile home when you move South, you will be in good company: there are more mobile homes in the South— especially in Florida, North Carolina, Georgia, and South Carolina—

than in any other region of the country. Most do not actually *move*, but remain stationary on small, privately owned lots, in quiet, out-of-the-way areas. Mobile home dwellers these days do not necessarily conform to the "trailer trash" stereotype. "Manufactured homes," as they are called, are sold these days mostly to retirees and to young marrieds who are not yet ready to buy their first real house. Some of the smaller models, the "single-wides," which are about 10–12 feet wide, are inexpensive; the "double-wides" (28 feet wide) and "triple-wides" (50 feet wide) can cost more than $100,000.

5. Do not underestimate the power of the sun. Parents should send their children outside with an even coating of waterproof sunscreen on their entire bodies, especially during the summer months. Hats are recommended as well: babies don't mind those floppy, large-brimmed hats, but toddlers and older kids prefer baseball caps. Even on cloudy days, the sun can still burn your skin.

Direct sunlight will fade furniture placed near windows. And outdoor garden furniture, children's plastic slides, and playhouses will fade outdoors in the South in no time.

CULTURAL QUIZ

Here are some potentially sticky cultural situations newcomers might find themselves in when they move South. Put yourself in the scenarios outlined below and try to imagine how you would behave. If you score badly, reread the book.

SITUATION 1

You have just been invited to your first dinner party at the home of a Southerner. When you arrive, you notice that among the beautiful furnishings and antiques that decorate the living room hangs an authentic Confederate uniform that you assume once belonged to an ancestor of the host. Your immediate reaction is one of shock and surprise, then offense, because you associate the uniform with the South's efforts to retain the system of slavery. Do you:

A   Say, "Forgive me, but can you tell why in this day and age you would dare to hang a symbol of oppression on the wall for all to see, and in such a prominent place?"

B   Clam up and feel uncomfortable for the rest of the evening?

C   Ask, in an inquisitive but gentle manner, "Tell me, what is the story behind that uniform?"

Comments

The first response would not only make your host uncomfortable, but would make you look ill-mannered and lacking in self-control. The second is silly—why ruin an evening when you don't have to? The third alternative is just right. It allows the host to tell a family story, and it prevents you from looking like a typical non-Southerner with confrontational political opinions that have no place in such a setting. Remember, many Southerners see the Confederate uniform and the Confederate flag as historical relics, not symbols of oppression.

SITUATION 2

You have been appointed as the chairperson for a fundraising event for your child's school. Your job is to oversee the activities of three other committee members who are supposed to sign parents up to help with the event, make baked goods, and organize advertising efforts. Two months before the event, you write a detailed checklist of everyone else's responsibilities and begin making calls to see if everyone is on top of things. They're not. Do you:

A   Call an emergency meeting to light a fire under the committee members' tails so they will understand the importance of getting everything done well ahead of time?

B   Tell the other people involved that, where you come from, people are much more efficient at organizing and fundraising?

C Relax, and write a letter to all parties letting them know that the event will be upon them before they know it and that by a certain date they should know who will be doing what? The letter ends with something like, "Let me know if there is anything you would like me to help you with."

Comments

Alternatives *A* and *B* represent everything Southerners dislike about outsiders: their urgency, bluntness, and "Where I Come From …" attitudes. Answer *C* is much more in keeping with the southern pace, while it also lets people know that you want to be friendly and helpful.

SITUATION 3

You are the only woman executive in your office. Your male colleagues constantly rise when you come into the boardroom, open doors for you, allow you to leave the elevator first, grab the lunch check out of your hands, and treat you like you need extra protection. You are used to being treated like an equal and fear that because you are a woman your opinions are not being taken seriously and your talents left unappreciated. Do you:

A Go into the bathroom and cry during lunch?

B Let it all boil up inside you and then rant and rave at a meeting because you can't take it anymore?

C Work hard, keep your emotions to yourself, and slowly let them see for themselves that you are of equal intelligence and abilities?

Comments

Showing a weakness for tears might get you typecast as a hysterical female. Neither is letting your anger overtake you and acting inappropriately in a formal business setting. The last option is the best, even though it takes incredible patience. It shows steadfastness and self-control and your commitment to working within the confines of a society that is still a bit uncomfortable with women taking leading roles.

SITUATION 4

You are a teenager who listens to cutting edge music. You arrive at a home of an acquaintance you made at school and the radio is set on the country music station. Your classmate and his family all sing along. Do you:

A Say "I can't believe you people listen to this stuff"?

B Say "I really know nothing about this kind of music. Tell me about it"?

C Leave early, feeling angry at your parents for forcing you to move to a land where your tastes are completely misunderstood?

Comments

The "you people" phrase is a definite no-no for anyone moving to another culture because it shows both closemindedness towards and disgust for the unfamiliar culture. The third response may be typical for a teenager, but it is not constructive. The second answer shows a willingness to experience new things as well as a desire to make a new friend.

SITUATION 5

You are invited to an impromptu dinner party during the summer. Your hostess says, "Just come casual." Does that mean you wear:

A The shorts and t-shirt you mowed the lawn in earlier that day?

B The sweatsuit with the Clemson Tigers logo on it?

C Nice pants, a button-down shirt and loafers if you are a man, or a skirt and blouse or similar outfit with nice shoes if you are a woman?

Comments

Casual does not mean purely comfortable in the South. It means make some effort to look nice, take care to make sure your hair is combed and makeup applied. Oh, and don't forget to stop by the liquor store or florist to pick up a hostess gift on the way to the party.

FURTHER READING

What follows is a brief list of well-written, amusing, and/or classic books about the South and southern culture, many of which I consulted countless times during the course of researching and writing this book. The titles by John Shelton Reed and Maryln Schwartz, as well as *The Encyclopedia of Southern Culture*, were invaluable to me, as were years of back issues of the *Atlanta Journal-Constitution* and *Southern Living*. Visit your local library stacks or bookstore shelves for many more selections on southern subjects.

GENERAL SOURCES

Auchmutey, Jim and Lea Donosky. *True South: Travels Through a Land of White Columns, Black-eyed Peas and Redneck Bars*, Longstreet Press, Atlanta, Georgia, 1994. A compilation of articles from the *Atlanta Journal-Constitution*'s "True South" column on a variety of particularly southern phenomena such as Big Hair, kudzu, and beauty pageants.

Kuralt, Charles. *Southerners: Portrait of a People*, Oxmoor House, Birmingham, Alabama, 1986. Lots of photographs accompanied by insightful text by the roaming southern journalist.

Naipaul, V.S. *A Turn in the South*, Alfred A. Knopf, New York, New York, 1989. A well-known author's intelligent impressions of the region and its people.

Reed, John Shelton. *My Tears Spoiled My Aim and Other Reflections on Southern Culture*, University of Missouri Press, Columbia, Missouri, 1993. An extraordinary study of the South and its people by a sociologist with a sense of humor.

————. *Whistling Dixie; Dispatches from the South*, Harcourt, Brace Jovanovich, San Diego, California and New York, New York, 1990. A collection of articles by the above (with some repetition).

Wilson, Charles Reagan and William Ferris, eds. *The Encyclopedia of Southern Culture*, University of North Carolina Press, Chapel Hill, North Carolina, 1989. A marvelous, 1,634-page tome covering everything about the South you'd ever want to know, with articles written by all the Southern Studies experts; sometimes available for a reasonable price from book clubs or in a two-volume paperback set.

SOUTHERN WOMEN

Abbott, Shirley. *Womenfolks: Growing Up Down South*, Ticknor and Fields, New Haven, Connecticut, and New York, 1983. A beautifully written memoir about a family of strong Arkansas women.

Fox-Genovese, Elizabeth. *Within the Plantation Household: Black and White Women of the Old South*, University of North Carolina Press, Chapel Hill, North Carolina, 1988.

King, Florence. *Southern Ladies and Gentlemen*, Stein and Day, New York, New York, 1975. A very funny and cutting account of the sexual and social lives of a variety of southern types.

McKern, Sharon. *Redneck Mothers, Good Ol' Girls and Other Southern Belles: A Celebration of the Women of Dixie*, Viking Press, New York, New York, 1979. A humorous survey of southern women, like King (above) but without the sting.

Scott, Anne Firor. *The Southern Lady from Pedestal to Politics, 1830–1930*, University of Chicago Press, Chicago, Illinois, 1970. A classic study of the southern female.

HUMOR

Batson, Ann Barrett. *Having It Y'all: The Official Handbook for Citizens of the South and Those Who Wish They Were*, Rutledge Hill Press, Nashville, Tennessee, 1988. A funny overview of all things southern.

Blount, Roy, ed. *Roy Blount's Book of Southern Humor*, W.W. Norton & Company, New York, New York, 1994. An extensive collection from the region's funniest writers, with a clever introduction by the editor.

Moore, Jack S. *The Official Redneck Handbook*, Larksdale, Houston, Texas, 1983. An occasionally amusing description of a favorite southern stereotype.

Schwartz, Maryln. *New Times in the Old South, or Why Scarlett's in Therapy and Tara's Going Condo*, Harmony Books, New York, New York, 1993. A witty Texas journalist's look at the New South and its impact on the old ways.

————. *A Southern Belle Primer, or Why Princess Margaret will never be a Kappa Kappa Gamma*, Doubleday, New York, New York, 1991. A hysterical account of the beliefs and practices of the archetypal southern belle.

Whaley, Bo. *Bo Whaley's Field Guide to Southern Women*, Rutledge Hill Press, Nashville, Tennessee, 1990. A kind of "bird watcher's" guide filled with anecdotes and digressions.

White, Bailey. *Mama Makes Up Her Mind and Other Dangers of Southern Living*, Vintage Books, New York, New York, 1994. A bestselling selection of short pieces about southern life and southern characters by a very funny writer and public radio commentator.

LOCAL COLOR/TRAVEL

Berendt, John. *Midnight in the Garden of Good and Evil*, Random House, New York, New York, 1994. A lively, true account of a murder in Savannah, Georgia, complete with insight into the lives of a host of southern eccentrics.

Cantor, George. *Historic Black Landmarks: A Traveler's Guide*, Visible Ink Press, Detroit, Michigan, 1991.

Hardy, Arthur, ed. *Arthur Hardy's Mardi Gras Guide*, 19th Annual Edition, 1995, Arthur Hardy Enterprises, Inc., New Orleans, Louisiana. A must have for those seeking information on parade schedules, routes, and historical details.

Hearin, Emily Staples and Kathryn Taylor deCelle. *Queens of Mobile Mardi Gras, 1893–1986*, Museum of the City of Mobile, Mobile, Alabama, 1986. A queen-by-queen guide to the royal court, complete with extensive gown description and photographs; available through the museum.

Jenkins, Emyl. *Southern Christmas*, Crown Publishers, New York, New York, 1992. A pretty book about southern Christmas traditions and present-day customs.

Redd, Lorraine. *Only in Mississippi: A Guide for the Adventurous Traveler*, Quail Ridge Press, Brandon, Mississippi, 1993. A guide to the more unusual sites and happenings of Mississippi.

Sexton, Richard and Randolph Delehanty. *New Orleans: Elegance and Decadence*, Chronicle Books, San Francisco, California, 1993. A gorgeous photographic journey through some of New Orleans' finest interiors; includes some artistic shots of Mardi Gras.

Steele, Phillip W. *Ozark Tales and Superstitions*, Pelican Publishing Company, Gretna, Louisiana, 1990.

Thum, Marcella. *Hippocrene U.S.A. Guide to Black America*, Hippocrene Books, New York, New York, 1991.

Timblin, Carol. *Best Places to Stay: The South*, Houghton Mifflin Company, Boston, Massachusetts, 1994.

SOUTHERN FOOD

Belk, Sarah. *Around the Southern Table: Innovative Recipes Celebrating 300 Years of Eating and Drinking*, Simon & Schuster, New York, New York, 1991. A useful and well-written cookbook with both traditional and contemporary southern recipes.

The Black Family Dinner Quilt Cookbook, The National Council of Negro Women, Inc., Simon & Schuster, New York, New York, 1993. Sequel to *The Black Family Reunion Cookbook* (see below).

The Black Family Reunion Cookbook, The National Council of Negro Women, Simon & Schuster, New York, New York, 1991. Wonderful soul food recipes contributed by black women all over the United States.

Claiborne, Craig. *Craig Claiborne's Southern Cooking*, Times Books, New York, New York, 1987. A good overview by an excellent chef.

Collin, Rima and Richard. *The New Orleans Cookbook: Creole, Cajun and Louisiana French Recipes Past and Present*, Alfred A. Knopf, New York, New York, 1975. The classic text on the subject.

Dupree, Nathalie. *New Southern Cooking*, Alfred A. Knopf, New York, New York, 1991. Great recipes by a southerner with her own TV cooking show.

Egerton, John. *Southern Food at Home, on the Road, in History*, Alfred

A. Knopf, New York, New York, 1987. If you love to read cookbooks, this is the one to buy; tremendously informative with lovely black and white photographs.

Flagg, Fanny. *The Original Whistle Stop Cafe Cookbook*, Ballantine Books, New York, New York, 1993. See the movie first, then use this humorous cookbook to fry your own green tomatoes.

Herbst, Sharon Tyler. *Food Lover's Companion*, Barron's Educational Series, New York, New York, 1990. An easy-to-understand dictionary of food and cooking terms; helpful for the inexperienced cook.

Magic: The Cookbook of the Junior League of Birmingham, Alabama, 1989 edition. A good example of a typical ladies' club publication with really good recipes.

Mickler, Ernest Matthew. *White Trash Cooking*, Jargon Society and Ten Speed Press, Berkeley, California, 1986. Honest, down home recipes by a member of the stereotype.

Pitzer, Sara. *Enjoying the Art of Southern Hospitality*, August House Publishers, Little Rock, Arkansas, 1990.

Taylor, Joe Gray. *Eating, Drinking and Visiting in the South*, Louisiana State University Press, Baton Rouge, Louisiana, 1982. A well-written history recommended by many southern scholars.

HISTORY

Cash, W.J. *The Mind of the South*, Vintage Books, New York, New York, 1941. The classic and controversial analysis of the southern psyche; a must read for Southern Studies 101.

Cobb, James C. *The Most Southern Place on Earth: The Mississippi Delta and the Roots of Regional Identity*, Oxford University Press, Oxford and New York, 1992. A thorough history of the Deep South.

Daniel, Pete. *Standing at the Crossroads: Southern Life Since 1900*, Hill and Wang, New York, New York, 1986.

Genovese, Eugene D. *The Southern Tradition*, Harvard University Press, Cambridge, Massachusetts, 1994. A history of southern conservatism from antebellum to present times.

Grantham, Dewey W. *The South in Modern America*, Harper Collins Publishers, New York, New York, 1994. A readable study of the post-Reconstruction South and its relation to the North, by a Vanderbilt University historian.

Tindall, George Brown. *The Ethnic Southerners*, Louisiana State University Press, Baton Rouge, Louisiana, 1976.

RACE AND CIVIL RIGHTS

Chafe, William H. *Civilities and Civil Rights*, Oxford University Press, New York, New York, 1980. An informative account of the Civil Rights Movement in Greensboro, North Carolina.

Curry, Constance. *Silver Rights*, Algonquin Books of Chapel Hill, Chapel Hill, North Carolina, 1995. A new biography of the ordinary people who participated in the Civil Rights Movement, those who registered to vote and sent their children to white schools, by a white member of the movement.

Greene, Melissa Fay. *Praying for Sheetrock*, Ballantine Books, New York, New York, 1991. A true account of a small, mostly black county in Georgia run by a cunning white sheriff; reads like poetry.

Lehmann, Nicholas. *The Promised Land: The Great Black Migration and How it Changed America*, Alfred A. Knopf, New York, New York, 1991. Personal narratives about the black migration from the Mississippi Delta to Chicago; see the made-for-TV series too.

NEWCOMER GUIDES

Hayward, Irva R. and David W. Coombs. *Welcome: A Foreigner's Guide to Successful Living in the Southern United States*, The Best of Times, Inc., Pelham, Alabama, 1994. A practical guide to life in the United States, with some specific information about the southern region.

Wanning, Esther. *Culture Shock! USA*, Times Editions, Singapore, 1985. A good general overview of life in the United States, with practical advice for the foreigner.

SOUTHERN ACCENT

Montgomery, Michael B. and Guy Bailey, eds. *Language Variety in the South*, University of Alabama Press, Tuscaloosa, Alabama, 1986. A technical study of dialect differences within the region.

Smith, Fabia Rue and Charles Rayford Smith. *Southern Words and Sayings*, Jackson, Mississippi, 1993. A small glossary of interesting southernisms.

STEREOTYPES

Kirby, Jack Temple. *Media-Made Dixie: the South in the American Imagination*, Louisiana University Press, Baton Rouge, Louisiana, 1978. An excellent discussion of southern stereotypes and the media's role in their creation and enforcement.

Reed, John Shelton. *Southern Folk, Plain and Fancy: Native White Social Types*, University of Georgia Press, Athens, Georgia, 1986. Reprint of a series of lectures on white stereotypes; funny and insightful.

Smith, Stephen A. *Myth, Media and the Southern Mind*, University of Arkansas Press, Fayetteville, Arkansas, 1985.

MANNERS

Martin, Judith. *Miss Manners' Guide to Excruciatingly Correct Behavior*, Penguin Books, New York, New York, 1982. A good starting point for the non-Westerner, written in an entertaining question/answer format; all books by this author recommended.

Stewart, Marjabelle Young and Marian Faux. *Executive Etiquette in the New Workplace*, St. Martin's Press, New York, New York, 1994. A comprehensive guide recommended for executive transfers.

MUSIC AND LITERATURE

Clarke, Donald, ed. *Penguin Encyclopedia of Popular Music*, Viking Press, New York, New York, 1989.

Gusikoff, Lynne. *Guide to Musical America*, Facts on File Publications, New York, New York, 1984.

See also Chapter 10: Southern Music and Literature: A Resource Guide

SOUTHERN COLLEGES

Insiders' Guide to the Colleges, Yale Daily News, St. Martin's Press, New York, New York, 1995.

NEWSPAPERS, JOURNALS, AND MAGAZINES

Atlanta Journal-Constitution: the news of the New South, with special southern culture columns in the Sunday "Dixie Living" section.

Oxford American: a bimonthly published by author John Grisham in Oxford, Mississippi, covering such topics as southern literature, photography, food, travel, sports, and leisure.

Reckon, The Magazine of Southern Culture: a brand new quarterly out of the Center for the Study of Southern Culture at the University of Mississippi featuring articles on regional customs, arts, myths, lifestyles.

Southern Exposure: a liberal journal published by Julian Bond out of the Institute for Southern Studies in Durham, NC, focusing on politics, black issues, arts.

Southern Living Magazine: a very popular monthly strong on recipes, gardening, decor, and profiles of Southerners.

THE AUTHOR

Jane Kohen Winter grew up in Florida and spent her summers in North Carolina. She has a master's degree in journalism from Northwestern University and has worked as a writer and editor in Singapore and Chicago. To date, she has written four books for young adults about different cultures: *Cultures of the World: Venezuela, Cultures of the World: Chile, Cultures of the World: Italy,* and *Women in Society: Brazil.* In researching *Culture Shock! USA—The South,* she traveled throughout the South. She lives in Evanston, Illinois, with her husband and three daughters.

INDEX